body movement
PERSPECTIVES IN RESEARCH

Advisory Editor: Martha Davis
Hunter College

body

BEHAVIOR DEVELOPMENT IN INFANTS

A SURVEY OF THE LITERATURE ON PRENATAL AND POSTNATAL ACTIVITY 1920–1934

BY

EVELYN DEWEY

ARNO PRESS

A NEW YORK TIMES COMPANY

New York • 1972

Reprint Edition 1972 by Arno Press Inc.

Reprinted from a copy in The Newark Public Library

Body Movement: Perspectives in Research
ISBN for complete set: 0-405-03140-8
See last pages of this volume for titles.

Manufactured in the United States of America

Library of Congress Cataloging in Publication Data

Dewey, Evelyn, 1889-
   Behavior development in infants.

   (Body movements: perspectives in research)
   Bibliography: p.
   1. Developmental psychobiology. 2. Infants--
Growth. I. Title. II. Series.
RJ131.D46 1972   155.4'12   72-343
ISBN 0-405-03142-4

BEHAVIOR DEVELOPMENT
IN INFANTS

A SURVEY OF THE LITERATURE ON
PRENATAL AND POSTNATAL ACTIVITY
1920–1934

BEHAVIOR DEVELOPMENT
IN INFANTS

A SURVEY OF THE LITERATURE ON
PRENATAL AND POSTNATAL ACTIVITY
1920–1934

BY

EVELYN DEWEY

PUBLISHED FOR THE
JOSIAH MACY, JR., FOUNDATION
BY COLUMBIA UNIVERSITY PRESS
NEW YORK: 1935

PREFACE

THE Normal Child Development Clinic is part of a research program of the Neurological Institute for the study of the correlation of the development of the brain with the development of behavior, under the direction of Dr. Frederick Tilney. This research covers the following representative animals: the opossum, the rat, the cat, the guinea pig, the pig, and man. The clinic's particular problem is the development of behavior in the human.

The present survey of the current literature on growth processes and infant behavior is the result of a suggestion of the Josiah Macy, Jr., Foundation and was made possible by its special grant for the purpose. The resulting condensed birds-eye view of what is being done by other investigators proved of such value to the Clinic that the Foundation is making it available in published form. The purpose of the survey was not to cover all the literature, but rather to select salient results and organize them according to the plan being followed in the study of growth by the Clinic.

The preliminary search of the literature was made by Miss Mary A. Ewer. Dr. Robert Patek gave valuable assistance in reading and abstracting foreign publications, especially the German. The manuscript was read critically by Dr. Frederick Tilney, Dr. L. Beverley Chaney, and Dr. Myrtle B. McGraw of the Normal Child Development Clinic. The author also wishes to acknowledge the assistance of Miss Ethel Minder and Miss Jean E. Moehle with the bibliography.

E. D.

NEW YORK
August, 1935

CONTENTS

PART I

GROWTH PROCESSES

I

GROWTH PROCESSES

ANY ATTEMPT to review what is known today about the development of human behavior requires a statement of what is meant by "behavior." For the purposes of this summary of the literature since 1920, behavior is defined as the neuromuscular and glandular reactions of living human organisms. The literature (chiefly periodical) for the fetal period and the first two years of life has been covered. We recognize that social and emotional development might be included under this definition, but we have not included these two phases of behavior since their very existence involves interpretations which lead us afield into theoretical speculations, and there is as yet no satisfactory theory of the processes underlying strictly objective neuromuscular behavior patterns. Therefore, the summary presented here is confined to the theories drawn from psychology and biology on the fundamental processes underlying growth and development of behavior, and to objective studies of fetal and infant behavior. The current theories of growth processes are based on two sources of objective evidence: data on human and animal behavior, and neurophysiological data on the correlation of structure and function. The first has furnished the basis for the psychological theories of the mechanisms of behavior, the second that for the biological theories. It has long been assumed that the time at which certain movements appear in an individual and in the evolutionary scale is an indication of a certain state of development in the nervous structures; and the functioning of the nervous system and of the specific nervous mechanisms in behavior are recognized as forming as fundamental a part of the picture as the behavior itself.

It is only by correlating and integrating the work in both these fields that we shall reach an adequate scientific understanding of what behavior is and of the ways in which development takes place. The literature on animal behavior offers many suggestive analogies for the study of human behavior, but it has not been possible to include it in this survey. Owing to the difficulties of investigation on human beings, our knowledge of the correlation of structure and function in behavior is drawn largely from studies on animals. It is chiefly from such data that the theories of behavioral processes advanced by neurophysiologists have been developed. Since an understanding of these theories is what gives meaning and background to the great mass of data on behavior during the first two years of life, a brief outline of the hypotheses and points of view of the main work that is being done in this field is presented together with some of the more important findings in recent investigations of the correlation of neural structures and behavior of animals. The literature on behavior proper has also been assembled from the point of view of obtaining an understanding of *growth processes*, that is by behavior patterns rather than by the usual method of what an individual or a group can do at successive age levels.

THEORIES OF BEHAVIOR DEVELOPMENT

THE BEHAVIORIST THEORY

The first strictly scientific psychological hypothesis of behavior growth based on objective, non-introspective data is that growth takes place by a process of expansion from the simple to the complex. This is the reflex-arc theory of behavior from which the behaviorists derive their theories. The exponents of this school state that animal and human behavior can be explained as a process of the interaction of the environment and a minimum repertoire of neuromuscular reactions which are present at birth. Growth takes place by a process of conditioning, or association of discreet new experiences with these primary reactions, which gradually brings about increasing complexity in behavior as the number of conditioned associations increases. Growth is thus a process of expansion and combination of certain primary reflex pathways into infinitely complex patterns through the action of the environment on the organism. Pavlov, a behaviorist, through controlled experiments in establishing conditioned reflexes and through his studies of the correlation of structure and function in dogs, has contributed the most exact scientific evidence in support of this view of the action of the nervous system. He says:

The nervous system is not only a conducting apparatus but a coupling machine, which creates new connections. Thus before the modern physiologist are two kinds of reflexes, constant and temporary, inborn and acquired, the reflexes of the species, and those of the individual. For practical purposes of distinction we call the first reflex *unconditioned* and the second *conditioned*. It is highly probable that newly formed reflexes (individual) under the continuance of uniform conditions of life during successive generations pass over into constant reflexes (generic). . . . The whole way along which the nervous impulse travels is, as is well known, called the reflex-arc or path. In the lower central nervous system there are recognized three parts of this arc: the receptor (a receiving apparatus), the conductor (conducting apparatus), and the effector (the apparatus which exercises the special activity). Add to "receptor" the word "analyser" (decomposing), and to "conductor" the word "connector" (linking or coupling apparatus), and you have the expressions for the corresponding anatomical structure and for the two fundamental activities which characterize the higher part of the nervous system. . . . As has been shown by many investigators, the conditioned reflex is unfailingly formed in the presence of a small number of definite conditions, and hence there is no basis for considering its creation as especially complicated. Always when some indifferent stimulus synchronizes with the action of some other stimulus which produces a definite reflex, then after one or many such coincidences, the formerly indifferent stimulus taken alone calls out the same reflex as the active stimulus which it previously accompanied. (152, p. 242.)

Thus the behaviorists believe that growth in behavior takes place by a process of conditioning or by the addition of new responses to the primary ones present at birth, that is by a process of association which sets up new connections in the nervous system. Thus learning takes place by trial and error; useful or purposive responses survive, the unsuccessful ones being gradually eliminated, since the successful bring a satisfaction to the organism and so gain an advantage over the unsuccessful. This process of growth from the simple to the complex is used in explaining all the reactions of man, his creative faculties, emotional life and even his temperament. Pavlov (152) gives an interesting explanation of temperament as due to the quality of the inhibitory mechanisms of the nervous system. He also believes that there is an external inhibitory element in the stimuli themselves, due to the relation between the strength of the unconditioned and the neutral stimuli. A corollary of this interpretation of the method of functioning of the nervous system is a belief in the localization of function. Pavlov (152, p. 384) states:

Each single afferent nerve fibre, running from some definite element of the peripheral receptive field, must be regarded as a conductor to the cortex of some definite element of one or other form of energy. In the cortex a special cell must stand in connection with the fibre, the activity of the cell being related to some definite element of one or another definite form of energy. This interpretation of the structure of the cortex rests on definite experimental indications: as a result of investigation of functional disturbances of the cortical cells, such a fragmentation of cortical functions is revealed as we could never dream of obtaining by an operative procedure. In my recently published lectures an observation was mentioned showing that it is possible to derange a point pertaining to a separate conditioned stimulus, namely the sound of a metronome, leaving points corresponding to other auditory stimuli undamaged. Succeeding experiments have confirmed that it is similarly possible to create a localized disturbance of the cortex, corresponding to a definite point in the tactile analyzer, without impairment of the normal functioning of any other parts.

Pavlov is quoted as illustrating the point of view of this school on the processes of behavior, since his experiments have included operative procedure on animals in an attempt to get definite evidence of the relation of structure and function. The school is supported by other physiologists in Russia (where it is especially popular at present since it fits very neatly into the current political theory of dialectical materialism), and by a number of psychologists in this country and in Europe.

A number of different points of view or of emphasis have developed within the school. One of the most interesting of these is Weiss's (208) analysis of stimuli and responses as biophysical and biosocial, thus emphasizing the importance of the relational element, or the interactivity of the organism and the environment, in the learning or growth process. He (208, p. 303) says:

Human behavior is the totality of the biosocial response systems which establish the individuals social status in the community of which he is a member. In the order of complexity the actions of individuals pass through simple movements, biophysical reactions, biosocial responses, temporary response series (for various ages and conditions of life), permanent response series (the career), the behavior life history.

Although the leaders in this school differ on some of the details of the reflex-arc explanation of behavior, they all appear to agree that "consciousness" or a mental factor in behavior must be ruled out and all accounts of behavior made in simple mechanistic terms of stimulus and response. Hunter (91) states: "Nowhere it is necessary to introduce the concept of consciousness, or experience, conceived as another mode of existence, or as another aspect of the physical world."

THE GESTALT THEORY

Another theory of the processes of behavior development is more recent and has swung to the opposite extreme. It is interesting that most of the physiologists and neurologists working on the correlation of structure and function at present tend, in their interpretations of results, to support the underlying principles of this theory—that growth or learning as a process proceeds, in general, from the whole to the part. Lashley,* for instance, concludes from his experiments on extirpation of the hemispheres of dogs that the amount of functional damage is proportionate to the extent of the extirpation and is not dependent upon the destruction of localized points in the hemispheres, and that lost functions can be relearned after the extirpation of their so-called centers, provided the total amount of cortical tissue removed is not too great. Thus the function of the cortex is to a certain extent generalized and not simply a connection center for specific

* See Bibliography, and "The effects of long continued practice upon cerebral localization," *J. Comp. Psych.*, 1921. Vol. 1, pp. 453-468; "The mechanism of vision," Vol. 4: "The cerebral areas necessary for pattern vision in the rat," *J. Comp. Neurol.*, 1931, Vol. 53, pp. 419-472; "A reanalysis of data on mass action in the visual cortex," *J. Comp. Neurol.*, 1932, Vol. 54, pp. 78-84; "Studies in cerebral function in learning," Vol. 3: "The motor areas," *Brain*, 1921, Vol. 44, pp. 255-285; "Visual discrimination of size and form in the albino-rat," *J. Animal Behavior*, 1912, Vol. 2, pp. 310-330.

nerve-fiber connections between specific afferent and efferent pathways.

In psychological terms, as explained by the Gestalt school, behavior must be explained as something more than the mere mechanical interaction of the environment and primitive response patterns, and the responses which become associated with them by conditioning. This plus element is not consciousness in the older psychological sense of the word, but is a function of the structures of the nervous system correlated, according to Koffka (106), with the neo-encephalon. It may be termed for purposes of illustration the ability to perceive, or the function of perception, as a fundamental property of the nervous system, which is present at birth and observable in an infant's behavior even then. Koffka's example of this is the fact that the infant does not react to simple auditory or visual stimuli first, but shows the first reactions to the human voice and face, both very complex stimuli. That is, in every reaction there is more than a simple mechanical stimulation of an afferent pathway and a motor discharge along the efferent; the stimulus is perceived as a whole and in relation to the needs of the organism. This perception is in the nature of a synthesizing or "configuration" activity in the cortex. By this synthesis is not meant the patterning of simple isolated sensations into a complex whole, but the actual reception of a stimulus in such a way that a whole is perceived. The common sense indications of this concept of perception are such familiar items as that the ability to distinguish the color or shape of an object is a later development than the ability to see and use the object as a whole. A nursing bottle is not seen by the infant as a cylindrical shape of something hard and white topped with a black nipple, and with a different quality of whiteness (milk) inside it, but as a total object which has a relation to his needs.

The Gestalt school believe that this quality of total perception in relation to the needs of the organism is an integral part of every stimulus-response pattern. Both analysis and synthesis are secondary functions which develop later from the relation or *stress* caused by the particular situation in the environment and the immediate need of the organism. Koffka (106) goes so far as to state that the forces which produce the first reaction ("instinctive activities") are not in the stimulus situation, but within the organism itself. According to this school, then, behavior development, or learning, takes place by a process of "transforming" or synthesizing and analyzing certain primary wholes experienced by the newborn infant, through the medium of sensory stimulation, into numberless larger and smaller wholes, each one determined in its configuration by the relation of the organism to the environment in terms of the needs of the organism. The relation of the whole to the need of the organism (or meaning) and the perception are but two phases of the same thing. The supporters of this theory admit that it implies the existence of consciousness, but maintain that it does not imply a non-physical or superphysical consciousness, and that all the processes involved in their analysis of behavior can be explained by the functioning of the nervous system.

Kohler (108, p. 147) gives the following account of the more usual methods of psychological analysis, which seems to suggest some of the reasons why the principals of Gestalt psychology seem hard to grasp, to those accustomed to thinking in the usual terms:

Our observations have followed a line which leads away from familiar ideas. One of the fundamental methods of natural sciences is *analysis*. The psychologist, therefore, confronted with a complex field of vision, for example, feels naturally inclined to analyze this field into smaller and simpler entities whose properties he may study with more ease and with more hope of clear results than an immediate consideration of the whole field would yield. Generally he does not ask himself what this procedure purports and if, perhaps, the term analysis is rather ambiguous, he simply analyzes down to very small parts of the sensory field—let us call them the "sense ions"—which do not contain differences, which show a minimum of area and so seem to constitute the simplest parts of the field.

Koffka (107, p. 136) gives the following outline of the learning process from the point of view of configuration psychology:

Our direct responses to stimuli are receptor processes which in many cases will be on the mental perceptual level; such a direct response is, however, only the beginning of the total response; the perception issues in action according to its constitution, the action is a natural continuation of the perceptive process and is determined by it and not by pre-established connection bonds. Change of responses to a constant stimulus does not take place by alteration in the function of ready-made devices, but it is a result of a change in the perceptive processes produced by the stimulus. Lastly: a stimulus upsets an equilibrium on the receptive side of the system; this upset equilibrium results in a movement which tends to bring the system to a new equilibrium and consequently the reaction must vary with the way in which the equilibrium was disturbed, that is the receptor process, with the phenomenal situation.

The same author (107, p. 131) reports an interesting experiment which bears out his point of view and seems to refute the reflex-arc explanation of behavior.

Marina dissected the inner and outer muscles of the eyes of monkeys and connected them crossways. An impulse sent to contract the external muscles of the right eye ought now to result in a movement towards the left eye and *vice versa*. Consequently in our experiment the monkey should react just as we predicted; it should look to the left when a bright spot appears at the right. Speaking more generally all the monkey's eye movements in the horizontal should have been the reverse of normal. In reality, however, nothing of the kind took place. As soon as the wounds healed the animal moved his eyes just as normally as it did before the operation. That means that in spite of changes made in the devices, the movements continued to be performed so as to produce the same sort of achievement.

Kohler in his accounts of experiments on apes reports many cases which seem unmistakably opposed to the trial-and-error theory of learning, and to indicate that in this infrahuman species there are definite indications of perception. Trial and error goes on for some time before the problem is solved and then suddenly the ape will make the correct manipulation, at which point, according to Kohler, his whole demeanor will change, his very expression seeming to indicate "Ah, that is the way to get the food," and after that the problem is solved without any errors. Richardson (169) quotes Kohler's experiments with a diagonal string stretched across the front of the ape's cage and attached so that the food could be reached only when the string was brought perpendicular to the front of the cage. Six apes were used and all six first pulled in the direction in which the string led; two then immediately solved the problem by passing the string from hand to hand outside the cage until it could be pulled straight down; two did not reach this correct solution until they had first tried to pull the string down inside the cage, and two did not solve the problem at all. The literature also contains some accounts of infant behavior which seem to bear out the thesis that there is a perceptual or mental element in learning, and anyone who has observed young children is familiar with the affective reactions which often accompany the first solution of a problem and which clearly suggest that the child has seen and grasped the point, or has consciously learned.

EVIDENCE FROM BIOLOGY AND NEUROLOGY

As suggested above, the most recent and scientific work of neurologists and physiologists on the correlation of structure and function of the nervous system, bears out, in outline, an interpretation of behavior which is in general agreement with the fundamental ideas of the Gestalt school of psychology, and which is called the *organismic* concept of the functioning of the nervous system. This theory holds that specific reactions evolve from more primitive total body responses, by a process of differentiation in the nervous system corresponding with its increasing maturation.

Coghill (43, 44), from extensive investigations of the correlation of structure and function in Amblystoma (salamander), has come to the conclusion that "all reflexes emerge as partial or local patterns within an expanding or growing total pattern that normally is from the beginning perfectly integrated." Even when reflexes have emerged out of the total behavior pattern, they are local or partial only overtly; they still remain inherently components of the total pattern, or are under its dominance. Individuation of reflexive behavior out of the total pattern takes place by processes of progressive restriction of the zone of stimulation adequate for the response, and of progressive reduction of the extent of muscular reaction. The growth of individual or of

specific patterns, as responses to local stimulation, involves a corresponding inhibition of the total reaction. When a reflex occurs,
there remains a "nervous equivalent" of the total reaction pattern
which does not assume overt form. Inhibition first begins as a
total pattern and dominates the whole animal; then it gives place,
more or less, to local excitation and permits local reactions, *i. e.,*
first as an overt reaction, then as a quiescent form. Coghill states
his "law of individuation of reflexes out of a total pattern" with
respect to inhibition as follows: "every definitive reflex is the
overt excitatory component of a total pattern that includes the
inhibition of all quiescent parts." This is borne out by the development of the nerve structures. The nervous mechanism of the
total reaction becomes functional first and in early life controls
all behavior. Secondary nervous mechanisms grow into and out
of the nervous matrix, but "this primary mechanism persists as
a clearly recognizable component of the nervous system, and still
sustains its typical relation to the effectors." From all sources of
sensory excitation, terminals grow into the nervous matrix. "Thus
a stimulus from any sense organ may excite the total reaction."
The mechanism of the total reaction is the instrument by means
of which the organism as a whole maintains the integrity of its
behavior pattern. This is accompanied by "the growth of neurones after they have begun to function as conductors." The
nervous matrix is, within the limitation of its intrinsic pattern of
growth, "autonomous in its reaction to its environment and in its
action upon its environment." The primary motor mechanism consists of longitudinal series of neurones on either side of the trunk
(in Amblystoma). They proceed from head tailward, and have
branches which form the motor nerves. The expansion of the total
behavior pattern follows the same cephalo-caudal direction as the
growth of the motor neural mechanisms. In Amblystoma, the
total reaction pattern begins as a contraction of the most anterior
part of the muscles of the trunk. This contraction spreads tailward with the growth of the individual. Particular reactions have
a similar beginning and progress. In the early period, a partial
reaction is not an individuation, but an incomplete execution of
the total pattern, owing to the fact that the mechanism of reac-

tion has not developed throughout the organism. When append-ages develop, the total pattern expands into them so that the appendages move only when the trunk moves. Later differentia-tion occurs, and the appendages acquire patterns of their own which, in response to local stimulation, are. known as reflexes. Motor neurones which control functional muscles, grow by means of new branches into non-functional muscle primordia. When muscles arise from the primordia they are under the dominance of the mechanism of the total behavior pattern.

Coghill (42) concludes that "behavior develops in man as it does in Amblystoma by the expansion of a total pattern that is integrated as a whole from the beginning, and by individuation of partial patterns (reflexes) within the unitary whole."

Coghill's theory of the neural process apparently does not dis-card the reflex-arc-pathway hypothesis entirely, but indicates that the reflex is not the primary neural activity, but a later develop-ment differentiating from the primary mass neural activity or total pattern. Lashley* goes further and believes that he has shown that behavior cannot be explained at all in terms of reflex-arc pathways. Although he finds specific reactions, they cannot be explained in terms of closely demarcated and delimited neural pathways. In all responses and stimulations, there is present a total action of the nervous system which is more than the neural "reflex paths." Coghill asserts that reflexes operate under the dominance of the total pattern, Lashley that the total neural areas function in any behavior. The two workers approached the prob-lem by different methods of investigation, Lashley reaching his conclusions from investigations of the behavioral results of ex-tirpating different areas of the cortex in animals. His work dealt with large fields of behavior patterns, such as maze threading. Coghill traced behavior in Amblystoma from its genesis, and found that in the early stages stimulation of the eyelid, for ex-ample, caused a reaction in the whole body, and that a specific localized reaction was a later development. Lashley, on the other hand, by extirpating various cortical areas, found that habits formed are not dependent upon specific neural areas, but that

* See above, p. 7, n.

there is an "equivalence of stimuli," and one of motor response, and concluded, therefore, that reflexes are not the mechanism of behavior.

Lashley (117) says that cerebral localization explains the results when brain areas are destroyed, but tells us nothing about the functioning of these areas; and he states that the general practice has been to introduce the concepts of association or of reflexes. "The essential feature of the reflex theory is the assumption that individual neurons are specialized for particular functions." Experiments, however, have shown that "a habit is formed by the activation of one set of receptors and executed immediately upon stimulation of an entirely different and unpracticed group." Such experiments have also shown that "The same motor elements are not necessarily used in the learning and the performance of motor habits and . . . motor elements can be utilized directly when no specific associations have been formed with them." He believes, therefore, that the important questions to answer are: How do specialized areas produce the details of behavior with which they are associated, and what are the functional relationships of the different parts and how are they maintained? He answers these questions by suggesting three principles of functioning. First, there are variable degrees of localization. "An area which is highly specialized for one function may play a more generalized role in another." For example, brightness discrimination is abolished in the rat by injury of the area striata only, but the maze habit is also abolished by destroying the same area or any other of equal size. Second, there are functional levels of organization. The fundamental organization for a function may be little altered except in the ease of its arousal. For example, cerebral paralysis in monkeys and in man may be lifted by great emotion. "The paralysis seems to consist of a greater or lesser difficulty in initiating movements whose organization is undisturbed. The emotional facilitation can restore capacity for movement." Third, functions have a relative fragility. "Animal experiments and the clinical material point to the conclusion that a given area may function at different levels of complexity and lesions may limit the complex functions without disturbing the simpler ones." For example, he found that the habit of threading a complex maze is seriously disturbed when more than 15 percent of the cortex is injured, but that the habit of a simple maze is left untouched by lesions of even 50 percent. There is a relational framework in cerebral functioning. "No logically derived element of behavior can be shown to have a definite localization; no single sensation, memory, or skilled movement is destroyed alone by any lesion . . . either a whole constellation of them is affected by the lesion or none at all." These constellations are determined "not by associative bonds but by similarities of organization."

Lashley (117) sums up his point of view in the following words:

Cerebral organization can be described only in terms of relative masses and special arrangements of gross parts, of equilibrium among the parts, of direction and steepness of gradients and of the sensitization of final common paths to patterns of excitation. And the organization must be conceived as a sort of relational framework into which all sorts of specific reactions may fit spontaneously, as the cells of the polyp fit into the general scheme of development. . . . The value of theories in science today depends chiefly upon their adequacy as a classification of unsolved problems, or rather as a grouping of phenomena which present similar problems. Behaviorism has offered one such classification, emphasizing the similarity of psychological and biological problems. Gestalt psychology has stressed a different aspect and reached a different grouping; purposive psychology still another. The facts of cerebral physiology are so varied, so diverse, as to suggest that for some of them each theory is true, for all of them every theory is false.

Irwin (96) says:

On the behavior side the organismic hypothesis waits for a body of experimental results from investigations in these two fields comparable to that on the morphological side. The problem of differentiation of behavior is analogous to the problem of the differentiation of protoplasm or of the nervous system; yet until psychologists specifically show what are actually the processes whereby differentiation of human behavior proceeds, the relation will remain that of mere analogy.

He believes that experimentation which may establish more than a mere analogy should concern itself with establishing the temporal order of differentiations of human behavior from the early mass stages, and with the nature of the transformation into their specific, more finely graded, and better-patterned aspects. His conclusions as to the probable processes of behavior growth, based on studies of such patterns as crying, grasping, feeding responses, and his own studies of neonatal activity, are that:

Patterns differentiate from a primitive general matrix of behavior called mass activity. Mass activity is at its maximum during the first fetal months, and during uterine existence the differentiation of activity into patterns is under way. After birth the processes of differentiation proceed with increasing degrees of specificity, definiteness, and preciseness of pattern until they attain the degree of maturity which we recognize in the adaptive behavior of the organism. However, the fact should be emphasized that experimental evidence for an organismic view from studies on human behavior are only beginning to accumulate. The organismic theory of human behavior needs the clarification which can come from detailed and separate investigations of the kind suggested. The crucial point of attack is an experimental analysis of the processes of pattern differentiation during the first year of life. A radiate theory of pattern differentiation is suggested as a tentative guide to this type of analysis.

He believes that evidence bears out the fact that this radiation of pattern differentiation, from birth on, proceeds in several directions. Grasping, for example, is the last stage in a process of differentiation which begins in the shoulder and upper arm, and the adult plantar response is the final stage of a differentiation that begins in the hips and progresses distally in the legs. He suggests that differentiation may also occur in an anterior direction from the trunk, and that in the trunk itself differentiation originates in the cervical region and progresses through the thoracic segments to the lumbar-sacral muscles. In other words, he believes that what behavioral evidence there is points to the fact that differentiation of behavior proceeds radially in the human, in the same way that maturation of the nervous system has been found to take place.

CORRELATION OF STRUCTURE AND FUNCTION FROM ANIMAL STUDIES

Studies of the correlation of structure and function in human beings are today so meager that it is to such studies on animals that we must look for practically all our information on the subject. The available evidence bears out the fact that in general outline the development of the nervous system of man corresponds to that of animals, and that the processes of growth are the same and follow the same general course in man as in animals.

Tilney is working on an extensive investigation of the correlation of structure and function in the brain of mammals (the opossum, rat, guinea pig, pig, cat, and man), in order to establish a sound neurological basis for tracing the development of behavior. Since the development of the cortex is greater in mammals than in other animals, he believes that many of the problems concerning the processes of growth will be solved if the phylogenetic and the ontogenetic development of this organ is established. Writing with Kubie, he says (195):

It is unquestionably true that all stages in the genesis and development of the brain must have important bearings upon the ultimate interpretation in the realm of behavior. These stages are the indispensable foundations upon which the maturing processes in the cerebrum are developed.

These authors point out that although the brain is the fundamental element in behavioral capacity, "the structures of the entire body must be given their proper values."

To date, the published results of Tilney's studies apply to some general work on the phylogenetic development of the cerebellum, to the cat and to the rat. His work is concerned with the specific details of the ontogenetic relationship between the structure of the nervous system and the behavior of the organism. He states (192) that it is probable that, with certain modifications determined by the order to which the animal belongs, the same control of behavior may be observed in the course of all mammalian development. He accepts Minkowski's eight stages in the development of reflex activity (given below, in the discussions of fetal behavior and of the plantar reflex), and says that two important considerations concerning correlations between structure of the brain and behavior should be borne in mind:

First, that a large integrative element operates in the neural control of all reactions and that each part of the neuraxis, including spinal cord, hindbrain, midbrain, interbrain, and endbrain, contributes its specific innervation to this control. Second, that the structures of the endbrain assume an increasingly important role in the regulation of behavior during the developmental process.

He considers the brain and the behavior of the animals studied, from this standpoint.

The cerebellum, he believes (193), "made its appearance at some critical period during the invertebrovertebrate transition in response to certain functional necessities which did not exist in the invertebrate," and that this mechanism has as its function the maintenance of posture in all types of motor activity. The cerebellum medialis governs the posture-maintaining function of inherent automatic associated movement; the cerebellum laterales governs the posture-maintaining function of acquired independent movement, especially in the arms and legs. "It has reached greatest development in man, whose capacity in acquired skilled acts with hands and feet far surpasses that of all other animals."

His paper on the rat (192) is the first report to trace the correlation of structure and function from the earliest embryological to the adult period. He states that: "A structural adequacy in the nervous system is essential to the several activities which make their appearance in the different periods of development and . . . such adequacy is founded upon the neural capacity for afferent conduction, neuraxial integration, and efferent transmission." In following the developmental processes of the brain parts, he found three significant phases in the development of the cerebral cortex, each representing a distinct period in the upbuilding of behavior. The first phase, *embryonic and fetal,* is one of general cortical differentiation. During this phase, the first reactions are circumscribed muscular twitchings, which then manifest more definitely reflex qualities, and are finally characterized by simple but distinctly integrated responses to stimulation. The structural immaturity in the hemispheres, interbrain, midbrain and cerebellum during this period warrants the exclusion of these structures in the control of behavior. Such influence as the nervous system exercises over the reactions of the animal he, therefore, attributes to the more advanced conditions of development in the segments of the spinal cord and in the caudal portion of the brain stem.

The second phase, that of *divisional cortical differentiation*, begins at birth in the albino rat, and continues into the fifth or sixth postnatal day. During this phase, the animal develops activities adequate for immediate adaptation to extra-uterine life, such as breathing, crawling, righting and sucking. The four major divisions of the cerebral cortex are now well defined, but too immature to permit of decisive activity in the regulation of behavior. Immediately after birth, reactions can be attributed to the spinal cord, to the caudal portion of the brain stem and to the tegmentum of the midbrain. Late in this phase, the rat develops greater vigor in its postural and situational activities, locomotion becomes more effective, although all the movements still retain the original neonatal paddling characteristics. Ineffectual attempts at scratching also appear during this phase.

The third phase, that of *local cortical differentiation*, begins on or about the fifth postnatal day and is well advanced by the tenth day. It results in the ultimate differentiation of thirty-one distinct cortical areas. Myelinization slowly advances in the nerve roots, spinal cord, caudal portions of the brain stem, and cerebellum. It then spreads to the midbrain and still later to the cerebral hemispheres. In the endbrain, the first fibers to be myelinated are the lateral olfactory tract, the septal fasciculi, the anterior commissure, the median forebrain brindle, and the mesial portion of the centrum ovale. Myelin appears later in the optic fibers, the lateral forebrain brindle, corpus collosum and intracortical radiation. The lateral portion of the centrum ovale and the intercortical fibers are the last to become myelinized. While local cortical differentiation is in process, the animal gradually increases the number and effectiveness of its reactions until it has acquired the full repertory of its postural, nutritional, locomotor, exploratory, play, sexual, parental, and protective activities. As it slowly emerges from this phase, it manifests an increasing number of adaptations in which discrimination is progressively more evident. The more rapid advances toward maturity seen in the neuraxial segments indicate the importance of the spinal cord and brain stem in fetal and early postnatal activities. Ultimate specialization in the hemispheres serves to expand and amplify these activities. In many respects the cortical differentiation in the adult albino rat is extremely primitive. This undoubtedly accounts for the comparatively limited rôle of the cortex in the neural integrations which control the somatic behavior of this animal. This general outline of correlation between structure and function in the rat, Tilney bases on careful detailed investigation of the animals from earliest fetal life until the adult stage of adaptation is reached. These correlations can be illustrated specifically by his investigation of tail compression at all the stages of development.

The eighteenth to nineteenth days of fetal life mark the transition from the inactive to the active period of somatic behavior, with a corresponding adequacy in the structural organization of the nervous system for segmental reflex response, and for a certain degree of intersegmental integration. At this stage, compression of the tail causes reactions similar to those evoked by any stimulation of the fetus, an extension of the head with opening of the mouth and a slight extension of the trunk, and a series of alternating rhythmical flexions of head and trunk to right and left. At this age, the spinal cord and caudal portion of the brain stem are provided with afferent and efferent connections, and sufficiently differentiated in nerve cells to account for the segmental reactions. At the twenty-first fetal day, just before birth, compression of the tail still gives reactions similar to those following stimulation of any segment, but they are now much more vigorous and sustained and are executed with more speed, and each lateral flexion of the trunk draws the head and hind quarters much closer together. Judging from the cellular organization in the different parts of the nervous system, the spinal cord and caudal portions of the brain stem still exercise predominant control over somatic reactions, though it is possible that the cerebral hemispheres may to some extent contribute to the regulation of behavior.

Compression of the tail on the first day after birth causes the animal to emit a sharp squeak, and it is at once thrown into a convulsive state.

Forceful clonic contractions affect the muscles of the neck, trunk and limbs. The young rat is turned over and sprawls upon its back, convulsively struggling to right itself. Should it succeed in doing so it makes violent efforts to move forward, only to be immediately overthrown again by the convulsive activity of the muscles. . . . Three characteristics in the response to this type of stimulation are noteworthy: (1) the apparent participation of the entire somatic musculature; (2) the violent, convulsive nature of the reaction; (3) the protracted duration of the effects produced by the stimulus.

At this stage, Tilney concludes that the midbrain is the most likely higher level of the neuraxis to participate in activities. The nature of the reactions to tail compression indicate that the nervous system is still devoid of selective inhibitory qualities, and points to a level of neural organization above that of the immediate, direct-reflex response, but below that of highly integrated reactions. On the fifth day, compression of the tail still elicits a convulsive reaction, but the head and anterior part of the trunk are not involved as vigorously as previously, and the forelegs also show less convulsive contractions. Selective restriction of the response has begun and, although some fraction of the stimulus has gained access to a higher correlating center, it is not yet sufficient to show what will be apparent later, that the response is in essence an avoiding reaction from its inception. Behavior now implies the participation of the thalamus, and probably of the corpus striatum and the paleocortex, as well as activities of the segmented portions of the neuraxis.

At ten days of age, compression of the tail gives reactions still further restricted to the rump and hind legs, most of the earlier convulsive character of the response being now limited to forceful wagging of the tail, and the disorganizing effects upon the motor stability of the animal being much reduced. The body response is a short start forward away from the stimulus, a sharp squeak and pelvic wriggling of short duration. This change indicates a more direct and adequate conduction of impulses to correlating centers, with a simultaneous diversion of much of the original segmental overflow; the effector response, however, Tilney states, must be attributed to correlation centers lower than the cortex, either in the striatum or the tegmentum of the midbrain. On the fifteenth day, the reaction to tail compression is a well-defined avoidance reaction accompanied by a slight squeak. The rat runs away from the stimulus, and, in some instances, after running a short distance turns around to face the source of stimulation. Structural organization shows that the parietal area of the neocortex has now assumed a rôle in the correlation of body sense, and that the cerebral cortex now plays a more decisive part in regulation of behavior.

By the twentieth day, the response to tail compression is entirely devoid of all the former diffuse wigglings, and the animal immediately turns to direct its head to the source of stimulation as if in readiness to fight; even the squeaking has now disappeared. Responses at this age show most of the characteristics of the adult rat, although there is still a greater degree of restlessness than at maturity. Investigation of the nervous tissues shows that, at this age, the cerebral cortex has at last assumed an unmistakable predominance in the control of behavior. In the adult rat, unless the tail is compressed with considerable force, there appears to be no response. When force is applied, the animal withdraws the tail and turns its head toward the stimulus. The tail of the adult rat is much tougher than that of the young animal and biting the tail is a very conspicuous feature of the play of rats, so that the stimulus value of compression appears gradually to diminish in importance until, unless it is severe, it does not enter into the discriminatory selections which influence behavior. Tilney says: "No single reaction observed in the development of the albino rat reveals more graphically the ontogenetic correlations between behavior and the structure of the nervous system than the response to compression of the tail throughout the several stages of growth."

Tilney has been criticized by some investigators as postulating that reactions are synchronous with the appearance of myelin in the controlling mechanisms, while they have shown that some of these reactions can be elicited in utero before myelinization has occurred. In his paper on the rat (192), Tilney explains his theory of the relation between myelin and function as follows:

Although it is unquestionably true that myelin is not essential to impulse conduction through the tract beds, the deposition of this ensheathing substance appears to bear a definite relation to the efficacy of transmission by means of the several conduction systems of the neuraxis. As a general rule those fiber systems of the greatest phyletic age are first to acquire their myelin sheaths. Whether these sheaths are merely an expression of the growth process in nerve fibers or are an index of their capacity for conduction, there can be no dispute that they are a late manifestation in the maturation of those neurones whose axis cylinders become myelinized. Viewed in this light, the myelin sheath affords valuable evidence concerning the degree of neurone maturity. The unmyelinized axone, belonging to a system which ultimately becomes myelinated, is part of a young and immature neurone. The myelinized axone is part of a mature neurone or one approaching maturity.

And later:

The transmission of impulses may occur through axones which fail to develop myelin sheaths as well as through axones before they have ultimately acquired such sheaths. The appearance of myelin in the intercortical fiber system, therefore, does not imply that the conduction of impulses between the cells of the cortex is primarily dependent upon myelinization. It does, however, indicate that the neurones of which such myelinated fibers are parts, have attained an advanced degree of differentiation and for this reason have increased their functional capacity. Consequently the appearance of myelinized intercortical fibers has critical significance as a gauge of cortical maturity.

Tilney and Casamajor (194) have published the results of their work on the correlation of myelinization and behavior in the kitten. The behavior studied at birth was the postural, the crawling approach, and sucking. The myelinized fibers were the ventral and dorsal roots of all cranial and spinal nerves, posterior longitudinal fasciculus, predorsal fasciculus, descending spinal tract or trigeminal nerve, and trigeminonaesencephalic tract, deiterospinal fibers, and the fibers of the acoustic system as far cephalad as the inferior colliculus. On the sixth day the myelinized fibers were the ventral and dorsal spinocerebellar tracts, ipsilateral fibers from the dorsal column nuclei of Goll and Burdack to the inferior cerebellar peduncle, the juxtarestiform fibers, the dentatorubral fibers entering the superior cerebellar peduncle, the rubrispinal fibers, the mesial fillet and spinothalmic fibers as far as the midbrain only, and the optico-oculmotor fibers. The reactions appearing on the seventh day were synergizing, primitive escape, and eye-opening. The authors mention as especially striking the synchronization of the myelin in (1) the spinocerebellar tracts, the vermis of the cerebellum, the superior cerebellar peduncle, and the rubrospinal tract with the synergizing reaction; (2) the spinothalamic tract with the primitive escape reaction; and (3) the optic nerves and tract with the eye-opening reaction. In the study published with Kubie (195), Tilney says that it is an "obvious fact that all structures of the body must attain adequate differentiation before they are capable of specialized reaction." The cells in the spinal cord and brain stem or segmental portions acquire myelin at an earlier period than those in the suprasegmental portions, especially those in the cerebral cortex.

In this same study Tilney and Kubie present the results of investigation of the developmental processes in the endbrain of the cat, resulting in the formation of the paleocortex, the archicortex and the neocortex. The processes pass through three and four-layer stages of ichthyopsid and reptilian conditions before attaining the mammalian six-layer cortex. They believe that the individual cortical layers have specific functions.

In our study of the developing fiber tracts we find much to corroborate this interpretation, more particularly as it applies to the efferent functions of the deep inner layers. It seems probable that a still more exact estimation of the functional significance of each layer will eventually be forthcoming. The sensory exigencies of mammalian specialization may, therefore, be conceived to explain the early development of the neocortex and the relatively late appearance of the archicortex. This viewpoint is supported by facts revealed in the genesis and development of the fiber tracts.

They find that the functional evolution of the neocortex in the cat, and presumably in all mammals, depends on (1) "the projection of the senses upon specialized neocortical areas, in which process general body sense precedes the special senses"; (2) "the bilateral association of these senses in the two hemispheres in

which again body sense takes precedence over the special senses";
(3) "intimate associations and elaborations within each type of
sense as well as interassociations between all of the senses"; (4)
"the efferent projection of sensory associations into the somatic
effector activities of the animal's behavior." They conclude that
the efferent projection system connected with general body sense
appears before the afferent projection system of the special senses,
as shown by the development of tract-beds related to the neocortex, and that the interhemisphereal fibers of the neocortex are
the last to appear in prenatal life.

Coghill* has made extensive investigations of the correlation
of structure and function in Amblystoma. He finds (32, 33) the
afferent system of this animal to be part of a definite reflex mechanism. The chief correlations he mentions are the "extension of
the root fibers of the trigeminal nerve into the immediate vicinity
of the motor centers in the lower portion of the medulla oblongata" with the first influence of the receptor field of that nerve
upon behavior, and that of response to light with the first fibers
of the optic nerve reaching the brain. He has disproved the accepted tradition that the floor plate of the vertebrate embryo is
non-nervous (34). He finds that it alone forms the commissure
and that the floor-plate cells continue to grow after they become
functional. "Nervous function does not preclude the possibility
of growth and differentiation in nerve cells," and "the development of the behavior pattern in Amblystoma involves definitely
and certainly the growth and differentiation of specific neurones
while they function as conductors."

The behavior pattern (35) develops in a regular sequential
order, and the progression of muscular contraction cephalo-
caudad, which makes locomotion possible, is explained by the
"structure of the primary motor track, which consists of neurones
with axones directed caudad and collaterals as primary root fibers

* See Bibliography, and *Anatomy and the problem of behavior*, Cambridge, Eng-
land, Univ. Press; New York, Macmillan, 1929, pp. xi-113; "Correlated anatomical and physiological studies of the growth of the nervous system of Amphibia.
VI. The mechanism of integration in Amblystoma punctatum," *J. Comp. Neur.*,
1926, Vol. 41, pp. 95-152; "The structural basis of the integration of behavior,"
Proc. Nat. Acad. Sci., 1930, Vol. 16, pp. 637-643.

to the myotomes." From his studies of the rates of differentiation and proliferation, he reports that there are definite centers for the steps leading up to and including locomotion; that there is a fundamental unity in the cerebrum, sharply differentiated from the rest of the central nervous system; that there is a fundamental unity of the rhombencephalon with the rostral seven to nine segments of the cord; that new accomplishments in behavior are acquired synchronously with marked acceleration in the cerebrum; and that growth, not functional conduction, is what stimulates further nervous development: "The stimulating influence of ingrowing nerve roots and tracts probably has origin in the growth phase rather than the conduction phase of metabolism."

Coghill (36) states that the entire pattern, including visceral, tegmental, somatic, primary motor, and floor-plate cells, develops in a series of eleven localized centers of differentiation, of which three are auditory and eight postauditory. Even in the non-motile stage, when there is no response to afferent stimulation, all but three of these centers can be seen. "The visceral and somatic systems are obviously differentiating under a common factor of controls which appears to be inherent in the nervous system." The center (37) which ultimately forms the cerebellum is one of those perceptible in the non-motile stage. He also points out (38) that the "cytomorphosis of the neuro-epithelial cell in its involvement with the external limiting membrane must be regarded as a dynamic process doing work" and, considering bio-electrical studies on other organisms, suggests the hypothesis that fluctuations in rate of differentiation involve fluctuations of electropotential along the external limiting membrane. Before (39) any afferent fibers come to the cerebrum there are at least two efferent systems, the motor and tectobulbar tracts. The primary development of both the association and the peripheral sensory systems is centrifugal, that is, toward the receptor field in sensory elements, and toward the motor field in the association of elements. This means that the "individual acts on its environment before it reacts to its environment." An integrated action (41) of fore and hind legs with action of the trunk is "a typical postural reaction and it occurs before a local reflex of the hind leg can be excited." The walking posture, and often walking itself, can be seen before it is possible to excite local exteroceptive reflexes of the hind legs. The plantar reflex begins as an action of the leg as a whole.

Coghill (40) believes that the fact that excitation of overt behavior by efferent nerves before stimulation by afferent nerves is possible, must mean that the efferent nerves are stimulated by products of the metabolism of the organism. "Behavior in response to such stimulation is spontaneous in the sense that it is the expression of the intrinsic dynamics of the organism as a whole." His study of behavior from its beginning "leads inevitably to the conception that the organism is primarily a unit, and that normality requires that all parts be approximately subject to the organism as a whole, or conversely, that the organism as a whole retain its power of activating the behavior of its parts." The mechanism of the total pattern is an essential component of the performance of the part, *i.e.*, the reflex. Behavior cannot be fully expressed in terms of stimuli-response bonds, nor can sensory-motor response be regarded as the whole function of the nervous system. He concludes that:

In so far as the correlation of nervous structure and function in the development of the individual has been carried, structural provision has been found for the perpetuation of spontaneity, autonomy, or initiative as a factor in behavior. Any theory of motivation, therefore, that attributes this function wholly to the environment, is grossly inadequate.

Tracy (196) has made a study of the toadfish, which has a very long period of endogenous activity as compared to Amblystoma, so that the movements occurring while the organism is still in the embryonic condition can be studied with ease.

In the case of these movements, we are dealing with activity which is obviously not a "tropism." . . . That there is a mechanism of motility activated from within can therefore be demonstrated and . . . subjected to observation and experimental analysis.

These endogenous body movements "form a continuous ontogenetic series with the 'voluntary' movements of the adult," and the motility type depends on a specific organization pattern peculiar to the species. Tracy suggests that the activity, which seems to react to excess or to deficiency of CO_2, is determined by metabolic conditions in the nerve cells and the surrounding fluids. Meanwhile, the afferent system grows gradually until it finally "captures" the primitive motor system. There are, therefore, two components of behavior: *endogenous* activity, the fundamental motility conditioned by inner physiological adjustments; and exogenous activity, the oriented activity which is a modification of endogenous activity enabling the organism to respond to external stimuli. Like Coghill, Tracy sees the endogenous activity as persisting and fundamental even after the afferent system has become functional. He finds that the segmental reflex is the last type of activity to develop. He also experimented with the cunner, which is free-swimming in the larval stage. On the first day of free-swimming, the embryo darts about in the water but gives no response to stimuli. On the second day one response only is present, an avoidance reaction to touch on the snout. Thus,

in this species we have a demonstration under natural conditions of a freely moving organism without an effective exteroceptive mechanism. . . . The young organism makes its first burst into freedom and begins active excursions at random in its environment at the behest of impulses which arise within itself.

Coghill (40) commenting on Tracy's work says: "Since the stimulating agency is a product of the metabolism of the entire organism, the motor nerve cells, being without definitive nervous stimulation, are purely means by which the organism as a whole drives its special parts to action."

Among the higher forms, the opossum presents the best opportunity for observation of immature individuals because of the relatively long fetal development in the pouch after birth. Langworthy (113) investigated the relation of myelin and function in this animal. He notes complex behavior in the newborn opossum before any myelinated fibers are present. The animals climb into the pouch, find and attach themselves to nipples and obtain nourishment, coördinate the forelegs, move the head widely from side to side, and perform other gross muscular movements. The appearance of myelin follows the order of phylogenetic development. The motor cells and nuclei are myelinated before there is any myelinated afferent connection. In sensory pathways, the primary neurone is myelinated first. Tracts seem to become medullated as they become functional, which Langworthy believes applies also to humans.

Swenson (187), from studies of the albino-rat fetus, concludes that each simple movement first appears in a definite position in a certain serial order of simple movements. When any simple movement has once appeared, "It persists in kind of movements, but its qualities change with the development of the animal." These movements go to build up the fundamental activities of progression, respiration and ingestion, which the newborn animal will need at once. He states (188) that there is a definite chronological order for the appearance of movements in the albino-rat fetus, and that these are obscured when one tries to study the kinds of movements and the qualities of movements at the same time. He classifies four stages of fetal behavior: (1) non-motile; (2) early motile, which is bilateral; (3) dorsoventral or extensor-flexor; and (4) rotation; and he believes that it is more satisfactory to study the fetus by these stages than by size or age.

Lashley has worked with the rat, correlating behavior with operatively induced brain lesions. He found (119) that summation of activities took place, no matter what association fiber groups were cut. For example, the rat's loss of capacity for learning visual habits, measured by difficulty of retraining, was found to be closely proportional to the extent of the cortical lesion and independent of the locus. He points out that the transfer of pattern discrimination—as when, for example, a rat which was conditioned to jump to a white erect triangular surface and to avoid an inverted one, chose the correct one without trial and error, when presented with the same shapes but smaller and in outline only—shows that there is no strict correspondence between neurones and functions. In a paper with McCarthy (120) he reports that in both seeing and blind animals there was perfect retention of the maze habit after the cerebellum was seriously injured. One animal with the cerebellum completely destroyed learned to run the maze without error. They conclude that "There is no evidence that the cerebellum plays any part in the performance of the maze habit." Lashley (117) regards it as futile to base psychological explanations on assumption of connections of reflex pathways, since (1) it can be shown to be indifferent, in a habit, which receptor cells get the stimulus and which motor cells execute the action, one set of cells learning the response and any other set performing it; and (2) extirpation and section experiments show that loss of habits depends more on the amount of destruction than on the severing of any possible definite conduction paths. He concludes that nervous tissue seems to exercise a facilitating effect on other nervous tissue, in addition to its specific function; for example, the maze habit was destroyed in a blind rat by a lesion in the visual cortex, but not in a normal rat by blinding.

Maier (131) has made an apparently somewhat similar study, but he expresses his conclusions in general terms as to the effect of cerebral destruction on reasoning and learning in rats. He states that reasoning ability was profoundly affected when the destruction exceeded 18 percent of the exposed surface of the brain, but that learning ability was not affected by lesions as great as 40 percent.

Angulo y Gonzales (3) found correlation between the stages of behavior development and the grouping of motor cells in the cord of the albino-rat fetus as follows:

Age 14 days: Non-motile stage: Motor cells in a cluster without grouping

Age 15 days: Motion of trunk: motor cells in three distinct groups in medial part of cluster

Age 16 days: Move trunk and fore limb: motor cells show grouping in lateral part of cluster

Age 17 days: Ventral flexion of trunk, extension of head: six cell groups visible, with indication of subdivision

Age 19 days: Discrete reflexes: motor cells now grouped are of adult type

At birth, he found (4), the motor cells showed no segmental arrangement corresponding to that of the spinal motor nerves. In transverse sections, they divide into fairly well-defined groups; in longitudinal sections, they form nearly continuous columns. Some columns extend the whole length of the cord, some are only in the cervical enlargement. From the fifth cervical to the first dorsal there are more columns than above that level. There is some fusion between some of the columns. He believes that the anatomical differentiation of these columns is associated with or governs the morphological differentiation of the musculature, and that, to determine their functional significance, study of progressive development in embryo is necessary. At eighteen days he found no response to tactile stimulation of hands, at nineteen days the response was present, and half a day later there were reflexes. At this time there was no response to tactile stimulation of hind legs. Ligation of the cord produced movements in parts not yet responding to tactile stimulation. He concludes that the motor nerve reaches parts before the sensory nerve, and that centers can be directly reached by CO_2.

Langworthy (116) found a correlation between decerebrate rigidity and myelinization in the rubrospinal tract in young rabbits, guinea pigs and kittens. Before myelinization, decerebration was followed by movements of progression and active reflexes. Laughton (121) found that for normal coördinated progression in the rabbit, the cephalic two-thirds of the pontine region must be intact. The shock of decerebration had a phylogenetic grading, being less in rabbits than in cats, and less in cats than in dogs. Kittens and pups show little shock. The cat and dog need the caudal two-thirds of the thalamus for normal progression. Laughton lays the difference between the controlling centers in rabbits and in cats and dogs to the fact that the carnivores need great precision in natural movements in order to be successful in stalking, springing and seizing their prey, as well as in defense; that is, it is the difference in habits that renders the rabbit brain more primitive.

East (54) concludes, from a study of the initiation of movement in rat embryos, that there is no significant correlation of initial movement with myelinization, with reflex-arc formation, with extent of distribution of nerve fibers, with the histological development of muscle, nor with "nissl bodies" or Nissl substance. She suggests that it is possible that nerve endings are the immediate essential factor, but that it is more probable that a chemical change, following a given morphological status, is the final cause.

Windle (211) correlated the developing movements in kittens from birth to the one-hundred-and-twenty-ninth day with the maturation of centers in the gray matter of the cord, as studied by the silver method. Precision and control of movements was correlated with pericellular plexuses, proliferation of fine fibers, end bulbs, and myelin sheaths. He calls attention to the fact that although the newborn kitten does not coördinate the fore and hind legs in crawling to its mother, it has the capacity for such coördination, which it shows if forced to swim. He (210) also finds the gradual development of spinal reflex-arcs correlated with the development of movement. "Just as the first reflex mechanism is largely a unisegmental one, the first movement is a simple one, and later activity involves a greater number of segments at the time when larger numbers of collaterals develop toward the medial end of the funiculus." Coincident with more complicated movements, come specialization of mantle-layer neurolblasts into groups and appearance of reflex-arcs with four neurones.

Windle and Griffin (213) found the first movement of the fetal cat to be ventrolateral neck-bending (at 16 mm.). This and the later supposed fishlike motions are prototypes of swimming, not of righting. The first prototype of the sucking reaction occurs at 60 mm. These authors agree with Coghill that growth is by individuation of the more discrete unit reflexes from the total patterns. "Functional motor differentiation proceeds cephalocaudally and proximodistally, and is followed similarly by the spread of sensory reception areas."

Windle and Fish (212) divide the righting reflex into two types, as Magnus does, one responding to exteroceptive and proprioceptive stimuli from the end organs of trunk, neck and head, and the other responding to vestibular stimuli. Testing by observations on a table and in water, and after destruction of the labyrinths and of section of the spinal cord, they conclude that the non-vestibular function matures before the vestibular.

Hinsey, McNattin and Ranson (87) have also studied the mechanism of walking, in the cat. They state that it is generally admitted that the thalamic cat and the midbrain rabbit exhibit fairly normal progression. They found that, by making sections at different levels through the brain stem of the adult cat, the most caudal plane of section that could be made and still leave the walking pattern intact, was one extending from the rostral border of the superior colliculi to the rostral portion of the mammillary bodies. Some of the prespinal centers which remained and which should be considered as possibly involved in walking and in the regulation of tonus were: the red nucleus and the hypothalamic centers remaining; the substantia reticularis; the tectum; the cerebellum; and the vestibular system. The authors conclude that the upper part of the mesencephalic tegmentum and possibly its continuation into the gyothalamus are necessary for the regulation of tonus and the maintenance of equilibrium which make locomotion possible.

Ranson (166) has studied rigidity, as caused by pyramidal lesions in the cat. He found that, after an extensive lesion in the pyramid of the medulla oblongata, the cat is still able to use the four legs in walking, and that the impairment of function is slight. Extensor rigidity was found only in special conditions, when the cat was not supporting its own weight. In another study, Ranson and Ingram (92) conclude that, while the red nucleus is important in regulating postural tonus, it is part of a more complex system governing this function. Ranson, Muir and Zeiss (167) found substantial, but not conclusive, evidence that the tone-inhibiting impulses reach the cord via the cortico-spinal rather than the rubro tract.

This is only a brief review of some of the more important work on correlation of structure and function in vertebrate animals. There are many interesting analogies from animal to human behavior, but a review of the literature on animal behavior is beyond the scope of this summary. However, the investigations of human fetal behavior are so few compared with those on animals that Coronios' (45) very general description of the growth of behavior in the cat is quoted. Carmichael (29) says from his complete survey of the literature that this presents a marked similarity with the fetal behavior observed in Amblystoma and all other animals that have been studied.

1. Before birth there is rapid, progressive, and continuous development of behavior in the fetus of the cat.

2. The development of behavior progresses from a diffuse, massive, variable, relatively uncoordinated state to a condition when many of the reactions are more regular in their appearance, less variable, better coordinated, and relatively individualized.

3. In the early stages of prenatal development the behavior appears to be progressing along a cephalocaudal course.

4. Behavior development appears first in the gross musculature and in the finer musculature later.

5. Behavior develops in each of the limbs from a proximal to a distal point; that is, the entire limb is first involved in the response and then gradually the more distal joints become, as it were, independent of the total movement.

It will be seen that these conclusions as to the course of the growth of fetal behavior correspond very closely to Minkowski's findings as to human fetal behavior, and to Irwin's conclusions as to growth, based on his studies of mass activity in the newborn and on the literature on neonatal behavior.

Part II

BEHAVIOR OF THE HUMAN FETUS

II

BEHAVIOR OF THE HUMAN FETUS

IF WE are to study behavior with any hope of acquiring definite knowledge of the progressive development of the various growth patterns and their relation to one another, we must start the study at the point where the life of the organism begins. The studies of animal and human fetal behavior and development have shown conclusively that life after birth is but a continuation of the processes operating in the growth of the embryo up to the time of birth. Minkowski's outline of the development of response to plantar stimulation, from the first reactions of the fetus to the adult form, is one of the few pictures of the sequential development of a growth pattern that has been made. There is, however, ample evidence that the responses which are found at the time of birth are, many of them, present in operatively removed fetuses sometime before birth takes place, and studies have shown that the reactions of infants born before term, yet old enough to be viable, are not different in kind from those of infants born at term.

Bersot (10) emphasizes the continuity of intrauterine with extrauterine life. Each function, reactivity, breathing, digestion, and so on, is slowly established in utero. By the change in the relationship of mutual dependency, it is transformed, perfected or regresses. The functions and reactions which take place after birth are only the continuation of those which take place in fetal life. Even the first breathing movement after birth is not a sudden apparition, but a continuation of the thoracic movements observed in the fetus. In a baby born before term, the great increase in number and diversity of external stimuli serves to awaken a greatly increased reactivity, just as it does in the infant born at term, an increase which is necessary for maintenance of life in the new medium. Kuo (110) states that "the development of

behavior is an absolutely gradual and continuous process," starting in embryonic life.

The moment at which the mental or neural behavior of an individual begins is still a matter of speculation among scientists.
Such behavior is the result of stages of development which have
preceded it, the development of the germ cells in the parents, the
fertilization, cell division, differentiation and migration, and the
organ formations which made the response possible. Carmichael
(29, p.33) says:

Thus, so far as the zero point of development is concerned, it must be
remembered that before fertilization events are occuring that are significant in building the new organism, and hence present a series of
possible zero points. After fertilization the first external movement is
also a possible zero point, but certainly not one that is absolutely placed,
for there is evidence that development occurs in a dynamic continuum
of relationships between organism and environment. Practically, then,
for all the difficulty of determination, the time of fertilization is probably best taken as the zero point of these processes which are to produce the new individual.

The exact age of a fetus, calculated from the moment of the
union of nuclei of the two parent cells cannot be absolutely determined. Different writers suggest different methods of calculat-
ing the time of union of the nuclei. Carmichael (29) states that
the present evidence points to the fact that fertilization occurs in
less than forty-eight hours after copulation. Estimates of fetal
age are given in the literature in terms of the month of pregnancy
and of the length of the fetus. Growth factors influence the size
of the fetus before birth just as they do after, and there is considerable variation in possible ages for a given length, especially
during the first weeks. Carmichael (29) gives Mall's table, published in 1910, and Needham's chart, redrawn from Scammon
and Calkins work, published in 1929, as the most reliable data on
which to estimate fetal age from length. The normal crown-heel
length at birth is given as approximately 500 mm. A further
variable in estimating fetal age is the large variation in the length
of normal pregnancies, which may be as great as 154 days.

The literature on human fetal behavior is rather meager, owing to the difficulties of investigation. The information which can be obtained about the living fetus within the mother's body is necessarily limited to her reports of the fetal movements which she directly experiences, and to sounds of heartbeats and a few other indications that can be obtained by palpation and the use of instruments on the body wall of the mother. Direct observations of the responses of fetuses to stimulation and manipulation are limited to material that can be obtained when a diseased condition in the mother makes artificial termination of pregnancy necessary. Minkowski, and Bolaffio and Artom, have published the most extensive reports of the results of direct investigation of living human fetuses. Minkowski's procedure is typical. The fetus is taken while still alive from the body of the mother, for whom such an operation is necessary, by Cesarean section under local anesthetic. The fetus is placed in a bath of physiological salt solution at normal blood temperature, in order to prolong life and make investigation possible. This procedure, however, cuts the fetus off from its oxygen supply and, according to Minkowski, the movements which are observed must be thought of as movements of an increasingly asphyxiated organism with increasing metabolites in the blood, which at first lead to hyperactivity and then to hypoactivity.

Primary Fetal Movements and Responses

The literature indicates that somatic behavior begins at some time during the first two months of intrauterine life. The germinal stage is considered to end at the end of the second week, when the true fetal period begins as the medullary groove begins to form. Shortly after this the cerebral and optic vesicles begin to be differentiated, and the earliest form of the heart appears. By the end of the third week the limb buds begin to appear; meanwhile, the fine structure of the muscles is differentiating. In 1877 Pfluger, according to Carmichael (29), demonstrated the heartbeat in the fetus as beginning in the third week, or in one of approximately 4 mm length. This point, however, cannot be taken as the beginning of behavioral life. Parker (149) states that the best evidence indicates that the early embryonic heartbeat is essentially an independent muscle contraction. Feldman (57), in summarizing earlier investigations on the fetal heartbeat, says that the phenomenon was discovered by a Swiss physician, and that its importance was first brought out by Kergaradec in 1822. The latter concluded that the fetal heartbeat could be heard through the body wall of the mother from the eighteenth week on.

According to Carmichael (29), the earliest recorded movements of operatively removed fetuses are a movement of the right arm, noted by Yanase in a fetus of 20 mm (about six weeks of age), and a case of extrauterine pregnancy reported by Strassman, who noted, through a rupture in the tube wall, slow backwards-and-forwards movements of the arms and legs of a fetus of 22 mm. Carmichael doubts the complete reliability of these two reports. Minkowski (141), however, observed a wormlike movement of the arms, legs and trunk in a fetus of 30 mm, about eight weeks of age. In two fetuses of 15 mm length, he reports (138) that it was impossible to bring about any muscular response to an electric current of even 40 milliamps. According to Carmichael, these are the two youngest fetuses about which the literature makes any statements regarding the activity of any part of the response mechanism. Yanase studied peristaltic intestinal movements in fetal animals and in man, and concludes that in man they begin in the seventh week.

Feldman (57) places the earliest time at which the mother may be conscious of the quickening of the fetus at the seventeenth week, and the time at which the physician may detect movements by the use of the stethoscope at the fifteenth or sixteenth week, although Sherman and Sherman (179) state that they may sometimes be detected as early as the fourteenth week. Feldman (37) deduces from the fact that in an eighth-week abortion the umbilical cord showed regular spiral twists and that these twists are not found in the cords of animals that carry many young and therefore give little room for movements, that movements of the fetus caused these twists. Carmichael (29), however, points out that these twists may result from passive as well as from active movements.

Most of the literature on the investigation of operatively removed fetuses, lists by length rather than by age the various preparations examined, and since the different authorities disagree as to the exact length at different ages, it is extremely difficult to arrange the material by age periods. Therefore the summary presented here is divided into the different types of reactions observed at different periods, or for fetuses of different lengths. Mall's table, printed by Carmichael, and Minkowski's (136) estimates agree that by the end of the second month, when movements and reactions can first be observed, the fetus has reached a length of about 40 mm. Minkowski gives 90 mm as the length at the end of the third month, 160 mm for the fourth month, and 250 mm for the fifth month. Mall's table gives the estimated lengths by weeks; twelfth to thirteenth weeks, 98 to 117 mm; eighteenth to nineteenth weeks, 215 to 233 mm; twenty-second to twenty-third weeks, 286 to 320 mm, as compared with 250 mm given by Minkowski for the end of the fifth month; and for the twenty-seventh to the twenty-eighth weeks, 358 to 371 mm. From this age to birth, the increase is to about 500 mm, but as a fetus is viable by this age and no great changes in reactions are noted between the seventh month and birth, the last three months can conveniently be considered as one time unit, as far as development of behavior goes.

The literature is in agreement that at about the end of the second month, spontaneous movements of the fetus can be observed and external stimulation begins to elicit responses. Minkowski (138) reports muscle contraction to a galvanic current in a fetus of 35 mm. In younger fetuses, there was no response to currents of even 40 milliamps. In a fetus of 40 mm (141), he observed spontaneous wormlike movements of the arms, legs and thorax, but no reactions to external stimulation were obtained, even on pinching. According to Carmichael (29), Woyciechowski observed a fetus of 42 mm, which was removed from a pathological mass of tissue. This fetus moved both arms and legs spontaneously and, in spite of cooling, active movements lasted for more than five minutes. When the fetus was touched with a finger, much stronger movements of the arms and legs occurred and the mouth was opened. The author refers to these as "protective movements."

In the next group of fetuses examined by Minkowski (139), which were in the third month of growth, a marked advance in reactions had taken place. Even at the beginning of the period, direct stimulation caused contraction of a few muscles, and sometimes of the antagonistic muscles. The muscles which react earliest, according to Minkowski, are, on the upper extremities, the biceps and the pectoralis, and on the lower, the adductoris femoris. Stimulation of the triceps leads to contraction of the biceps. Examination of these two muscles in a 40-mm fetus showed that the neural structure of the biceps had begun to develop while the triceps was still in an undifferentiated state The reactions to muscular percussion persist and can be obtained often for an hour or longer, while spontaneous movements and other reactions fade out in ten or fifteen minutes. He concludes from this fact and from the differences in neural organization of the different muscles, that the stimuli are conducted either along the bones or along the neural tracts. Bolaffio and Artom (18) also found reactions to direct muscle stimulation at this period, observing them even in limbs which had been torn from the fetus by the delivery forceps.

In a fetus of 50 mm (134, 141) extracted by Minkowski, plantar stimulation, immediately on extraction, gave a plantar flexion of the toes. Two or three minutes later there was at first no response to stimulation, and then a slow dorsal flexion of the foot and a lifting of the inner edge of the foot. After ten minutes there was no reaction. He believes that the dorsal flexion observed after a few minutes was undoubtedly an idio-muscular reaction, and that the immediate plantar flexion is one of the first potential neural reactions. (This is especially interesting in view of the clinical signs of plantar reactions.) This he calls the *embryonic*, or *neuromuscular, transition phase* of the plantar reflex, during which the reactions are variable and inconstant in form, and the transition is taking place from idiomuscular to neural excitation. Bolaffio and Artom (18) disagree with this, however, stating that the skin of the fetus at this time is very thin and that it is difficult to be sure that what is believed to be cutaneous stimulation does not really involve deep stimulation of the underlying musculature.

Minkowski (139) says that in the second to third months the nervous structures necessary for reflexes—peripheral nerves, spinal ganglia, anterior and posterior roots and medullary area— are present, but are still in a thoroughly embryonic state. At two and one-half months of age, there are no medullated fibers, the outer zone of the cord is slightly differentiated and poor in cells. In the gray matter, there are many fat cells in a diffuse protoplasmic syncytium; the anterior horns are larger, richer in protoplasm and better differentiated. The medullary stem is in condition to transmit, but only in a general manner, the impulses radiating out in all directions.

In fetuses of 50 to 55 mm (137), estimated by Minkowski as in the first half of the third month, the spontaneous movements observed were asymmetric, arhythmic, uncoördinated, athetoid movements of the head, body and legs. Movements in response to stimulation usually spread simultaneously over several limbs, over one whole limb, or sometimes over one section of a limb. In this period, every area of the skin serves as a reflexogenous zone for various and remote reactions. Many motor reactions may be obtained by passive movement of the body; usually the reactions involve the whole body and vary widely. These reactions Minkowski believes are the first appearance of the labyrinth reflexes, which have their origin in the semicircular canals. They become more regular with increasing age, and will be described more in detail in the next age group. He believes that, at first, parts of the reactions are aneural and due to the elastic tension of the skin, which is sufficient to move the small extremities, as they are in a liquid medium and have practically no weight. Bolaffio and Artom (18), who noted the same responses at this period, attribute them to stimulation of proprioceptors in the neck. In a fetus of 65 mm length, Minkowski (139) obtained a contraction of the quadriceps femoris on percussion of the patellar, with spreading of the reaction to other muscles on the stimulated leg and to the other extremities. He points out, however, that at this age the tendons are so small that it is impossible to isolate the stimulation to them. Bolaffio and Artom (18) state that tendon reflexes do not appear until the sixth month. Minkowski (135) states that extirpation of the cerebral hemispheres did not change the skin and labyrinth reflexes in a fetus of 60 mm. Sectioning the medulla just above the cord region abolished the labyrinth reflexes, but those of the extremities persisted. He concludes that the skin reflexes from stimulation of the extremities are spinal in origin, but that the labyrinthine involve the medulla. He (139) states that the labyrinth is completely differentiated in a fetus of 40 mm length and that it plays an important rôle in the liquid medium of the fetus.

Bolaffio and Artom (18) report that dropping a fetus of 55 mm a few centimeters to a table gave contractions of the flexor muscles of the limbs. Energetic responses occurred to tapping the table lightly with the fingers, involving elevation of the scapulae, movements of the arms, flexion of the thighs and of the legs. While the fetus was active, the skin of the abdomen and breast was stimulated with a blunt rod, with no response. After the cessation of activity, direct brain stimulation gave no muscle response. In two fetuses of 70 mm, stroking and tapping gave slow, local contractions of the limb muscles in one, and in the other, light stimulation of the skin of the whole body gave no responses. Percussion of the forearm, however, gave flexion, adduction and internal rotation of the arm. On the lower limb, it led to flexion and adduction of the thighs, with slight flexion of the legs. With light percussion, the contractions were limited to the homolateral limb, with stronger percussion, there were also contractions of the heterolateral limb. Percussion on the breast gave homolateral responses in the pectoral muscles, and on the abdomen it gave bilateral contractions in the abdominal muscles. These authors state that to the end of the third month, muscle stimulation gives slow contractions that have a tendency to diffuse and generalize. With development, the contractions become faster and the tendency to diffusion lessens, disappearing toward the beginning of the sixth month.

PATTERNS OF ACTIVITY

ELECTRIC MUSCLE STIMULATION

Minkowski (138) has investigated the reactions to electric stimulation, with both faradic and galvanic currents, of fetuses from 55 mm in length to 342 mm in length. His conclusions are that from the third month on, the muscles react to both kinds of stimulation. The reactions to faradic stimulation were always tetanic, like those of adults to similar stimulation. Galvanic stimulation, however, gave various reactions, some of which differ from those of adults. In a number of cases, he got a very fast jerk and a slower relaxation of the muscle. But in most cases there was a tetanic contraction of the muscles until the current was interrupted. He concludes that from the fourth month, the fetal nerves are able to transmit electric current to the muscles, although the fibers are still unmedullated. The early variable reactions to galvanic current are a primitive form of direct aneural stimulation. The quick adult jerks, he believes, are seen only after the myofibrillae appear. These develop only in a few muscles, such as the biceps. He comments on the fact that Bolaffio and Artom did not observe the tetanic reaction to galvanic current, but that he himself has seen it as late as the seventh month in a 340-mm fetus. He states that a young fetus shows the same reaction to weak and strong currents, but as the myofibrillae develop, a differentiation in reactions to currents of different strengths appears. Bolaffio and Artom (18) state that until the sixth month, the cortex and the pyramidal tracts are not excitable by electric or mechanical stimulation, while the pons, the bulb and the medulla are; at birth the motor zone of the cortex is likewise excitable.

PLANTAR RESPONSES

Minkowski (141, 134) traces the development of the reactions to plantar stimulation in fetuses from the end of the second month to adulthood. This sequence is especially interesting, since he believes reactions to plantar stimulation are one of the earliest

forms of neural reactions observable. The first reactions he observed have already been given. In the third and fourth months,
as shown by fetuses of 55 to 140 mm, dorsal flexion is dominant.
Plantar flexion, which is latent under normal conditions, appears
as the fetus weakens. This he calls the *spinal* phase. In the fifth
and sixth months (160 to 320-mm length) of 14 fetuses, the 10
that were extracted under local anesthetic all showed dorsal
flexion immediately after extraction. Those that showed plantar
flexion from the beginning were all extracted under general
anesthetic and showed no spontaneous movements, and only short
reflexes could be obtained. During this period, the rôle of the
big toe in the flexion was variable, just as it is in the adult
Babinski reflex. He believes that this change to a dominantly
Babinski type of response indicates a cerebral component that
favors this type above the earlier plantar responses; this component is probably in the midbrain. This he calls the *middle
fetal*, or *tegmento-spinal phase*. The late fetal stage lasts from
this time until birth, and is probably *pallido-rubro-cerebello-
tegmento-spinal*. The reactions of premature infants to plantar
stimulation are extremely variable in this period, and all variations are observable, but perhaps plantar flexion is favored over
the earlier stage. The next stage Minkowski calls the *neonatal*
or *initial cortico-subcortico-spinal* stage. The reactions are similar
to those obtained in the prematures; both types of flexion occur
alternately and approximately equally, sometimes even on the
same infant. Probably with the beginning of myelinization in the
motor centers, there is a change in favor of dorsal flexion. Bolaffio
and Artom (18) report that they could not observe the onset of a
dorsal or Babinski type of response to plantar stimulation in the
fourth month, and they report it as still lacking in a fetus of
280 mm. In a fetus of 340 mm, which was old enough to make
weak crying sounds and breathing movements on extraction, they
observed for the first time plantar flexion of the toes to stimulation of the sole. In slightly larger fetuses, plantar stimulation
led to toe movements and flexion of the toes. They state that
plantar responses begin between the sixth and seventh months,
and are then present until birth, in two forms: (1) response to

superficial stimulation, which is a slow extension of the big toe and extension and abduction of the other toes; (2) response to deep stimulation of the muscles or bones, which is slow flexion of all the toes.

Bersot (10) traces the responses to plantar stimulation in fetuses born prematurely, apparently without special efforts to prolong life. He emphasizes the fact that the total response should be studied, not simply that of the toes and foot, and that the variability of the response is the significant thing. Fetuses born at four or five months show only a flexor movement of the toes, slow but very clear, involving particularly the last four toes, while the big toe often remains immobile. The last four toes seem to get longer while they execute a light plantar flexion. There are no reactions in any other parts of the body. The reaction ceases after six to eight stimulations, suggesting that fatigue comes on rapidly. Fetuses born at twenty-seven to twenty-eight weeks of age show a withdrawal of the limb by flexion at the pelvis and in the knee, in response to plantar stimulation. This movement is slow and weak and soon ceases with repeated stimulation. The toes flex and extend, with the big toe remaining immobile or following the others. A contralateral reflex of crossed extension also sometimes occurs, sometimes with a slight dorsal flexion of the foot. In fetuses born at thirty-four to thirty-six weeks, the response to plantar stimulation is much like that to any external stimulation of the lower extremities. The last four toes flex at the first phalanx and extend at the last two, the big toe sometimes follows the other toes but more often it extends as in the Babinski sign. There is a dorsal flexion of the foot, and flexion of the leg on the thigh, and of the thigh on the pelvis. There are several muscular contractions, and the opposite limb is extended with the toes flexed at the first phalanx. These are the most frequent responses of the legs, but sometimes both flex simultaneously, or show alternate movements of flexion and extension. The contractions are very slow, so slow that the position of the toes and extremities continues for a few minutes after stimulation ceases.

LABYRINTHINE REFLEXES

Minkowski (137) reports that in a fetus of 190 mm, third to fourth month, moving the body from a sitting to a lying position and vice versa gave bilateral symmetric motions in both arms, or in both legs, or in all together. These movements lacked the tonic character of those observed by Magnus and de Kleijn on decerebrate animals. Moving the head to the right in relation to the body caused the right arm to abduct and the left one to adduct, and movement of the head to the left caused the opposite responses in the arms. These reactions were tonic in character. The elastic tonus of the extremities caused them to return to their normal position when they were passively moved. In his general discussion of the labyrinth reflexes, Minkowski (139) states that changing the position of the head in relation to the thorax results in movement of the arm toward which the head is moved, and sometimes also in movement of the diagonal arm. The character of the movements is variable, but tends to become regular with increase in age. The movements are tonic in character and last as long as the head position is maintained in relation to the thorax. The reactions to changing the position of the body in space are chiefly bilateral, symmetric movements in the upper or lower extremities, or in both. The reactions start sometimes by a bending of both arms or of both legs, and sometimes by a stretching of the extremities. There is adduction, abduction and rotation of the limbs in or out. The movements are quick and the limbs soon return to the original position, even if the new position in space is maintained. These reflexes he compares to Magnus and de Kleijn's semicircular-canal-labyrinth reflexes.

SPONTANEOUS REACTIONS

Minkowski (139) summarizes the spontaneous reactions observed in a large number of fetuses from two to five months of age, or from 50 mm to 230 mm in length. Most of these fetuses made head, thorax and limb movements which were more or less vigorous. The head was turned from side to side, and lifted and lowered. The thorax was bent and stretched, and the extremities were bent, stretched, adducted, abducted, and rotated in or out. These motions were slow, asymmetric, arhythmic and uncoordinate, and had little locomotor effect. They involved one or more articulations, the proximate or distal limb section and one or more limbs moving simultaneously. Occasionally single motions of fingers or of one finger alone, the thumb or first finger, were observed. These small, slow motions are sometimes interrupted by jerky choreatic movements, especially in the older fetuses, or if external stimulation is applied. The duration of these spontaneous movements is very short, never more than a few minutes, sometimes not more than from one-half to one minute. The same movements can be elicited later, however, as reflexes, by external stimulation. Minkowski reports having observed in two fetuses in the fourth month (160 and 180 mm) spontaneous dorsal flexion of the big toe, although there was no response to touch on the sole of the foot; spontaneous movements of all the extremities and the head were present before the umbilical cord was ligated. About the end of the fourth month is the time at which the mother begins to be able to feel fetal movements and, shortly after, movements and heartbeats can be detected by the use of a stethoscope on the body wall of the mother. It is at about this time that Minkowski noted in a fetus of 230 mm, for the first time, the continued rhythmic contractions that are usually called Ahfeld breathing movements. In an earlier study, Ahfeld described these rhythmic contractions of the fetal thorax, which can be felt through the mother's body wall, as important in the transition from uterine to extrauterine breathing. Carmichael (29) says that these movements have been known at least since 1798, and that there has been considerable speculation as to the way in which they are related to the change at birth from the gaseous interchange between the blood stream of the mother and that of the fetus, to true respiration. In a fetus of 280 mm, Minkowski (139) reports faint sounds made after exposure to the air. Carmichael believes this fifth-month fetus to be the youngest for which the literature reports sounds. Bolaffio and Artom (18) report superficial respiratory movements, which ceased after a moment or two and then reappeared, in fetuses

of 310 and 330 mm. And in another fetus of 330 mm, they report
weak cries and spontaneous movements, more feeble than those
of an infant born at term. They also report that in fetuses of this
size and larger, from the sixth month on, the movements are so
lively and strong that it is very difficult to give specific descriptions of behavior.

SKIN, MUSCLE AND TENDON REACTIONS

Minkowski (137) states that during the fourth month and
into the fifth, reactions are, in general, about the same as in
younger fetuses. The motions become more rhythmic and coordinated, however, and both arms or legs flex and stretch
rhythmically. Reactions irradiate less over the whole body and
are confined to typical motions, but there are still many variable
reactions, and they occur in other extremities than the one
stimulated. In a fetus of 190 mm, short, long and diagonal reflexes were obtained, and in another of the same length stroking
some of the abdominal muscles caused contractions. In another
190-mm fetus (139), stimulation of one foot gave rather constant movements of fingers or of the little finger alone, in the
diagonal hand. At this time, light pressure on the foot or touching
it with a brush, may cause, not only shortening or other movements of the stimulated leg, but also flexion, stretching or adduction in the bilateral limb, and bending or stretching of both arms.
Touching the hand of a fetus of 135 mm caused flexion of both
arms, repeated opening and closing of the mouth and retraction
of the head. In fetuses of 110, 160 and 215 mm, stimulation on
the lower lip or chin caused repeated opening and closing of the
mouth. A touch on the eyelid before the eye slit was formed,
caused contraction of the orbicularis muscle. Reactions to percussion of the muscles can often be obtained for a long time after
spontaneous motions and responses to external neural stimulation
have ceased. The biceps, triceps, pectoralis and adductoris femoris
are still the easiest muscles to stimulate. In a fetus of 135 mm,
stimulation of the triceps caused a contraction of the pectoralis,
and in one of 215 mm, it caused contraction of the biceps or
the pectoralis. Percussion of the extensors in the hand may cause

contractions of the flexors. He concludes that the stimuli are still conducted either along the nerve tracts or along the bones. In fetuses of 130 and 160 mm, pressure and pinching of the sole of the foot gave a plantar flexion of the foot with a passive dorsal stretching. Pinching of the foot of a 190-mm fetus resulted in flexion of the stimulated leg and stretching of the diagonal limb. If the other leg was then stimulated, it contracted, while the leg which had been flexed, stretched.

In a fetus of 230 mm, Bolaffio and Artom (18) observed localized muscular contractions about the limbs and other specialized muscle groups, from superficial stimulation. Strong and deep stimulation gave flexion of the whole limb. Stroking the ridge of the tibia gave a lively adduction of the homolateral thigh. Stroking the pectoral muscles gave adduction of the contralateral limb, and increase in the stimulus caused contraction of the whole corresponding limb. As the vitality of the fetus diminished, the contractions disappeared first in the lower limb and later in the upper. Removal of the hemispheres gave more vivid responses, and stimulation of the medulla gave violent respiratory movements, involving the cervical, thoracic, abdominal, and diaphragm muscles, and led to elevation of the shoulder and adduction of the arms. These experimenters explored the cortex of a 260-mm fetus, with electric stimuli, and got no response, even with intense stimuli. Not until the pons was uncovered did they get responses, which were from the muscles inervated by the facial nerve. Stimulation of the medulla gave strong respiratory movements. Stimulation of the cervical cord caused elevation of the shoulder and flexion of the upper limbs, and that of the lumbar cord gave movements of the lower limbs. In a fetus of 280 mm (sixth month), they found that every muscle reacted to stimulation, even to percussion, by contraction; these specific responses were more marked in the head than in the leg regions. They also found a bilateral patellar and an Achilles reflex on one side. In slightly larger fetuses, they found the same specific muscle contractions on percussion, and the tendon reflexes were more marked. In the larger fetus, the biceps, triceps and Achilles were elicited. They believed that no cutaneous reflexes were elicited in these fetuses, either before or after removal of the brain. In another fetus of 330 mm, the cortex was electrically, directly stimulated, with negative results. When the lower centers were stimulated, however, there were specific responses such as increased breathing rate and shoulder, arm and finger movements. In fetuses a little larger, these authors report that percussion of muscles gave responses not limited to the single muscle. The patellar was present and bilateral, the Achilles was not always obtained. The abdominal reflexes were absent. The sucking reflex was obtained only by stimulating the tongue, but in larger fetuses the zone had spread to the external surface of the mouth. On applying pressure to the palms, there were energetic grasping movements. Bolaffio and Artom state that the grasping reflex occurs only on deep stimulation, and that, from this time on, superficial stimulation of the palms gives inconstant and variable responses.

During the seventh month Minkowski, and Bolaffio and Artom report the appearance of the abdominal reflexes. Bolaffio and Artom state that they are weak, inconstant, and almost always asymmetric, and that the cremasteric reflex is weak, variable and asymmetric during the last two months. As we have seen, the plantar reflex has developed to much the same form as that found at birth. The corneal reflex is present and by birth is constant and strong, and the conjunctival reflex is more or less constant, according to Bolaffio and Artom. Infants born prematurely, even before this age, can survive, and studies indicate that during the last two months of pregnancy development in behavior is in the nature of increasing specificity and differentiation of responses. Bolaffio and Artom report that during this period the muscular reflexes prevail decreasingly over the tendon reflexes, and that by the end of the ninth month the tendon reflexes are so well established that they prevail over special muscle reflexes. They make an exception of certain of those of the upper limbs, which they say are elicited with difficulty because of the smallness of the limb. They state that these reflexes are produced independently of the central nervous system, though inhibited by a mechanism of the cerebral hemispheres.

Responses to Sensory Stimulation

The literature presents some evidence of the development of the special senses during prenatal life. Testing these senses when the fetus is within the mother's body, or even in operatively removed fetuses which live for a few moments only, is, however, extremely difficult, and most of our evidence is drawn from the developmental condition of the neural mechanism of the senses before or at the time of birth. Conditions within the uterus are so constant that sufficient differences to allow of stimulation can hardly exist for most of the special senses. Peiper (155) states that the infant must be capable of receiving sensory stimuli before birth, since he can do so at birth. Taste, smell and light stimuli cannot reach the infant in utero, but hearing, touch and labryrinthine stimuli possibly may reach him. Langworthy (114) states that the sensory endings of the skin, and on the muscle and the vestibular and even the cochlear nerves, may receive adequate stimuli in utero, but that the optic and olfactory nerves can hardly be stimulated until after birth, and that myelinization of their fibers does not occur until that time. The behavior of fetuses examined outside the mother's body, makes it clear that even had the investigators tested for the special senses, the movement or response ability of the fetus is so restricted that responses, if obtained, would be very difficult to interpret. Observations on premature infants furnish some of the available data on sensory development before birth. But it should be remembered that the presence of a response in a premature infant does not mean that the response has been or could be called out in a fetus of the same age which is still within the uterus. The amniotic fluid, for instance, in the fetus's mouth and nostrils probably would prevent the reception of stimuli of taste and smell and, since this fluid is practically constant during the whole of pregnancy, it cannot be considered a stimulus in itself. Temperature and light conditions within the uterus are also so constant that stimulation of these senses cannot be said to occur until birth. Plain stimuli within the uterus are of course a possibility, but responses to such stimuli in premature infants are practically lacking.

TASTE AND SMELL

There is probably no adequate stimulation of the organs of taste or smell until birth. Evidence from premature infants indicates that sweet can be distinguished from salt, sour and bitter, and that premature infants at least in the last month are able to smell substances when air enters the olfactory cavity. The data on taste and smell in the newborn and premature is presented below, in the section on the senses in the newborn.

VISION

Bolaffio and Artom (18) state that the pupillary response is present from the seventh month on, and that by the time of birth it is constant, but slow. Pratt, Nelson and Sun (164) summarize the literature on early reactions to light and conclude that there is evidence that even at normal birth the neural mechanism for sight is not fully developed. Some eye reactions are, however, developed fairly early in fetal life, as noted above. Hess (81, p. 74) says:

Over the eyes of the youngest prematures occasionally there can be seen more or less well marked vestiges of the pupillary membrane. The cornea is inclined to be somewhat thicker, the anterior chamber less deep and the iris less pigmented. Strong impressions are followed by reflex closure of the lids, but sudden movements are not followed by such closure as the reflex is psychic, depending upon fear. The *eye movements* of the premature infant are uncoordinated, motion being most often in a horizontal direction, occasionally outward, but more often and in a comparatively strong manner, inward. It is not uncommon to see this tendency to convergence present until the second month. The *light reflex* is present before birth and the pupil, when exposed to a strong light contracts only to dilate again, in two or three seconds. The secondary dilatation is particularly well marked in the premature as a result of the poor development of the nerve fibres which are easily fatigued. The convergence reflex is absent in prematures as well as in the more mature infant because fixation does not occur.

Studies of eye responses in the newborn show great differences in the responses of premature and newborn infants with those of even slightly older infants, with evidence of early developmental increments.

The auditory mechanism has long been considered to be developed before birth to a point where it could function. Early investigators, however, considered that the infant remained deaf until, by breathing and crying, the Eustachian tube was opened and the fetal fluid in the middle ear drained out. This view has apparently led some authors to report infants as deaf immediately on birth or for some time after it, when stimulation did not bring obvious responses. In 1924, however, Peiper (155) found changes in the breathing curve on auditory stimulation in six neonates. He therefore decided to test fetal movements through the body wall of the mother, as a method of discovering whether sound would cause changes indicating a response. The mothers were trained not to respond to the stimuli, so that as far as possible the recorded movements should not be due to passive movement of the fetus. A loud sound was selected so that it should penetrate to the fetus. The mother's breathing curve was also taken as a check on whether the recorded movements were truly fetal. In more than a third of the cases definite fetal responses to an automobile horn were recorded. The most common response was what seemed to be a drawing together of the whole body of the fetus. There were individual differences, and the response was sometimes found on one day and not on the next. Continued stimulation led to a diminution of the response. Forbes and Forbes (59) report one somewhat similar case. A pregnant woman was lying in a tin bathtub, thirty-one days before the birth of the child. By accident a small child playing beside the tub struck it with a glass jar. The mother instantly felt a sudden jump of the fetus unlike its ordinary movements. Later the experiment was repeated by an adult observer who clearly observed a quick rise of the mother's abdominal wall, while she reported feeling the same jump that had occurred the first time. The authors state that the mother was completely relaxed, was not startled by the noise and felt no vibration through the skin from the blow on the tub. The mother's tactual sense was tested later, and it was found that a vibration of the intensity of the blow on the tub was felt only by those portions of the skin which were in contact with the tub. The authors believe that this was a true auditory muscular reflex in the fetus, but add that the possibility of reception through the skin cannot be entirely ruled out. Peiper also cites instances of mothers who said that they had noted, during the last months of pregnancy, that the fetus was very active during a concert. It seems probable that the mechanical blocks to hearing in the fetus and the just-born are so great that a stimulus to be heard by the fetus must be loud enough to pass through them, and that further experiments with loud sounds will show whether old fetuses and very young infants can really hear or whether such responses as those cited above are due to tactual stimulation.

SUMMARY

It is impossible to make, from the mass of data on fetal behavior, a clear summary of growth in intrauterine life. The most that we have been able to do is to give an idea of the difficulties in studying behavior at this period, of the limited amount of material on the subject, and a general picture of the fetal responses that have been observed at the different age levels. The one growth pattern which may possibly emerge from the mass of details is Minkowski's outline of the development of response to plantar stimulation.

By the time of birth, the human fetus has developed an extensive repertoire of responses, so that birth is simply a transition from life in a protected liquid medium to life in a varied environment where countless stimulations affect the organism, not a moment at which the ability to perform new reactions suddenly appears. Spontaneous movements of operatively removed fetuses occur at about the end of the second month of pregnancy. These are probably aneural or idio-muscular in character, and at this age external stimulation apparently evokes no reactions. The first aneural spontaneous movements are wormlike contractions of the arms, legs and thorax. After the second month the movements are slow, asymmetric, arhythmic and uncoördinated, and very variable as to the parts of the body involved. The reactions to external stimulation are of the same character. With increasing age the movements become less variable, and there is a progressive increase in specificity and coördination, until by the time of birth most of the commoner special reflexes have become more or less established. Every area of the skin may at first serve as a reflexogenous zone for various and remote reactions; as growth proceeds, the reactions become more regular and localized to the simulated area or the proximate parts. In a fetus in the third month, Minkowski observed plantar flexion of the toes in response to stimulation on the sole of the foot. He traces the development of the plantar reactions from this time to birth. In the third and fourth months, he found a transition from the early variable plantar reaction to a phase in which extension, or the Babinski type of response, begins to predominate. In the fifth and sixth months, dorsal flexion has become dominant, and the big toe often opposes itself to the others in a simianlike reflex of prehension. The reactions are still variable and continue so, with flexion occurring about as frequently as extension, until sometime after birth, and both types of reaction can often be observed in the same individual. Bolaffio and Artom believe that the dorsal type of flexion does not become established until the end of the sixth month.

About the end of the third month, the tonic neck and labyrinth reflexes begin to appear, though at first some of the movements appear to be due to the elastic tonus of the skin. The reactions are variable at first and become more regular with increasing age. Because of the small size of the fetal members and the thinness of the fetal skin, it is difficult to distinguish skin and tendon stimulation from muscle stimulation. Percussion of a muscle gives contraction. Lighter stimulation gives variable and diffuse reactions. In the fourth and fifth months, diagonal reactions are often observed. Minkowski believes these are related to the trotting reflexes observed in animals. The corneal reflex is established very early, contraction of the orbicularis muscles occurring in the fourth month, before the eye-slit is developed. In this month, Minkowski also observed contraction of some of the abdominal muscles on stroking. He seems to agree with Bolaffio and Artom, however, that the true abdominal reflexes do not appear until the seventh month. About the end of the fourth month, the mother begins to feel fetal movements, and shortly after movements and heartbeats can be detected by a stethoscope on the body wall of the mother. About the same time Ahfeld breathing contractions can be noticed in extracted fetuses. Bolaffio and Artom report the tendon reflexes as present in fetuses in the sixth month, the patellar and Achilles being the first to appear. They also report that during the last months of pregnancy the muscular reflexes prevail decreasingly over the tendon, until at birth the tendon reflexes are dominant. In the sixth month the sucking reflex is present only on stimulation of the tongue. The grasping reflex is well developed sometime before birth.

Very little is known about the possibility of the reactions of the special senses in utero. It is probable that the neural mechanisms are sufficiently developed by birth so that reactions can occur almost immediately thereafter. Evidence indicates that pain is not felt to any extent for sometime after birth. There is some evidence that loud auditory stimuli may sometimes reach the fetus through the body wall of the mother; this evidence is quite inconclusive, however. Langworthy (114) states that, in the case of man, birth serves as a great stimulus to the deposit of myelin in the nervous system.

In the first few weeks after birth the optic and olfactory systems acquire myelin sheaths, and myelinated projection fibers from the thalamus extend to many areas of the cerebral cortex. The question arises as to the changes at birth that account for this increase in the deposit of myelin. Probably it is the result of increased stimulation of the sensory organs.

He mentions the evidence indicating that human sensory pathways are myelinated at the time when sensory endings receive adequate stimuli. He believes that the optic and olfactory nerves cannot receive stimulation in utero, and points out that myelinization of their fibers does not begin until after birth. His conclusion is that the increased number of stimuli reaching all sensory end-

ings after birth may well account for the great increase in myelinization at that time, but that the fact that the optic tracts of the
guinea pig are myelinated by the time of birth is an objection to
this conclusion.

Minkowski (140) says that what is seen, in the kind of experiments he has performed with fetuses, are really artificially
elicited fragments of functions which are severed from their
natural environment. These experiments are valuable, but do
not necessarily give true replicas of natural behavior. He states
that a reflex cannot be simplified and reduced to basic elements.
At least in a latent way, the whole organism participates in every
reaction, and so what we call a reflex is only the overt part of
the whole. Thus there is no real distinction between instincts
and reflexes, or unconditioned and conditioned reflexes. Reflex
movements and integrative processes are so bound up with different inner and outer stimuli that under usual biological conditions
they lead to objectively purposeful reactions, serving the common interest of individual or species. What distinction there is is
one of degree, not of kind. The reflexes which in early stages are
aroused diffusely, later become differentiated and specialized.
And what are called conditioned reflexes are simply the responses
of the organism not only to single stimuli, but also to complexes
of stimuli of varied nature and origin, which are partly synchronous and partly appear in a determined order, and which
act on the earlier reflexes, or instinctive life, in many ways and
combinations. Bersot also points out in his discussion of the
development of the plantar reflex that it is the whole organism
which responds, that the baby tends neither to localize his reactions nor to vary them with the stimuli.

Coghill (42) has summarized the available studies on human
fetuses and discusses the results in comparison with his findings
on Amblystoma. He enlarges upon the interpretation of Bersot's
and Minkowski's observations by pointing out that the real
significance of the type of reflex activity observed by them in
the young fetus is the existence of a total reaction pattern similar
to that observed in Amblystoma. He says that although Bolaffio
and Artom maintain that the cortex, under six months, is without

function, yet they report a strengthening of reflexes after decerebration in a 70-mm fetus.

It appears therefore that from the beginning of the process of development of reflex specificity of receptors and the individuation of reflex patterns, the cerebral cortex of man operates with the rest of the nervous system as a unit. . . . In conclusion I am convinced by a study of all available records of movement in human fetuses of the first six months, that behavior develops in man as it does in Amblystoma by the expansion of a total pattern that is integrated as a whole from the beginning, and by individuation of partial patterns (reflexes) within the unitary whole.

He states that the difference between instinct and reflex is in magnitude of pattern of reaction; they are not two distinct categories of behavior. The purpose or end-result of both is the same—the adaptation of the organism to the environment. Reflexes emerge as partial or local patterns within an expanding total pattern that is normally perfectly integrated from the beginning. Even after they have appeared they are only overtly local or partial; they still remain inherently components of the total pattern or are under its dominance.

Although, with the possible exception of the plantar reflex, we cannot yet give the course of the various behavior patterns for which development starts in utero, Minkowski has given a general outline of what he believes to be the course of this growth, and the general processes underlying it.

Minkowski (140) believes that the development of reflexes in the human fetus, in general, corresponds to the history of reflexes in animals, given by Winterbert. The first movements are idiomuscular, that is aneural, and are characterized by regular and constant rhythm. A neuromuscular phase follows, in which some parts of the organism come under the influence of the nervous system while other parts do not, or else the neural influence is only intermittently observable. Finally the nervous system becomes the dominating influence in reactions and the movements become more and more localized and specialized. He states that in the youngest fetuses he examined, those of 40 to 50 mm, he could not observe complete lack of neural activity, but that it is probable that before the end of the second month such a stage exists. In fetuses (135) of from two to five months of age, idio-muscular reactions and neural reactions exist side by side, the former persisting after the disappearance of the neural reactions and after the ablation of the medulla. Minkowski says that the primitive or idio-muscular excitability never ceases and can be found in adults, but that the muscles of the normal adult are much more under the dominance of the nervous system than those of a fifth-month fetus, and so the aneural reactions show much less easily and regularly. The neural motor reactions which are found in second- to fifth-month fetuses and are transmitted through the central nervous system, are movements of the head, body, extremities, the long and short skin reflexes, the cervical reflex, the labyrinth reflex, and the phenomenon of reflex inhibitions. These movements and reflexes are characterized, on the one hand, by their great variety, their faculty of irradiation and generalization, and on the other hand by their tendency to assume, with progressing age, more and more specific biological characters of defense, of locomotion, of orientation in space, of reciprocal inhibition, of coördination, of correlation, and so on. The early neural stimuli (140) are visceral-humoral, and general and special proprioceptive. Apparently the different anatomical-physiological components develop in a determined order, but also have periods of more and of less rapid growth, so that a change may be due to development or to a resting stage in some component part. Minkowski cites as an illustration of this the numerous changes in the plantar reflex in the course of development. The less highly differentiated a part of the nervous system is, the nearer the embryonic condition it is. Differentiation is always relative, however, and it is always possible to regress to a more primitive and more generalized type of reactions. Development and regression both take place in temporal layers.

We do not give the various neural mechanisms governing the responses found in the fetus, because these have not been worked out. Minkowski has done considerable work on the correlation of structure and function, but it cannot be organized into a picture which shows the various stages of the relationships. Like the work on animals, only details have been collected for the developmental state of certain parts of the nervous system in relation to certain specific reactions. Minkowski (135) states from his neural work that the skin reflexes from stimulation of the body and the extremities are essentially spinal, since they persist after section of the spinal bulb near its inferior limit, and that the labyrinth reflexes must be located in the bulb since they disappear after the bulb is sectioned at its inferior limit and persist after ablation of the brain, the optic seat and meso-cephalon. Facial reflexes, closing of the mouth and lifting of the chin at a touch on the lower lip or tongue, or contraction of the pupil at a touch, have an anatomic basis in the development of the nucleus of the seventh pair. Head movements with a labyrinth origin correlate with the development of the vestibularis in the labyrinth and of the vestibularis nerve in its entire course from the labyrinth to the bulb. This can be traced in a fetus of about two months. The early development of the vestibular mechanism he (129) attributes to its necessity to the life of an organism living in a liquid medium of the same specific weight as itself, so that movements are easy and the limbs without weight. Myelin (135) in the spinal cord and nerve stems starts to develop in the fourth fetal month. The irradiation of responses which occurs before this time is due to the lack of any myelin sheathing.

Infants known to be prematurely delivered may throw light on the later stages of fetal life, but it should be remembered that a normal fetus of the same age as a premature infant may, owing to the marked environmental changes, react very differently from the infant. Change from life in the amniotic fluid to life in air, from placental to pulmonary respiration, from the relatively constant external stimulations of intrauterine life to the varied and continually changing ones of life after birth, and so on, all have a necessary influence upon the sensory responses and activity of the organism, regardless of its age. Therefore, the behavior of premature infants cannot be taken as an indication of the potential activity ability of fetuses of the same age. Bersot (10) states that the premature infant seems to have an advantage in development over the one born at term. A baby born at thirty weeks has by thirty-five weeks a larger, quicker and more extended repertoire of responses than the one born at thirty-five weeks of age. Everything indicates, Bersot states, that the premature infant shows the effect of the training which the external stimuli, received since the minute of birth, have been giving him. Since the anatomical development must be nearly the same for both babies, he concludes that functional and anatomic development must be linked by a relative correlation, and not by direct causality.

In general, the responses of premature infants born near enough term to be viable are the same as those of infants born at term, and it is from this source that most of our ideas of growth or development in utero are drawn. That is, the infant shortly after birth shows such and such behavior; therefore the development which leads up to this behavior must have taken place in utero, and the neural mechanisms also must have developed in utero to the point where the reactions which take place afterwards are possible. The relations between the reactive ability of the newborn baby and the effect of the increased stimulation of the organism in an extrauterine environment is not known.

The behaviorist view, of course, emphasizes the rôle of the environment in initiating behavior, and holds that, with the exception of a few responses labeled *unconditioned*, all postnatal responses are learned. The Gestalt view seems to swing to the other extreme and holds that at least the background for behavior patterns is present at birth, and that specific behavior develops from a fundamental relation, oriented within the organism, to the external world. That is, growth or maturation is interdependent in behavioral development with learning, or the rôle of the environment. The organismic concept of the physiologists also favors the latter view, but in general the supporters of this view seem to hold a less rigidly all-or-none theory of the relative rôles of learning and the nervous system than the psychologists. Whatever the truth will ultimately prove to be, we do know that some types of behavior have developed completely in utero, other types have begun to develop in utero and have reached different levels of growth by the time of birth, and still other types which are normal to the adult are not present at birth and do not develop until later. A very fruitful field for investigation would seem to be the attempt to discover whether differentiation or the organismic principle governs all these types, or whether exercise and practice may not play a rôle, and possibly a large one, in the behavior patterns that emerge after birth. To state the problem another way, does this one principle of growth apply at all the behavioral levels in the same way, or is the organismic concept inadequate to explain behavior at the spinal, midbrain and cortical levels? Is myelinization perhaps not necessary for the *emergence* of a pattern, but essential for the fully developed pattern? We have not enough information, either on the neurological or the behavioral side, to answer this question at present. It will be seen that, although we know much more about the behavior of infants after birth than we do about that in utero, the same difficulty applies to the studies of infant behavior that confronts us in fetal behavior. Few studies have been made which trace the development of a single behavior pattern from the earliest reactions to the fully developed ones of the full-grown organism.

PART III

NEONATAL BEHAVIOR

III

NEONATAL BEHAVIOR

THERE is no exact agreement among investigators as to the length of the period covered by the term *neonatal*, but in general it covers the interval from birth until the umbilicus is healed. Behavior and reactions occurring during this period are generally assumed to be part of the behavior equipment of the individual at birth. The most recent and most careful studies, however, indicate that behavior growth is taking place in these first weeks of extrauterine life, but that the changes which occur are comparatively slight and that no emergence, marked development or regression of patterns takes place. At least until data are more refined than they are at present, therefore, behavior equipment at birth can conveniently be taken as that which occurs during the first two weeks or until the umbilicus is healed.

As already noted, if we are to trace growth processes and discover how they take place, we must follow behavior from its genesis. The difficulties of investigating fetal behavior are so great and the techniques for it so new that, aside from the general knowledge that development is progressive in utero and that birth does not bring any change in the nature of growth, we are still forced to begin the details of our picture with birth. A great deal of work has been done to determine what behavior is possible at birth and shortly thereafter. A review of the literature on the subject from the point of view of growth processes suggests a classification of reactions under two heads: reactions which are developed by the time of birth to practically their adult form, and reactions which are partially developed at birth and which grow or regress and modify after birth. While it is necessary to know what patterns are completely developed at birth, a pattern is not significant in tracing the development of behavior, once it is fully adult. It is the other patterns, those which are partially developed or which change after birth, that are important. During the neonatal period these patterns are largely specific reflexes, mass activity, and the reactions of the special sensory mechanisms. The progressive modifications of the specific reflexes are traced here, since they are steps in total patterns which play a rôle in life from the time of birth. A number of reactions which regress sometime after birth appear to be part of such total progressing patterns, but there is a marked change in the character of the reactions at the early reflex level and their later emergence in a purposive or adaptive form, and the mechanisms for their transformations are not known. Therefore, these reactions are included in their early form under *neonatal behavior*, and in their later purposive form under *behavior during infancy*. The reactions of the special senses, especially sight and hearing, for which the literature is full, are also included under both sections, since their investigation is reported in the literature in this way. But it should be emphasized that there is no real break between the neonatal period and infancy proper, and that behavior growth is taking place in an apparently steady but irregular stream from the appearance of the first neuromuscular reactions in utero to the final establishment of each pattern in its adult form, at a great variety of ages from before birth to a chronologically adult age. It will be seen, however, that the literature emphasizes the break between the two periods. The number of studies which traces any one pattern from its overt genesis to the adult form is small; most studies have been made by age periods.

The same kind of contradictory statements, as to the ages at which certain reactions appear, that occur in the literature on fetal behavior, occur also in the studies of postnatal behavior. Lack of definition of terms seems to account for these differences. In general, investigators have focused their attention on fixing the age at which a certain reaction appeared instead of noting the sequence of reactions in the development of a total pattern. The few studies which have been made by the latter method indicate clearly that much of the confusion as to age levels will be cleared up when it has been applied to all types of behavior. For example, even the layman is aware of the fact that a child who cannot hold up his head, cannot sit up, and the same principle appears to apply in a much more closely correlated series of reactions in the development of any one behavior pattern. A number of investigators have devoted considerable time and effort to determining the age at which infants normally hold up their heads; yet the most careful studies of newborn infants indicate that most infants momentarily hold up their heads from the time of birth. Therefore, to be understood, each report of the age at which the reaction occurs needs a careful and complete description of just what is meant by holding up the head. It is generally agreed by most investigators that growth takes place as a gradual and steady process. Thus, unless we know the course of development of any one reaction, the age of its appearance may refer to almost any point in the total course, and so become more or less meaningless. Bersot and Minkowski have brought this point out clearly in their discussion of the plantar reflex during fetal life; Shirley has worked out the tentative sequence of gross motor development from birth up to and including walking, and Halverson has studied the sequence of arm and hand reactions leading up to fine prehension but his work does not begin until after the neonatal period. With the exception of Shirley, none of these authors has correlated the reactions studied with other coincident behavior patterns, and Shirley's work is partial and very general.

REACTIONS FULLY DEVELOPED AT BIRTH

Immature as the human infant is at birth, there are a number of activities he performs practically as well as an adult, and which he continues to perform in much the same way throughout his whole life. In general, the reactions that are present in adult form from birth, or very shortly thereafter, seem to be largely visceral, the stimulus coming from within the organism, and both stimulus and response being concerned with simple life processes, such as digestion and breathing. Some of the specific deep and superficial reflexes which are elicited by external stimulation are also present from birth. The literature is in substantial agreement as to the reactions which are fully developed at birth and, since we are here interested in the development of behavior, we shall confine ourselves to a brief listing of these reactions. No attempt has been made to give a complete review of the work of all those who have written on the subject, and the authors who are cited are selected simply because their work contributes to the picture of the equipment of the newborn. In order to investigate the development of behavior in the infant, it is necessary to have this picture in mind, so that the distinction between those responses which are changing or growing and those which are already established will be clear.

SLEEP

Sleep is undoubtedly part of the infant's equipment which is present from birth in a completely developed form. Habits of sleep change, but there is no reason to believe that the sleep itself is of a different character at birth than later on. Sleep plays a very large part in the life of the newborn baby. Bryan (22) reports that infants usually stay awake the first two hours after birth, and Bühler (23) that over twenty-one hours of the young infant's day is spent in sleep or dozing. She also found that the sleeping periods of the newborn are short and that they increase gradually with age, and as the length of the naps increase their frequency decreases. Pratt, Nelson and Sun (164) found that movements during sleep increase with age during the first two weeks of life, just as they do during the waking periods, but that the infants moved more when awake than when asleep. A number of authors note that the smile which they report as present from birth usually occurs during sleep.

CRYING

Crying is another activity that is present from birth; in fact the infant's first cry is considered an important factor in establishing respiration. At first the stimuli for crying are limited to the simplest and most immediate environmental factors and to the proprioceptive stimuli from hunger, pain or discomfort. But as behavior becomes more and more complex, the number of things which may stimulate it increases, while at the same time other ways of reacting to stimuli develop, so that crying decreases with age, after complex behavior begins. There is a difference of opinion as to the age at which crying with tears begins. Taylor-Jones (189) reports tears on the first day of life in one or more of the seventy-five babies she tested, and Blanton (14) reports them during the first week. Bühler (23) states that they do not appear until the end of the first month. It is difficult to account for this discrepancy since Bühler observed her subjects for twenty-four hours of the day. The mouth sounds accompanying crying are considered, by a number of authors, as the starting point for the development of speech. This aspect of crying will be discussed under the development of speech. The other vocal sounds noted in the newborn are vocalized sighing and grunting and mouthing sounds.

YAWNING, SNEEZING, ETC.

The longest list of the spontaneous reactions which can be observed in the newborn in fully developed form is that given by Taylor-Jones (189). She observed the following, in one or more of seventy-five infants on the first day: yawning, sneezing, hiccuping, sighing, coughing, stretching, smiling, salivation, vomiting, urination and defecation, besides sleeping and crying. Shirley (180) lists among those patterns which are present at birth yawning, sneezing, hiccuping, stretching; she also refers to vomiting. Gesell (65) refers to the ability of the newborn to yawn, cough and sneeze on the first day. Bühler (23) mentions yawning, stretching and vomiting. Gilmer (67) took moving-picture records of four infants, for a short time each day, for the first ten days of life. He describes the bodily accompaniments of stretching and sneezing. Stretching occurred with the mouth and usually the eyes closed; the legs were always flexed and the forearms were drawn toward the head and shoulders with an upward pull at the shoulders rather than at the forearms, or the arms were straightened above the head. In a number of cases of extreme stretching, the infants reared up on the backs of their heads and arched their backs. With slight sneezes, no arm and leg movements were recorded. The eyes were always closed on inspiration and stayed so until expiration; the mouth and nose were wrinkled, and the mouth was open or closed; in strong sneezes the forearms were jerked upward and inward and the legs flexed at the moment of expiration. This complete description made from camera records of these two reactions shows that, although the specific reaction is present in much the same form in which it is found in adults, the bodily accompaniments of the reactions are the same sort of generalized, more or less total body reactions usually found in the newborn, even to specific stimuli.

GASTRIC HUNGER CONTRACTIONS

Gastric hunger contractions are another mechanism that appears to be fully developed in the newborn infant. Carlson and Ginsburg (28) studied puppies and newborn infants. The subjects swallowed rubber balloons attached to a catheter, before the stomach had ever contained food. Gastric tonus and hunger contractions were found very soon after birth. They differed from those of adults only in being more frequent, and occurred every ten to fifteen minutes. The periods ended in an incomplete tetanus which these authors take to be a sign of youth and a vigorous stomach.

PUPILLARY REFLEXES

The literature indicates that the pupillary reflex, a contraction of the pupils when a bright light is flashed in the eyes, can be elicited in the newborn if the stimulation is carefully applied. It is hard to get immediately after birth because the infant's eyes are usually closed, and when open there is often a film over them for some time after birth, but when conditions permit the test, the reflex is usually present. Chaney and McGraw (31) mention the need of a more accurate technique for the qualitative study of this reflex. They found a positive response in 91 percent of the 100 neonates and in 64 per cent of the 25 partunates tested. Taylor-Jones (189) found the reflex present in all the 75 infants she tested on the first two days of life. Rolando (172) found it in 78 of 80 neonates he tested. Sherman and Sherman (179) report on 26 infants tested during the first few days. They found a good reaction in only 6 infants, but a sluggish one in 15 others and no reaction in only 2. Cotelessa (46) mentions the pupillary reflex as among those common to the newborn. De Angeles (2) tested 88 infants during the first two weeks, the majority on the first and second day after birth. He reports that 17 percent had obstinately myotic pupils, with a barely perceptible oscillation toward the light; 20.5 percent showed enlarged pupils and slow eye movements, and 62.5 percent showed a series of alternations beginning with a contraction provoked by a luminous stimulus and followed by a dilation. Nakaoji, Kubara, Inamatu and Imoto (144), however, present results curiously at variance with those cited. In an investigation of over 2,000 infants under two years of age, they found that during the first two months there was practically no pupillary reflex; that it begins to appear in boys in the second month, and in girls in the third, and that by the fifth and sixth months it is present in 75 percent of girls and 80 percent of boys. They may be talking of the blinking response on approach, or their results may be explained by the way their tests were made, or by their lack of exactness in explaining what they mean by "practically" no response.

The other eye reactions which are found fully developed at birth are the corneal reflex, which is elicited by a slight touch on the eye; and the conjunctival, which is a blink or jerk of the lids elicited by a touch on the corner of the lid. Rolando (172) reports a positive corneal reflex in 78 of his 80 neonates, and the conjunctival in 76 of the 80. De Angeles (2) found a very vigorous corneal reflex present in all of his 88 subjects. Gonzales (69) says that the conjunctival reflex disappears during sleep in infants under one year of age. Gutman (74) says the corneal reflex is present from birth and the conjunctival is elicited less regularly.

DEEP AND SUPERFICIAL REFLEXES

With the exception of the plantar reflex, which changes in character with age and is the subject of much controversy, the literature on the state of the cutaneous and tendon reflexes in the newborn is meager. We shall summarize here only the literature dealing with those reflexes which are established and fully developed by birth, and refer only to those reflexes which have been most frequently investigated in the newborn. Wide individual differences are found in the response to skin and tendon reflexes in the newborn, just as in all early behavior patterns; therefore, the absence of the reflex has not the pathological significance it has for the adult. Chaney and McGraw (31) point out that the differences in muscle tonus in newborn infants affect the nature and amount of activity resulting from stimulation. They observed that the abdominal reflexes seemed difficult to obtain in infants over half an hour old, when there was tension of the abdominal muscles; and that they were difficult to elicit in infants under half an hour old, even when the muscles were flaccid. On the other hand, the hypotonia of these very young infants seemed to facilitate responses to tendon stimulation. These findings are interesting, in the light of Bolaffio and Artom's (18) statement that the tendon reflexes prevail over the muscle in fetuses by the time of birth. Rolando (172) states that by the use of a definite method, all the more common and important nervous reflexes can be provoked in the newborn, but that the systematization of the responses is difficult because of the wide variety of behavior they present. Therefore, the presence or absence of one reflex cannot be taken as an indication of the status of the nervous system and the probability of the presence of an organic or functional change. De Angeles (2) says that variations in the responses make repetition of a test to reach precise, definite conclusions, difficult. After several stimulations, a kind of muscular fatigue, or an adaptation to the stimulus, results, so that in protracting observations the examiner excites a reflex entirely different in quality and intensity from the first one. Vigorous stimulation elicits not only the reflex which is sought, but a series of muscular contractions which are extraneous to those peculiar to the reflex, and which interfere with its interpretation.

The literature indicates that further investigation of the relationship of muscle tonus and the presence or absence of specific reflexes is needed. The most that can be said at present seems to be that at birth certain responses can be elicited in a sufficient number of infants to establish the fact that the mechanisms for the reactions are fully developed by the time of birth, or very shortly thereafter, and that failure to provoke the response does not indicate any necessary abnormality in the individual infant, because of variables in the condition of the infant which have not yet been thoroughly investigated.

Chaney and McGraw (31) found that a larger percentage of responses to the tendon stimulations was elicited from the partunates than from the infants over half an hour old, while a much larger percentage of responses to cutaneous stimulation was elicited from the infants over this age. The biceps, triceps, Achilles and patellar reflexes were stimulated by five successive taps on each tendon. No definite evidence was found that a repetition of stimulations materially increases the probability of a response. The positive responses to these stimulations ranged from 46 percent for the triceps in the neonates to 92 percent for the biceps in the partunates. De Angeles (2) says that the results from his tendon stimulation on 88 infants were doubtful for all tendons except those in the knee; for this he obtained a normal response from 20.4 percent, an exaggerated response in 54.5 percent, a much exaggerated one in 21.6 percent and no response in 3.5 percent of the cases. He found a difference between the two knees in the intensity of the response, this being common in the premature infants. Sometimes the response was present in one knee and not in the other. Cotelessa (46) lists the patellar and Achillean reflexes as among those that are common to the newborn. Hayashi (79) says that the patellar response is almost always found on the first day, and that the Achillean increases during the first year to be always present by two years. Burr (25) tested the deep and superficial reflexes of 96 infants one hour to ninety days of age. He found a positive patellar response in 61 of 66 infants, 3 of whom were less than one hour old. He states that the patellar response is as good in young infants as it is in adults. The response to Achilles stimulation, however, was absent in 30 of 52 infants, and was in general weak and required many stimulations. He says that it is not known how late in life this reflex may appear in a normal individual. He concludes that deep and superficial reflexes may be present at birth, but that the absence of one or all is not an indication of disease, and that when they appear after birth there is no regular order for their appearance.

Chaney and McGraw (31) got a positive response to cutaneous abdominal stimulation in 33.3 percent of the neonates and in only 2 percent of the partunates tested. Rolando (172) reports positive abdominal responses from 24 of the 80 neonates he tested, and a positive response to cremasteric stimulation from 6. De Angeles (2) says that the abdominal reflex is elicited with difficulty and must be tested during sleep or nursing. He found it hardly perceptible in 77 percent of the 88 neonates he tested, rather intense in 16 percent and absent in 7 percent. The cremasteric he found present in 92 percent of the infants, and he states that it varied in intensity with the descent of the testicles. Hayashi (79) states that the abdominal reflex increases with age and is always present by two years, and that the cremasteric is found in 90 percent of children by three years. Cotelessa (46) lists the abdominal and cremasteric reflexes as common to the newborn. Burr (25) found a positive response to abdominal stimulation in 20 out of 27 infants, and says that it can sometimes be elicited in young infants only by stimulation of the lowest third of the muscle. Troemner (197) found that the abdominal reflexes were present in a decerebrate infant he examined, which lived two days.

LIFTING HEAD

Another behavior pattern which is generally conceded to be developed by birth is the ability to turn the head to free the nose for breathing, and to lift the head at least momentarily when lying prone. Blanton (14) noted turning the head at birth. Shirley (180) says that all the 25 babies she tested were able to turn the head to free the nose, and that most of them lifted the head at least momentarily during the hospital period. Gesell (65) lists lifting the head when prone, as a developmental item noted the first week. He places this as a reaction which is fully established by four months, but this discrepancy is probably due to the fact that his tests begin at four months of age, and that by that time the normal baby should be able to hold his head up more than momentarily when in this position. Bryan (22) states that 10 of the 66 infants she tested, lifted their heads off the table when prone, during the first twenty minutes of life. There is an observable difference between the way the baby holds his head up just after birth and the way he does so later, when the reaction has developed as part of a more complex and co-ordinated pattern of bodily movements, but this difference is hard to describe in objective terms.

REACTIONS DEVELOPING OR REGRESSING AFTER BIRTH

THE SPECIAL SENSES

The literature on the sensory development of newborn infants is in general agreement that the neural mechanisms for the senses are developed to the point where there are differences in reactions to different sensory stimuli. These reactions, however, are not like adult reactions, a fact which seems to have led some of the earlier investigators to conclude that the senses were "dormant" in the newborn, while the fact that differential reactions are found, seems to have led others to the view that the sensory mechanisms are well developed by birth. Recent investigations, carried out under carefully standardized conditions and making use of quantitative measures of reactions, suggest that all these earlier conclusions need revision, and that measurements of the sensory reactions of the newborn which justify definite conclusions are just beginning to be made.

There is much speculation in the literature as to the possibility of sensory stimulation during intrauterine life. The general opinion is that with the exception of tactual, and possibly auditory stimuli, external conditions in the uterus are too constant to permit of effective sensory stimulation. The evidence for tactual stimulation is drawn from the position of the hands and the probability that both passive and active movements bring them in contact with each other and also possibly with the lips and face.

The evidence for auditory stimulation is presented in two recent accounts of apparent reactions by several fetuses to loud external sounds. Many authors, however, state that the infant is deaf at birth and for sometime thereafter, because of the amniotic fluid in the Eustachian tubes, and the gelatinous fluid in the middle ear. The difficulty here seems to be that of eliminating the possibility of the conduction of the vibrations from the sounds used as stimuli.

Similar difficulties have confused much of the testing for other sensory reactions. In 1913 Canestrini (27) pointed out another difficulty — that of drawing conclusions about sensory reactions from facial expressions of infants. It is well known that facial movements are well developed at birth and that they take forms which in older children can justifiably be interpreted as expressing emotional reactions, but it does not follow that the same psychic interpretations are justified for infants. Canestrini believes that much of the confusion, in the literature, about these reactions in the newborn has arisen because facial movements were the reactions noted and the observer read an emotional reaction into them.

Methods of restricting the stimuli to the particular sense organ to be tested are just beginning to be worked out. Results with these methods indicate that vision and eye movements are perhaps further developed at birth than has been commonly supposed, and that the other special senses are sufficiently developed to give differential reactions to certain stimuli: that is, they are neither dormant nor yet well developed. Troemner (197) tested the reactions of a decerebrate infant that lived two days. It gave no response to light, sound, smell, taste or touch. There was, however, a definite response to pain, trembling to cuts and pricks, and a response to cold, though none to heat. The eyelids moved weakly, but the pupils and cornea not at all.

The evidence seems to indicate that some progress in maturation of the sensory nerve tracts, or at least in many of them, has occurred in utero. Birth gives a great spurt to this process, just as it, for the first time, brings stimulation of many of the special senses. Therefore, it would seem that the more fruitful approach to investigation of the senses in the newborn is one which attempts to discover what sensory behavior is present and how this behavior develops with increasing age, rather than that which has dominated the literature for so long, which attempts to interpret sensory reactions as either present or absent. It is now generally accepted that other forms of behavior are in a developing state at birth, and all the evidence points to the fact that the special senses are not an exception, but show progressive behavior also.

The work of Canestrini (27), published in 1913, is accepted as the first significant statement of the sensory equipment of the newborn which is based on data gathered from thoroughly controlled and scientific procedure. As the work which has been done since has usually used Canestrini's work as a point of departure, his findings are summarized here.

In Premature Infants.—Peiper (154) tested three premature infants, one of 370 mm length and two of 420 mm length. The first was three days old; the other two, fourteen days old. The infants were tested for reactions to sound, light, pain, and cold, by noting changes in the respiration curves on stimulation. Differential curves were obtained to all these stimuli, and Peiper concludes that the premature infant is not less sensitive to stimulation than the infant born at term. He states that the infants must be kept perfectly quiet, and considerable rest periods given between stimulations, as rapid consecutive stimulations create a state of adaptation to the stimuli and the infant fails to react. Peiper points out the danger of ascribing changes in the curves, due to fright or body movements, to sensory stimulation. The changes in the curves on stimulation were clear and quick and were alike for all the different stimulations. There was a pause, lasting up to nine seconds, before restoration of the respiratory rhythm, when the reaction was a lowering of the curve. The intensity of the stimuli were kept as constant as possible, but there was considerable variation in the irritability of the sense organs. Peiper checked his results on these premature infants by experiment on one sleeping older child, and got the same results. He also tested a microcephalic infant thirteen months old with the light and sound stimuli, and got curves like those obtained with the premature neonates.

Taste.—Canestrini (27) tested the senses of newborn infants by noting the changes in curves obtained from pneumograph records of fontanelle pulsations and abdominal respiratory movements. He tested the taste reactions to sweet, salt, sour and bitter substances. He got calming reactions to sweet, as shown by a lowering of respiratory and brain-volume curves. Salt also seemed to be distinguished; the curves showed restlessness, and cessation of sucking was also observed. Sour and bitter gave changes in the curves as compared with sweet and salt; both showed marked irregularity in fontanelle and breathing curves. He found no difference between reactions to mother's and to cow's milk. He states that taste is the sense best developed at birth and compares favorably with that of adult animals. He makes a distinction between primitive and refined taste, and says that the latter is acquired.

Shirley (180) noted the facial and bodily reactions of 14 infants, during the first two weeks, to sweet, bitter, sour, and salt substances. The reactions to sour, bitter and salt were, in the majority of cases, those of rejection, as shown by turning the head from side to side, screwing up the face or making a wry face, crying or fussing, pushing the applicator out of the mouth with the tongue, or slashing the arms so that they knocked the applicator out of the mouth. Twelve of the infants sucked contentedly on the sweet applicator, although there were some facial reactions with the sucking. One baby sucked on the bitter and salt applicators and cried at the same time, and another sucked on the acid. Shirley reports that some of the babies kept their mouths tightly closed after the first taste, so that the mouth had to be pried open for the second. Bryan (22) tested 66 infants during the first ten days and found no differences in reactions to different milks when presented as a taste or as an odor. Lactic-acid preparations, however, gave facial contortions. Taylor-Jones (189) tested 75 infants on the first two days of life with salt inside the lower lip, and reports mouth motions, smacking lips, running tongue out, and salivation. This test, however, seems

inconclusive since there is no mention of comparing these reactions with any other taste or with a neutral substance.

Pratt, Nelson and Sun, and Jensen have recently tested taste
reactions by a more thorough scientific procedure and by meas-
urement of the reactions in quantitative form. Pratt, Nelson and
Sun (164) used a stabilimeter with a polygraph record of bodily
movements in a control cabinet, with supplementary records by
an observer and the experimenter. The stabilimeter was locked
when the experimenter handled the infant or touched him in applying the stimulus. The infant's mouth was opened for insertion
of the taste applicators by a touch on each corner of the mouth,
and the authors note that this stimulus alone often started sucking movements. In reports on the sucking reflex, this fact is often
noted, and it is significant of the loose procedure used in much
of the investigation of taste reactions that this is the only study
found where a distinction is made between the sucking reflex
and responses to taste. Twenty-eight infants were tested, each
an average of 8 times, from birth to the fifteenth day. The stimuli
were applicators dipped in solutions of sugar, salt, quinine, citric
acid, and water, given in this order. Reactions were noted to 85
percent of the stimulations. There was little variation with age,
although the number of specific reactions was greatest on the
first day and lowest from the fifth to seventh days. Recorded
body reactions increased from 7 percent on the first day to 13
percent on the eleventh day; head and facial reactions also increased. There was an increase in sucking movements for sugar
and water from birth to eleven days, and a decrease for quinine
and citric acid. Sucking reactions to the different stimuli were
as follows: 49 percent to sugar; 36 percent to salt; 32 percent
to water; 22 percent to quinine, and 7 percent to citric acid. The
number of reactions to water would suggest that the infants do
not react to taste alone, but partly to the presence of something
in the mouth. The total number of specific movements occurred
as follows: 25 percent to citric acid; 24 percent to quinine; 19
percent to sugar; 17 percent to salt; and 15 percent to water.
When sucking is excluded, the infants reacted least to water and
sugar. The infants did not react to the taste solutions in the

same way as adults. The citric acid solution seemed weak to the adults (2.14 percent) yet the infants reacted strongly. The quinine solution seemed strong to the adults (0.27 percent) yet the infants' reactions were relatively weak. The authors conclude that when the taste solutions are of about equal strength and not too strong, there is not much specificity in reaction, and that intensive stimuli should not be used for infants, as some investigators have done, if characteristic reactions to different types of taste are to be isolated.

Jensen (98) has employed an elaborate technique for measuring differential reactions to tests and temperature by means of changes in an objective record of the feeding reaction. He states,

The absence of language responses in the newborn infant has restricted the investigation of just those problems which are the basis of adult behavior. . . . In seeking an objective procedure which might serve, at least as a partial substitute for such language behavior, a new experimental technique was developed which involves the use of a fundamental behavior mechanism, the feeding reaction, as an indicator of the infant's responses to controlled stimulation. This technique consists in comparing sucking reactions to various experimental stimuli with a control sucking reaction, all curves being objectively recorded. The controls being identical, any deviation from the control curve by the experimental curve was interpreted and described as a differential reaction.

A specially constructed nursing bottle was used, and a calibrated nipple connected with a carefully developed manometer which registered changes which were recorded on a polygraph. The control reaction was milk at 40° C. The taste reactions obtained were for sterile water, 6-percent glucose, acid milk, and 0.900, 0.450, 0.225, and 0.200-percent salt solutions. With 973 salt stimulations on 14 infants, all infants failed to show a differential reaction to the 0.200-percent solution; one showed it to the 0.225-percent solution; 6 to 0.300, while only 3 failed to give it to the 0.450-percent solution, and only one to the 0.900-percent solution. The differential reactions secured were gradual deviations from the control curves, becoming more marked as the percentage of salt solution was increased. They began with a slight break in the curve and increased up to the point where vigorous avoidance movements were made and the child cried hard. Differential reactions occurred 95 percent of the time without marked facial expressions, but when these did occur they were always with differential reactions. Twenty trials on 3 infants with acid milk gave no differential reactions. Seventeen infants gave no differential reactions to glucose. Eighty-two stimulations on 15 infants gave no differential reactions to sterile water. The difficulties of isolating gustatory reactions are shown by the fact that differential reactions were found in every one of 604 cases of 17 infants sucking on air.

The results of the different investigators cited here show that no method has yet been developed which makes possible unequivocal statements as to the taste of newborn infants. The evidence does seem to indicate, however, that infants give a positive reaction to sweet, and that salt, sour and bitter may give negative reactions. It seems to be conclusive that the taste reactions of the newborn are not like those of adults, which suggests that definite statements cannot be made until further work has been done with more different kinds of taste stimuli and with solutions of different strengths. A further difficulty is that almost any stimulation of the oral cavity and of the lips and cheeks of the infant gives mouth reactions or sucking. Continued quiet sucking, however, seems to furnish adequate evidence of positive taste reactions; and very marked continued facial reactions, accompanied by violent body-wide movements and crying, whether combined with a cessation of sucking or not, seem to be adequate evidence of negative reactions.

Smell.—The earlier writers on the sense of smell in the newborn believed this sense to be well developed at birth. The concensus of the more recent work is, however, that it is not well developed. Canestrini (27) suggests the possibility that the earlier workers were influenced by the facts that smell is highly developed in animals and that the myelinization of the olfactory tracts begins comparatively early in fetal life. In his work, he carefully confined the stimulations to smell alone, and used twenty odorous substances. He obtained changes in the fontanelle or respiratory curves in 47 of his experiments, and no change in 54. The changes noted were an increase in fontanelle pulsations, increased respiration, and deeper and more irregular respiration. He found no reaction to lukewarm cow's milk. Crying infants were sometimes quieted by bad-smelling substances. His conclusions are that much of the experimental stimulation of the olfactory nerves really serves as a stimulant of the "trigeminal components of the sense of smell," and so is tactual rather than olfactory. This is illustrated by the common, adult reaction to ammonia. Parker (150) calls this kind of olfactory stimulation the *common chemical sense*. In the effort to get differential reactions, investigators have used extremely strong substances of the sort which set off other than olfactory reactions, such as sneezing. Canestrini notes that the positive reactions he obtained were largely in response to such substances.

A recent study, which was not made under controlled scientific conditions, is that of Taylor-Jones (189). She tested 75 infants on the first and second day with mother's milk on a cotton pladget held near the nose. She found no reaction in sleeping infants, but in those awake and near the nursing time she observed dilation of the nostrils and mouth motions. Fifteen infants were tested in the same way with ammonia; those asleep jumped, drew back the head, cried, blinked, dilated the nostrils, and made mouth motions; those awake turned the head away, cried, made mouth motions, sneezed, and brushed a hand across the face. The sneezing which was observed in several infants is interesting, in the light of Canestrini's belief that much of the testing has evoked tactual rather than strictly olfactory reactions.

A recent very carefully controlled experiment is that of Pratt, Nelson and Sun (164). Smell was tested during the investigation for 48 infants, on the stabilimeter in the control cabinet. Capsules containing two drops of valerian, acetic acid, oil of cloves, and ammonia were used, and a control capsule without any odor. The odors and the control air were forced into the infants' nostrils by an olfactory pump which released the odors through a glass tube at the moment of stimulation. There was slight variation in the number of reactions for infants of different ages until the eleventh day, and after that there was a drop in the number of

reactions, which was 49 percent on the first day and 44 percent
on the eleventh and after, the average being 48 percent. The
number of specific movements was largest on the first day and
smallest on the eleventh. These reactions, among the infants who
were asleep and dry, were 28 percent general body movements,
26 percent movements of the extremities, 13 percent head movements, 10 percent mouth sounds, 9 percent facial movements, 5
percent sucking reactions, 6 percent eye movements, and 3 percent mouth movements exclusive of sucking. The sucking reactions decreased from 13 percent on the first day to 4 percent on
the eleventh. Fifty-nine percent of the activity was to ammonia,
32 percent to acetic acid, 5 percent to valerian, 3 percent to cloves,
and 1 percent to air. The puff of control air was a stimulant to
the older infants; the activity to oil of cloves was less than that
to air alone for these infants. The authors conclude that the newborn infant does not react to olfactory stimuli in the same way
that adults do. They cite the fact that to the experimenters the
ammonia seemed much stronger than the acetic acid, yet the
infants' reactions to these two stimuli were about equal. If the
ammonia and acetic acid are eliminated on the ground that they
stimulate the common chemical sense rather than smell alone, it
is obvious that few and weak reactions were found in this study.

Pain.—Observations of the tactual sense of newborn infants
fall into investigation of the superficial reflexes, which are summarized elsewhere, and a few experiments on pain stimulation and
the temperature sense. Pain due to proprioceptive stimuli is practically impossible to investigate in the newborn, though the older
literature contains considerable speculation as to what pleasant
or unpleasant sensations are possible to the newborn. There are
some studies of the reactions of infants to experimentally applied
painful stimuli. The general opinion is that infants at birth do
not react to these stimuli in ways that give evidence of experienc-
ing much discomfort. Carmichael (29) reports Genzmer's conclusion, drawn from work on premature infants, that pain is very
little developed in the fetus. A premature infant stimulated on
the first day of life until the blood came, gave no response. He
goes on to state that in work with animals, it has been found

that very strong and even destructive stimulation may or may not give a response that is different from one obtained by strong stimulation of the same point with a stiff hair.

Canestrini (27) reports very poor reactions to pain stimuli, as registered by changes in the fontanelle and breathing curves of neonates; 8 out of 10 give some reaction to the prick of a needle. The lips were the most susceptible area. Peiper (156), however, states that neonates react to pain if in good general condition, and that they could not be operated on without an anesthetic. Koffka's (106) general statement is in agreement with Canestrini's, that the infant's pain sensitivity is subnormal. Sherman and Sherman (179), in their study of 96 infants from one hour to twelve days of age, found positive reactions to a needle prick on the first stimulation, in all infants after the seventy-sixth hour. To a prick on the face, all infants over forty-one hours of age responded the first time the stimulation was given; all responded from birth before ten rapidly increasing stimuli were applied, the number of stimuli necessary to start the reaction decreasing with age. From the first to the eighth hour, three infants did not respond at all to the pricks on the leg.

Temperature.—Studies of the temperature sense of newborn infants give results in much less ambiguous terms than those on pain, although investigation has not yet proceeded far enough to give definite information as to the temperature thresholds for specific reactions. Canestrini (27) found that of a number of tactual stimulations applied to different parts of the body, cold stimuli produced with ethylchloride, alcohol and cold metal gave strongest reactions, as measured by increased respiration and brain-volume curves, and restlessness. The reactions were much more marked than those to needle pricks.

Pratt, Nelson and Sun (164) investigated temperature reactions in their controlled study of infants during the first days of life. The stimuli were a cold cylinder applied to the forehead and to the inside surface of one knee, and water of different temperatures put into the mouth with a medicine dropper. Twenty-one babies were stimulated with the cylinder, the average temperature of which was 11° to 12° C., with a stimulating area of 50 sq. mm. The infants were about as sensitive asleep as when awake; there were reactions to 93 percent of the stimulations when awake and to 91 percent when asleep. The reaction was segmental, 64 and 52 percent head movements to stimulation on the forehead, and 88 and 74 percent flexion and extension of the leg to stimulation on the knee. These reactions were the most specific ones obtained in their testing of the various senses. Thirty infants were tested with water at 8°, 13°, 18°, 23°, 33°, 43°, 48° and 53° C. There were reactions to 87 percent of the stimulations. Sucking as a reaction decreased from 30 percent on the first day to 16 percent on the eleventh day and later. The body reactions increased with age, from 17 percent the first day to 23 percent on the eleventh. The infants reacted more strongly to the temperatures that were colder than the body than to those that were warmer.

Jensen (98) tested the temperature sense of 17 infants by means of sucking curves obtained from milk warmer and colder than body temperature, fed the infants through a special nursing bottle which gave a polygraph record. A total of 450 stimulations was given. The thresholds for differential reactions to the warm milk varied with the individual from 50° to 85° C., and for the cold milk from 5° to 32° C., but tended to remain constant for each individual for the period of the testing. Reactions to 55° and to 15° C. were secured on eight infants the second day. With 12 infants the reactions for temperatures above 50° C. were identical for those below 23° C. Sometimes as long as six or eight seconds elapsed before the change from the normal sucking curve began. Jensen cites this as an indication that reliable results cannot be obtained with the medicine-dropper technique. The differential reactions appeared as a gradual deviation from the normal curve, which became more marked as the temperatures were raised or lowered from the body temperatures. He explains the fact that he got just as marked reactions to warm stimuli as to cold, while Pratt, Nelson and Sun did not, as due to the fact that, as shown by his threshold determinations, they used only one temperature above his upper threshold, and that one only three degrees warmer than the threshold, while they used four temperatures below his cold threshold, two of them very strong.

Hearing.—The number of observations and controlled studies of hearing in neonates is much larger than that made on the special senses already reviewed. The reports are, however, again conflicting. Some investigators report reactions to sounds very shortly after birth; others state that the infant is deaf at birth and for sometime thereafter, giving as the reason the presence of fluid in the Eustachian tubes and of a gelatinous substance in the middle ear, temporary closure of the auditory cavities, immaturity of the auditory neural tracts, and absence of bone conduction. The reports of two studies furnishing possible evidence of hearing by fetuses have been cited. The possibility that the reactions observed in these studies are due to conduction of vibrations also applies to some of the studies on hearing in the newborn, where very loud clanging noises close to the infants' ears have been used. Pratt, Nelson and Sun (164) give us the probable reasons for the conflicting evidence, the lack of uniform technique, lack of similarity in the stimuli used, dominance of individual differences in the infants, and the lack of specific reactions to sounds. The more recent literature, which will be summarized here, seems to indicate that reactions which are definitely the result of auditory stimuli can be observed very shortly after birth.

Canestrini (27) took the breathing and fontanelle curves of 70 neonates, from six hours to fourteen days of age, to a number of auditory stimuli, such as the shot of a toy gun, the sound of a whistle, the music of a mouth organ, and the sound of a bell. When the infants were asleep, stimuli which were not loud enough to waken them, even on the first day, caused a slowing down of the breathing curve with a temporary increase in cerebral volume and an increased pulse rate, which he says is analogous to the attentiveness symptoms of an adult. For infants awake, he found a flattening of the respiratory curve and, to intense stimuli, irregularity in the respiratory curve and increase in the brain pulsations, which he points out are analogous symptoms to those of fright in the adult. There was an immediate quieting effect on crying infants, as shown in the curves, to vocal or mouth-organ stimulation. He found a decrease in the reactions when the stimulus was repeated after a fifteen-second interval.

Peiper (155), who investigated fetal reactions to a loud automobile horn, states that to observe the sound reactions of neonates their breathing must be studied after a period of quiet rest, and that moving and handling the infant cause motions which make it impossible to observe reactions to specific stimuli. He got responses to auditory stimuli in 4 of 6 neonates, the youngest of whom was twenty-five minutes old, as indicated by changes in the respiratory curve.

Bryan (22) used a hand bell of 512-vibration frequency and a Galton whistle with a pitch of 10,000 to 35,000 vibration in testing 66 neonates during the first ten days of life. She concludes that the newborn infant gives no evidence of hearing ordinary sounds during the first two days; reactions began on the third to the seventh days. She believes that some of the infants listened to vocal sounds before the tenth day. Koffka (106), in reviewing the knowledge about newborn infants, confirms Bryan's view that infants react early to the voice. He believes that it is the first differentiated reaction shown to sounds, and that it occurs in a specific form during the third week.

Shirley (180) reports that 7 of the 24 babies she tested during the first two weeks of life did not react at all to sounds, and that no reaction whatever to sounds occurred in 62 percent of the examinations. The commonest reaction of those who did respond was a blink, which occurred in 32 percent of the tests; jerks occurred in 7 percent of the tests; none of the babies showed any symptoms of fear. Taylor-Jones (189) in her tests on 75 neonates during the first two days, used a snapping beetle as a stimulus; this eliminated currents. Twenty-seven of 29 infants who were crying stopped when stimulated in this way. Only 2 responded when asleep; 26 who were awake and not crying responded by blinking, flinching, quivering and turning the eyes; 6 gave no response.

Irwin (95) measured the latent time of the body startle of twelve infants from fifteen hours to fifty-three days of age. The stimulus was a loud tone from a loud-speaker four inches behind the infants' head. The sound was loud enough to cause a startle in adults. Several stimulations were given to each infant. The response was either a body startle or a closing or tightening of the eyelids. The eyelid response occurred even when there was no body startle. Irwin says that the latent time of the 163 body startles obtained is comparable to that of simple auditory reaction time in adults. There was little change in the mean latent time from day to day. The mean time was 0.18 seconds, with a standard deviation of 0.03 seconds, and the shortest time was 0.07 seconds.

Bühler (23) states that during the first two months, infants give no signs of responding to auditory stimuli which are weak or of limited intensity. Haller (75) investigated the reactions of infants to changes in the intensity and pitch of pure tone. She concludes that the effect of an auditory stimulus depends upon the physiological conditions of the infant and all the internal and external stimuli that are operating at the same time. The reactions obtained are reflex, undifferentiated responses definitely related to the intensity of the stimulus, and which do not usually persist after the removal of the stimulus. Her specific conclusions are that pure tones of a high vibration rate are more disturbing to infants than those of a low vibration rate, and that infants show more positive and varied expressions of discomfort than of comfort to auditory stimuli. She sees no reason, however, to attribute these reactions to fear.

Aldrich (1) reports an interesting case of obtaining auditory response from a young infant who gave no signs of responding to usual tests. A conditioned reflex was established by ringing a bell out of sight of the infant and scratching the sole of her foot with a pin, hard enough to cause pain. This procedure was carried out every half hour throughout one night and into the morning. By mid-morning the child gave the reaction, which she had been showing to the pin, when the bell was rung without scratching her foot. Aldrich suggests the conditioned reflex as a possible method of testing other sensory reactions of the newborn.

Pratt, Nelson and Sun (164) tested the hearing of neonates

in experiments carried out with the infants on a stabilimeter in a control cabinet. An empty one-pound coffee can was struck on the bottom as a method of getting a sharp, loud sound; a snapping sound was made by a mouse trap arrangement which released a metal spring on a wooden base, an electric bell with a 600 to 800-cycle frequency was rung about 12 inches back of the infants' heads; a Chinese wooden bell with a sharp shrill sound of 1,500 to 2,000 cycles was used, and a 350-cycle tuning fork mounted on a box-type resonator. These stimuli were checked for loudness before using them; the can was the loudest and the tuning fork the weakest. Fifty-nine infants were given 461 tests and 5,836 stimulations with the can, snapper, wooden bell, electric bell and tuning fork, in this order. Reactions were obtained to 46 percent of the stimulations; 2 percent of these were pacifying reactions. There was an increase in the amount of activity per stimulation, as measured by the stabilimeter, with increasing age from birth to eleven days and older. The specific movements observed were: movements of the extremities, 35 percent; eye movements, 34 percent; general bodily movements, 26 percent; sounds by the infants, 3 percent; facial and head movements, one percent each. The can elicited 31 percent of the specific movements, the snapper, 26 percent; the electric bell, 25 percent; the wooden bell, 13 percent; the tuning fork, 8 percent. The measurable activity was 47 percent to the can, 21 percent to the electric bell, 16 percent to the snapper, 9 percent to the wooden bell, and 7 percent to the tuning fork. From these two measures they conclude that the reactions were only partially determined by the loudness of the sounds, as determined by adult reactions. There was practically no variation with increasing age in the number of times an infant reacted to the sounds. The pacifying reactions were to the tuning fork, the electric bell, the snapper, the can and the wooden bell, in this order, and the duration of the stimuli was also in this order, which, the authors suggest, may be significant. Head movements increased with age and constituted only 36 percent of the total specific movements, from which they conclude that reactions to sound are no more specific than those to other stimuli. They state:

The analysis of the three factors (number of reactions, specificity of the reactions, amount of movement) shows that each type of sound stimulation has a stimulating effect of its own, but the variety and difference in force of the reactions was such that for these early ages the reactions to the type of stimuli used were not very specific. Further experiments on the separate variables, tone, noise, loudness, duration, would yield significant results for the auditory mechanism, which, as one of the factors of speech, becomes of such great importance at later ages.

Pratt (161) has also studied the effect of repeated auditory stimulations upon the general bodily activity of 28 infants from two to eleven days of age. The stabilimeter was used and the auditory stimuli were automatic blows of a constant intensity upon the bottom of a coffee can, presented at intervals of 10, 30 or 60 seconds. Activity during the experimental period was compared with that during a control period in the cabinet. The total bodily activity increased during the periods of auditory stimulation, and was in the nature of immediate response to the individual stimulations, rather than the result of a heightened general irritability and restlessness, as shown by the polygraph records and electrical-counter readings. The total activity of a period increased when the number of stimuli was increased, but the decrease in the interval between stimuli caused an average decrease in the effectiveness of the individual stimulations. Pratt concludes from this study that the newborn infant is able to adjust himself to situations of the type presented by a process which reduces the magnitude and extent of his responses to recurring stimuli, and that the character of the responses indicates that we are not justified in characterising them as emotional responses of fear.

Loewenfeld (124) says that the newborn infant does not hear during the first few hours after birth, owing to mechanical blocks, but that he does hear after this. He cites Demitriades' tests on 105 neonates in which the earliest reactions to sounds were obtained between three and four hours after birth. He himself tested 3 children for the first seven days and 6 during the second week of life; after sixteen hours of age all reacted, and without any observable difference in the type of responses from those found in tests made throughout the first month of life. During the first three days of life reactions were noted to one-third of the stimulations, and to the seventh day to 50 percent of the stimulations, and to the end of the first month to 62 percent.

Eye Movements, Sight and Color Preferences.—Practically all investigators of the behavior of newborn infants have observed and reported on some of the many possible eye reactions, and there has been much speculation as to the extent of the visual acuity of these infants. Wide differences of opinion are found as to the ability of infants to fixate on light, to focus, to follow moving objects, to make color distinctions, and so on. The literature, however, shows that a great variety of eye reactions have been observed, even though definite and conclusive results have not been obtained. Any interpretation of the behavior of the newborn is complicated by the fact that it is impossible to substantiate conclusions as to the psychic experience, or feeling tones, which may be said to be part of the reactions. In investigating sight, this difficulty is increased, although there is general agreement that infants do not see in the sense that adults do. Statements as to how much they see, and how what they see appears to them is related to consciousness, must be taken as purely theoretical.

Gesell (65) says that an infant on the first day of life shows a rhythmic tensing movement of the eyelids, and the eyes move back and forth continually with a slow semirhythmic regularity. Koffka (106) states that the eye reflexes of the newborn are bilateral from the first, that at first the infant keeps the lids closed against the light, and that the lids do not blink at the rapid approach of an object. Eye movements are of two kinds, coordinated and uncoördinated, and fixation is possible even on the first·day. Other authors comment on the uncoördinated character of many of the spontaneous eye movements of very young infants; one lid will open while the other remains closed, and even the eyeballs make frequent movements which are independent of each other. Gutman (74) observed asymmetric lid movements, but states that movements were coördinated when the infants looked up or down. Bryan (22) reports that 15 of the 66 infants she tested, opened their eyes immediately after birth, and that an infant usually remains awake for the first two hours after birth.

The eyes soon adapt themselves to light. Taylor-Jones (189) tested 75 babies on the first two days of life and reports that all moved the eyes with rotary movements, up and down and back and forth. She also observed temporary nystagmus and sometimes strabismus, and states that she observed definite evidence of focusing in 23 babies.

A number of authors have commented on the eye blink found in the newborn as contrasted with the blinking reflex, which does not appear until later. A newborn infant will not blink at a threat stimulus, that is when the hand or an object is moved rapidly toward the eyes, but will sometimes blink at a touch on the eyelids, nose or face. Gutman (74) reports a screwing up of the lids to a hand-approach in an eight-day-old infant. He also reports a squinting and screwing of the lids at an electric bulb, from birth on. Valentine (198), in his observations of his son, got a blink to touch and to blowing on lids from the tenth day on, and believes the blinking reflex at a threat is conditioned from these earlier blinks to air movements, since, in the care of the infant, an air current and a sudden approach must often occur together. Jensen (98) reports the observation of nystagmus in 5 infants tested for reactions on the day of birth. Shirley (180) reports blinking as the most frequent reaction to sound, occurring in 33 percent of the tests she made on 24 infants during the first two weeks of life. It is probable that these contradictory statements on the presence of blinks in the newborn are due to differences in the exactness of meaning given the word, rather than to differences in observing a reaction which may be described more or less accurately as a blink. Gutman (74) states that some neonates show convergence fixation and conditioned eye movements in following a light in all directions, from birth on, while, in the majority of cases, these reflexes are probably acquired after birth.

Schaltenbrand (177), in his classification of the tonic neck and labyrinth reflexes, lists optic nystagmus under the reflexes of movement which are temporary in character, and which he states are probably reactions of the semicircular canals. He tested over 120 children from birth to eight years of age. The infant is held erect by the examiner, who then turns his body around, thus getting a test situation which is the same as using a revolving stool for adults. He found that eye-deviation and nystagmus appeared immediately after birth. Some infants, during the first few days of life, reacted to the turning with nystagmus-delirium of the eyes, but after this time the reaction was always typical, that is the eyes alternately lag behind and catch up until a certain speed of turning is reached. As the turning is retarded, the nystagmus returns, but in the opposite direction. Peiper and Isbert (159), in their study which followed Schaltenbrand's, report that all neonates showed adjustment of the eyes to changing posture. In infants born at term, the reflex began to fade in the second week. In premature infants, it lasted throughout the first three months, but was missing in all infants after the first half year. Shirley (180) also tested for eye coördination by swinging a tape horizontally, vertically and in a circle before the eyes of the infants she tested. Eye following was observed in all but 5 of the infants at least once during the first two weeks; for some it was noted consistently from birth on. Positive reactions were obtained in only 40 percent of the examinations. The percentages were as follows: eyes closed, 14; followed light, 40; did not follow, 26; doubtful, 18. She noted nystagmus only 6 times while making 129 examinations. Bryan (22) tested 66 infants with a flash light. She reports no following of the light with the eyes, and stronger reactions when the infants were asleep than when they were awake. The reactions were more acute during the first three days of life than later. She observed fixation on whiteness or brightness for considerable periods of time.

The more exact quantitative studies give fuller results. Canestrini (27) noted the changes in fontanelle pulsations and respiratory curves, in 70 neonates, to bright, medium and very weak electric lights, and to Bengal colored flames. Infants were tested while awake and while asleep, and, with the exceptions of one who had fallen into a sound sleep, observable reactions were obtained to all the experiments. The responses varied with the condition of the infant, whether hungry or just fed, and whether tired or just awakened from a nap. Allowing for these conditions, the stronger the stimulation, the stronger the reaction obtained; reactions are obtained in sleeping infants and in those who are crying, if the stimuli are strong enough. The reactions to strong and sudden light were similar to fright reactions in adults, but Canestrini warns against reading adult feeling tones into infant reactions. He found some evidence of the summation of stimuli in the changes in breathing and brain curves. His experiments with the colored lights were too few to enable him to say more than that the reactions were like those to the white light of comparable intensity.

Gurnsey (72) tested 25 infants, from eight hours to six months of age, with a standard differential pupiloscope. He found that the average size of the pupils increases in small increments with age. Rapidity of pupillary expansion and contraction was markedly less for the young infants than it is for adults. He obtained 6 examples of extremely slow contraction without observable stimulus in infants under two months of age. Five subjects showed simultaneous difference in the width of the pupils. Uncoördinated right-left eye movements occurred in 60 percent of the cases of infants under two weeks of age; in 30 percent at six weeks, and in one case at four months and twelve days of age. This was the only case with no consistency in the dominance of either eye. Three cases of uncoördinated eye and lid movements were observed in infants under sixty hours of age. Blinking reflexes were obtained in 80 percent of the cases, but only in response to contact or to intense light stimulation. Fixation was lacking well into the second month. Therefore it was difficult to determine differences in focal and peripheral sensitivity. At three months preferential sensory adaptation—that is to say, turning the head, the eyes, or the body—occurred to a light stimulus at 50 degrees from a similar stimulus equidistant in the visual median plane.

Sherman and Sherman (179) tested for eye coördination 96 infants from one hour to twelve days of age. The infants were in a darkened room and a dim flash light was moved one foot at a distance of about 15 inches from the infants' eyes. Fifteen eye movements were observed and the error in coördination expressed in the percentage noted in these fifteen movements. At two and one-half hours of age the percentage of error was 62.5, from the tenth to the thirty-fourth hour it averaged 13 percent, and above that age there were no errors.

Beasley (8) has recently made a study of visual pursuit on 109 white and 142 Negro infants from birth to twelve days of age. These infants were tested for horizontal, vertical and circular pursuit, under careful, standard conditions, with a dim light, with the hand with fingers moving, and with a wooden cylinder. The stimulus was sometimes prolonged as much as ten minutes in order to get fixation; once it was obtained, pursuit often followed easily. He also found it necessary to vary the distance from the eyes to suit the subject. "Is it not likely that there are variations in accommodation present at this age that would determine partly at least optimal distances for objects of any size?" The Negro infants excelled the whites, showing some type of pursuit in 93 percent of the tests, while the whites showed it in 61 percent. Horizontal pursuit was more successful than vertical, and vertical than circular. The Negro and white infants were about equal on horizontal pursuit, the Negroes were a little better on vertical pursuit and markedly so on the circular. The data, when arranged according to age, showed an improvement in performance with age, which was greater for the Negroes than for the whites. This seems to be one of the best and most conclusive experiments on the vision of neonates which has been made, and seems to indicate clearly that when adaptations are made to suit individual differences, which all investigators report to be marked in the newborn, the evidence for considerable skill in the use of the visual mechanism is definite.

McGinnis (129), however, does not agree with Beasley as to the age at which pursuit appears. He made a very thorough and careful study of optic nystagmus in the newborn. He points out that many of the writers who have observed eye movements in young children have been unfamiliar with the work on eye movements in adults, and that therefore they do not describe their results in a manner consistent with the accepted practices in classification, or in a manner that makes it clear just what type of movements were observed. He states that true nystagmus is the response of the eyes to a succession of moving objects and consists of two phases—a slow deviation in the direction of the movement of the object and a rapid jerk in the opposite direction. The slow phase is considered to be the same as pursuit eye movements, and the rapid phase the same as the movements termed *saccadic* by some workers. Six infants from the first to the forty-third day of life were tested. The infants were placed in a crib designed so that they lay in a trough which kept their bodies and heads in line with the view of the camera, yet allowed free movements. This crib was pushed into a cylinder lined with white cardboard to which were attached eleven black cardboard bars. This cylinder could be rotated about the child to stimulate nystagmus, or oscillated in harmonic motion on its axis to give conditions for studying visual pursuit. There was a narrow slit around the cylinder against which the lens of a moving picture camera was placed, which was focused on the infants' eyes, and photographs were taken of eye movements. The bars were on one side of the cylinder so that either the clear or barred field could be turned before the child. During the first two weeks experiments were made whenever the infants seemed to be in a favorable condition for them. Time was given the infant, and an effort made to have him focus on a dim light in the cylinder. Photographs were taken while the cylinder was oscillating at slow, medium and rapid speeds with the clear and barred fields, and with the bars at an angle of 40 degrees, and while it was rotating at slow, medium and rapid speeds as each bar passed the camera.

McGinnis's results are quoted in full below. We should also note his comment that the number of subjects was too small to permit of generalizations as to the age at which visual pursuit first appears, and so on.

Optic Nystagmus and Eye-Movements

1) Optic nystagmus occurs the first time each subject opens his eyes in the experimental situation while the cylinder is rotating at slow or medium speeds (even during the first 12 hours after birth, and even in an infant who is born one month prematurely).

2) Both the large saccadic eye-movements, which make up the quick phase of optic nystagmus, and the slow, gliding pursuit movements

(composed of several small saccadic movements), which make up the slow phase, occur during the first occurrence of optic nystagmus.

3) A few coördinate compensatory eye-movements occur within a few days of birth, but they occur too infrequently to permit any further generalizations concerning them.

4) The technique used on sleeping infants fails to produce optic nystagmus.

5) The number of eye-movements occurring during optic nystagmus is influenced by the number and the speed of movement of the bars on the visual field, and also, but to a smaller degree, by the age and experience of the child.

OCULAR PURSUIT

1) Successful ocular pursuit is not exhibited by any subject during the first two weeks of life. However, before ocular pursuit is possible (even in the first two weeks), the majority of the movements of the infants' eyes occur in the direction of the movements of the stimulating object; but many eye-movements in the opposite direction occur.

2) With increasing age there is a gradual increase in the number of eye-movements corresponding in direction with the movements of the stimulating object, and a gradual decrease in the number of movements in the opposite direction.

3) At the same time there is a marked increase in the number of head movements occurring in the direction of the movement of the stimulus.

4) All the subjects, when six weeks old, are able to respond to the movements of the apparatus with an ocular pursuit which has many of the characteristics of the ocular pursuit of an adult, and which is practically free from gross ocular movements which do not correspond with the movements of the stimulus. (Non-corresponding movements make up only 5.5 per cent of the total number at 5 weeks, and only 3.1 per cent at 6 weeks. Ocular pursuit first appears in the subjects during the third and fourth weeks.)

5) The number of ocular adjustments during the pursuit of a moving object under our experimental conditions is inversely related to the speed of movement of the apparatus (as is true in the case of optic nystagmus); but, under conditions otherwise comparable, the proportion of eye-movements in the correct direction is usually greater for the rapid speed than for slower speeds of the apparatus.

6) Inasmuch as the number of eye-movements occurring during optic nystagmus is only influenced to a relatively slight degree by the age and experience of the child, and inasmuch as age and experience produce a pronounced effect on the infants' ocular pursuit of a moving

visual field, the investigation of the latter ability appears to offer greater value for normative studies of infant development than does the study of optic nystagmus.

There seem to be at least two possible reasons for the difference in conclusions on ocular pursuit reached by Beasley and McGinnis. Beasley adjusted the distance of his stimuli to obtain the apparent optimal distance for each infant, while apparently the distance between the eyes and the stimulus was constant in McGinnis's experiment. McGinnis, with his motion-picture technique and fixed field with ruled bars, was able to make a much more detailed analysis of the eye movements involved in the various responses than was Beasley with his methods. It is possible that what Beasley observed as pursuit is the same reaction that McGinnis gives as the one occurring in the first two weeks, where the majority of the movements occur in the direction of the stimulating object. It is also possible that the differences are due to the small number of subjects tested by McGinnis, and to the fact that Beasley made a great effort to obtain fixation before he started moving the stimuli, while McGinnis apparently waited only a few seconds.

Peiper (157) studied the color sensitivity of premature infants. He used Tscherning photometric glasses of neutral grays which can be combined so as to give an accurate measure of the brightness of the light, and these were combined with color filters, enabling him to control the light value of the colors. The reaction stimulated was the eye reflex on the neck, that is the throwing back of the head when the eye is stimulated by a light-beam. The reflex depended upon the brightness of the light. The lowest light value at which the reaction occurred with the gray glasses was obtained. The gray glass was then replaced by colored glasses of known color values and the infant stimulated until the reactions were obtained, thus giving the individual color value for each infant. Peiper used red, yellow, green and blue. He found that these colors had the same relative light values for premature infants and for adults. An increasing light sensitivity against light of different wave lengths with dark adaptation was also found, indicating that the relative light value of colors shifts toward the purple end of the spectrum. Peiper says that neonates show reactions on stimulation of all the special senses, but that it is unknown how far the sensations aroused are like those of adults. It is possible that there are no true sensations, since the cortex is not yet active. In speaking of the sensations of the newborn, we must remember that they are much simpler than those experienced by adults, although it seems proper to conclude that infants have sensations similar to those of adults if they react as adults do. In any case differences in sensations can be measured by the differences in reactions. He points out that most of the work on color sensations in infants has been done by attempting to test for color choices, a method that cannot be used on young infants and that gives doubtful and conflicting results with all babies.

Pratt, Nelson and Sun (164) tested 24 infants with white and colored light from a flash light held about three inches from the infants' eyes, and flashed three times. The colors were yellow, green, red and blue, obtained by using color filters made up into slides on the same flash light that was used for the white light. Variations in luminosity were controlled by dimming the white to correspond with the luminosity of the colors, but the colors still presented such wide variations that the authors state that the results are ambiguous. To the white-light stimulations, the number of reactions, number of specific movements and the amount of stabilimeter activity rose and fell at nearly every age level, independently of one another. To the colored-light stimulations, the infants showed a fairly steady increase with age in the number of reactions and a decrease of from 81 to zero percent in the amount of stabilimeter activity from the first to the eleventh day. The number of specific movements, however, remained fairly constant with age. The total number of reactions showed no increase with age. The number of specific movements to the colors decreased in the following order: white, yellow, green, red, and blue, which is the same order as the luminosity grading of the colors, indicating that the effect was probably due to differences in luminosity, rather than to color discrimination. Since the color stimulations and the white stimulations were not given to the same infants, further analysis of the differences could not be made. The number of reactions of the head also decreased with age, from 13 percent the first day to zero percent the eleventh day. The authors conclude "That the light stimulations release not only reactions of the eyes but also movements of many other parts of the body, seems to indicate that the sensory elements at birth are so diffusely connected with many other motor elements that when an infant reacts at all, it reacts segmentally with various degrees of energy for the different segments."

Pratt (162) has made a study of the effects of repeated visual stimulation upon the activity of 28 newborn infants two to eleven days of age, similar to the study of auditory stimulation cited above. He found that the type of stimuli used, a rather dim electric light presented in the stabilimeter, did not appreciably increase the bodily activity, nor were there any specific responses of the gross musculature of the body. There was some indication of a Moro type of response to the first one or two stimuli presented to the youngest infants. He suggests from this that the Moro fear reaction may not be a conditioned or learned response on auditory stimulation, but one which is elicited only on stimulation of a greater intensity, as age increases.

POSTURE

One of the posture reflexes in newborn babies which has been observed and reported by a number of investigators is the spontaneous assumption, when the infant is placed in a prone position, of a posture similar to that of the fetus during intrauterine life. Shirley (180) noted this posture soon after birth in all of the 24 babies she tested. She states that it was outgrown by all but 2 of the infants during the first three or four weeks, "as the legs relaxed from their flexed neonatal posture." Eckstein and Paffrath (55), in an analysis of movement types in the newborn, attribute this posture to the tonus of the musculature and not to the intrauterine position. Peiper and Isbert (159) also state that this posture is not a continuation of the intrauterine position, and that it disappears gradually with age. In pathological conditions it sometimes persists until about two and a quarter years of age. The perusal of the literature suggests that it is while in this position that the crawling motions mentioned by a number of authors can be elicited. Shirley also describes the normal posture of the newborn baby while sleeping on his back. The knees are somewhat flexed, the arms are flexed at the elbows with the upper arms close to the sides, the hands lying at the shoulder level with the palms outward and the fists closed.

Shirley (180) noted an active postural reaction which is in the nature of an adjustment of the body to the environment. When prone, all the babies were able, from birth on, to turn the head to free the nose for breathing. During the first two weeks all but 7 of the 24 infants were able to lift their chins off the table at least momentarily and a very few were able to lift their chests as well. Gesell (65) gives, in his list of developmental items for the neonatal period, lifting the head when prone, at one week. Bryan (22) notes that the movements preparatory to lifting the head when prone appear to be the same in all infants, and that they seem rather more purposeful than random. Studies of motor development in infants after the neonatal period also refer to the infant's ability to lift his head or head and chest when prone, as a sign of development. This apparent contradiction appears to be due to the fact that this movement is present as a reflex at birth and like the grasping, stepping and crawling reflexes, gradually disappears in the reflex form as it develops as a controlled voluntary movement. The neck muscles are the first over which the infant gains control, and therefore the interval between reflex activity and controlled movement is short, and the distinction between the two reactions has not been clearly brought out.

Dennis (52) has recently called attention to two responses of the newborn infant which he believes should be added to the list of unlearned human responses which are present at birth. These he calls the posture of nursing and the posture of defecation.

GENERAL MOTILITY

Many authors have observed the spontaneous activity, or general motility, of babies during the first few days of life. The reactions which we have placed under this heading, for our purposes, are those general movements of the whole body, or of its segments, which occur independently of specific external stimulation, and which show definite characteristics during the first ten days or so of life, and can be distinguished from these reactions which are fully developed at birth. A general knowledge of the newborn infant's spontaneous bodily activity is a necessary background to testing for special reflexes, in order to avoid the pitfall of recording as a response a movement that merely happens to occur immediately after the stimulation. In fact, the mass activity of the very young baby is so great at times that in testing for specific responses every precaution should be taken to see that the subject's muscles are relaxed and that his limbs have assumed a passive posture before the stimulus is applied. Nearly every investigator of the behavior of infants has given a description of and commented upon the highly active, diverse and generalized movements that are observed. The whole body is involved in many of these random activities, and, at the same time, the movements of the separate segments are highly uncoördinated; the two arms and even the fingers of one hand move in opposition to one another and constantly show patterns that an adult cannot duplicate without the most difficult, conscious muscular effort. Mass activity, however, has not been proved to be the only total response of newborn infants. Reactions to plantar and Moro stimulation and the proprioceptive reactions observed in crying and hunger often involve the whole body to some extent, and appear to be in the nature of mass activity. Further investigation and more refined methods of distinguishing between mass activity as such and that which occurs as part of a definite response to a stimulus, are needed before definite conclusions can be drawn as to the rôle mass activity plays in infant behavior.

Dennis (51) notes that when an infant is hungry, mass activity may be a striking feature of behavior merely because of its frequency. Weiss (208), however, believes that the mass activity during hunger is not convulsive in nature, nor yet is it purely random muscle exercise, but that it is the infant's first reaction to his social environment, and that the biosocial as well as the biophysical aspects of behavior should be taken into consideration before reactions are finally labeled as non-specific or useless

Irwin and Weiss (97) have compared the mass activity of the newborn to adult pathological behavior due to lesions which render the cortex non-functional, and they, with other authors, look upon this manifestation as evidence in favor of a positive relation between behavior and immaturity in the neutral structures of the newborn.

Eckstein and Paffrath (55), in a study of premature infants, ascribe motor discharges to proprioceptive stimuli, and state that regularity of periodic movements, which can be followed for hours and is not present in older children, is a characteristic of premature infants. They describe the movements of a premature infant on the twenty-first day after birth, and ascribe the slowness of the movements to strong muscle tonus. In stimulating premature infants, they say, strong stimuli must be used to offset this. With weak stimuli, they found a long interval—three seconds— before a slow contraction set in. This was followed by a corresponding slow stretch, then a four-second interval of rest, and then another less vigorous and shorter contraction. They report that a single stimulation gives a sequence of movements, followed by rest. With a strong stimulation, they obtained a rapid contraction of the leg after half a second. This was followed by a slow after-motion, a four-second rest, and then a still slighter movement. The speed of the reactions increased with the strength of the stimuli.

Studies of general motility have been made by several methods: descriptions of movements observed during longtime observation or during shorter periods of testing; by motion-picture records supplemented by longer observation; and at the Ohio State University by means of a stabilimeter in a control cabinet where the infants were protected as far as possible from changing external conditions, and the rôle of the experimenter was reduced to a minimum.

Bühler (23), who used the observational method, refers to the characteristic, uncoördinated, purposeless movements of infants without external stimulation, as spontaneous impulsive movements of all the limbs "in motley confusion, in inimitable array, and in irrepeatable succession." She considers this kind of activity

to be a sort of bodily exercise which continues until practice leads
to coördinated movements serving to link the child to his environment, and appearing when the child's needs turn toward it. These
are the activities which, she states, do not end in themselves, but
turn out toward the object. Gesell (65) describes the spontaneous
activity of the newborn in greater detail. The hands make random
rotating motions near the mouth; if one touches the mouth or
cheeks, the mouthing motions of the lips are increased; the head
moves from side to side, the legs also move, the whole body
squirms and there is facial grimacing, the fingers are flexed and
straighten independently of each other, the fingers and toes fan
or are contracted. Shirley (180) gives an account of the random
activities of the 24 babies she studied from birth. The gross bodily
activities were jerking, squirming, waving, kicking and tremor.
The movements were little affected by the type of situation or
the stimulation. When awake, the babies turned their heads freely
from side to side, and did much random kicking and squirming,
particularly in crying. Between the first and eleventh days, 6
babies turned completely from back to side, and 5 turned from
their sides to the back or stomach, which she calls a passive
reaction probably caused by losing their balance. The kicking
was fairly strong and some babies almost turned over by this
method. At ten days one baby kicked his feet alternately and
rhythmically. She says that the rolling and turning could not be
attributed to precocious motor development, as the weak and
smaller babies were the ones that rolled most.

Gilmer (67) studied the spontaneous responses of 4 infants
from one to ten days old by means of motion-picture records and
observation. He notes grimacing, smiling, and opening the mouth,
which was not crying, sucking or yawning, and also isolated arm
or leg movements. The latter, he says, were never as vigorous as
those movements in which the total organism was brought into
play. He did not record these general movements in detail, but
claims that

the newborn's behavior organization is body wide, his responses are
total bodily responses. The body segments do not act in complete iso-
lation. Our study supports Dennis' claim that mass activity is not the

only total bodily response of infants, but that, on the contrary, there are many total bodily responses.

The fullest and most scientifically controlled and recorded studies of the spontaneous activity of newborn babies have been made at Ohio State University, using a stabilimeter in an experimental cabinet. Movements were recorded in millimeters and seconds on a polygraph, and the infants were observed through a peep hole. Pratt, Nelson and Sun's (164) study was of 25 infants from birth to seventeen days of age, the infants being stimulated for sensory responses and observed during a control period in the cabinet. The results of records of the control period are as follows: 72 percent were asleep and 28 percent awake; 55 percent were dry and 45 percent wet (in the usual nursery sense). Movements in millimeters were figured per kilogram of body weight and per second. For both measures, an increase in activity with age was found; that in seconds was more regular than that in kilograms. The sleeping infants were moving 21 percent of the time, those who were awake 42 percent of the time, those who were dry 21 percent, and those who were wet 30 percent. The most stable group were those who were asleep and dry; they moved 18 percent of the time. They also found more crying among the wet group than among the dry, when the infants were awake. They explain this as due to the stimulation from evaporation over a large area, which produces increasing activity until the child is awakened and shortly begins intermittent crying, and then continues crying with every part of the body in motion. Those infants who were observed very soon after feeding were asleep and very quiet, so quiet that often not a single stabilimeter movement was recorded. Babies taken shortly before their next feeding were awake, restless and fussy. There was some evidence that infants are more active in the afternoon than in the morning. The stabilimeter did not distinguish between movements of a limb or of the body, so that there is no record of how much of this activity was in the nature of total bodily responses and how much was movements of isolated segments.

The same year Irwin (93) also made a study with the stabilimeter of 4 infants as soon after birth as possible. He attempted to obtain a record of the amount of activity, the nature of the reactions and the localization of the internal stimuli to which the infant was responding. The polygraph was used and also an observer's record of the body segments involved in the movements. His findings agree with those of Pratt *et al.*, that the dry infants were quieter than the wet ones. He also found, as did the other investigators, that the percentage of babies who were wet and not crying increases with age. The greatest increase in movements during the first ten days was found in the body movements, the least increase in head movements. The greatest decrease was found in leg movements. The arm movements remained about constant. At the end of the ten days, an increase in the dominance of fore-body segmental activities over hind-body activities had taken place. There was also an increase in the use of vocal mechanisms. The infants were more active just before nursing than just after nursing. They were least active about noon and most active early in the morning. The least activity was found on the first day; the greatest on the tenth. He found that mass activity was at a minimum on the first day, and at a maximum on the seventh, with a decrease on the eighth and ninth days and a second increase on the tenth day. On the basis of his findings, Irwin divides behavior of the newborn into specific movements and mass activity. Vocal sounds, with the exception of faint throat sounds such as gurgling, were components of mass activity. He concludes that when external stimuli are as constant as they were in this experiment, well-integrated behavior patterns are not frequent. The ones found were as follows: sucking, when fingers or covers touched the lips, and without contact when the baby was hungry; a characteristic sleeping posture; usually alternate leg movements crudely resembling movements of progression; and possibly a characteristic hunger cry. He believes that the stimuli under these conditions are proprioceptive, probably from the alimentary canal. He also makes the suggestion that behavior is speeded up as soon as the change from placental to alimentary feeding is well established. He states that mass activity is probably a result of neurological immaturity, and also suggests, with Weiss, that mass activity may serve a social purpose.

Pratt (163) has reported on the relation of bodily activity to temperature and humidity changes, for about 70 neonates, during the control period in the stabilimeter. The range of temperatures was from 74° to 88° F. Increase in temperature appeared to cause a slight decrease in the amount of time the infants engaged in bodily activity involving shifts of position; the correlation coefficient between the time of activity and the degree of heat was —0.205 ±0.024. The relation of activity to the humidity changes was not at all clear. Pratt concluded that the changes were probably due to the changes in temperature, not to those in humidity.

Galewood and Weiss (64) studied the sex and race differences in activity of 78 white and Negro infants under two weeks of age, during a control and an experimental period in the stabilimeter. They found that the Negro infants were less active than the white, and the males were less active than the females, with a greater difference between the sexes for the Negroes than for the whites. During the control period the largest percentage of movements for all groups were those of the body, next of the legs, the arms, vocalizations and head movements, in this order. There was a drop in activity for all groups except the Negro females from the second to the fourth days. During the experimental period, responses to light, sound, temperature, odor, holding the arms and holding the nose, were measured by the breathing changes. There was a decrease in frequency of body, arm and leg movements during this period as compared with the control period. There was an increase of stretching movements with age, and the decrease in these movements during the experimental period, compared with the control period, became marked with increasing age.

REFLEXES OF MOVEMENT AND POSITION

A number of investigators have studied the responses of the newborn to movement, or to postural manipulation of the whole body, or of parts of the body, and have observed that responses to these manipulations fall into more or less definite patterns which change with increasing age. The infant's responses to movement of his limbs and trunk, to strained posture and to sudden movements of the whole body, undergo marked changes during the first year of life, until, by the time locomotion is established, the reflexes have disappeared or changed into forms related to the maintenance of normal adult posture and locomotion. Peiper and Isbert, and Shaltenbrand, who have made the most thorough studies of such reflexes, follow the classification of reflexes made by Magnus from his studies on animals. The latter suggests that some of the reflexes may be atavistic survivals, since they are similar to those found in four-legged animals. It seems clear that most of these reflexes are of the same nature as the early creeping, stepping and swimming movements which are present at birth as reflexes and which fade, to reëmerge in a coördinated and purposive form.

Moro Reflex.—In 1918, Moro (142) published a paper on the physiological importance of the first three months of life. In it, he described the reflex which is known by his name. When an infant is laid on his back on a table, and the table is struck on either side of the infant, the arms are spread apart and then brought together to form a bow; at the same time the legs make similar movements. Moro found this reaction only during the first few weeks of life; it became gradually less distinct until it was hardly ever seen after the age of three months, except in premature infants. Moro says that the response is sometimes elicited when the infant is unwrapped or awakened and is doubtless connected with fright. He compares the response to the "clamping instinct," described by the zoölogist Dorflein, and found in young animals which are born fairly well developed but which continue to depend upon the mother for care and food. He expresses the belief that it is the remainder of a strong reflex of our tree-climbing ancestors. He shows a picture of the young infant reacting in this way, and one of a young orang-outang clamped to its mother, and points out the similarity of the two positions.

Schaltenbrand (177) found that the Moro reflex could be elicited by shaking the infant's support, tapping on the abdomen, extending the legs at the hips, blowing on the face, and moving the infant in any way. His study was made on more than 120 infants and convalescent children. He found the progressive lessening of the response during the first three months noted by Moro. Peiper and Isbert (159) suggest a change in the usual method of stimulating the Moro reflex, which permits repetition of the reflex as often as desired. The infant is balanced on one of the experimenter's hands and the head is supported with the other hand; this hand then hits a hard blow on a table beneath the infant. They found the reaction always present during the first quarter year. During the first week, it was accompanied by tremor of the arms, but during the second week the tremor begins to disappear and is found only sporadically. The reflex is seldom found during the second and third quarters of the first year and never during the fourth quarter.

Freudenberg (61) gives a list of the different stimuli which elicited the Moro reflex in 70 neonates he investigated. It was found if the body of the infant was moved quickly through space, and also with a rapid transfer of the body into a new position. The movement is the stimulus, as, if the change in position is made slowly, the reflex is not found. All movements of the vertebra in the neck region give it, such as laying the infant down without head support and turning or bending the head to the side. It is not found, however, on ventral flexion of the head. Forceful stretching of both legs at the hips and knees, and so overcoming normal physiological bending, also elicits the reflex; stretching of one leg is not sufficient. The usual hitting of the surface on which the child is lying is also listed; the author notes that the surface should be springy. A tap on the abdomen will produce the reflex. Cold or warm applications on the chest or abdomen will release the reflex, but cold or warm irrigations of the ear will not. Touching the body will not give the response, but blowing on the face will. Acoustic and optic stimulation will not give the reflex; even a light so strong that the pupillary reflex and squinting showed clearly, failed. If one arm is held the reflex is not inhibited in the other limb. Freudenberg found that the reflex can be elicited into the fourth, fifth and sixth months, especially in sleeping infants and in those who are weak. It is sometimes found in the second year, and he found it in an idiot five years of age. Cerebral illness defers the disappearance of the reaction. Freudenberg states that the Moro reflex is not a labyrinth reflex, although Magnus describes the reaction of an infant when laid down backwards as a labyrinth reflex. The Moro reflex is a response to motion, while the labyrinth reflexes are responses to the position of the body, and the form of the two reflexes differ. The Moro reflex does not show a lasting change in the tonus of the limbs, but is a rapidly disappearing reaction of movement showing only a tonic component.

Gordon (70), in tests on 85 infants during the first month of life, also found that thermal stimuli will elicit the response, and that aural and optical stimuli will not. He says that the response is strongest during the first two months of life, disappearing at the end of the fourth month. He states that absence of the response on one side or the other indicates either motor paralysis or injury on that side, and that persistence of the reflex after six months of age signifies cerebral or pyramidal injury. Sanford (172) criticizes Gordon's conclusions as to the cause of asymmetric response. Sanford tested 465 infants, from a few hours to ten or fourteen days of age. He found the Moro response often absent for several days in an infant, but never asymmetric for more than the first twenty-four hours except in cases of fracture of the clavicle, when there was no response on the side of the fracture for the entire two weeks, or until the callus was well formed. He concludes, therefore, that, contrary to Gordon's statement, an asymmetric response to Moro stimulation is not necessarily an indication of neural injury. Troemner (197) reports the presence of a kind of Moro reflex in a decerebrate infant he studied.

Rolando (172) reports a positive response in 42 of the 80 neonates he tested. Chaney and McGraw (31) tested 100 neonates in the manner described by Moro, with a blow on the bed beside the infant, which was repeated after several minutes. This they call the *Moro interval*. They also tested by repetition of the stimulus at five-second intervals, which they call the *Moro consecutive*. In more than half the cases they obtained a typical response to the interval stimulation, with practically no difference in the number of responses to each of the three stimuli.

There was a partial response in about 35 percent of the cases, and no response in about 10 percent of the cases. With consecutive stimulation, they found a typical response in 43 percent of the cases, a partial one in 38 percent, and no response in 18 percent of the cases. They suggest that the Moro reflex is a response to the suddenness of a stimulus, and that on repeated stimulation there is a fatiguing of the reflex mechanism and therefore lessened frequency of response. They also gave the stimulus to the infants in a prone position; 53 percent responded by an elevation of the buttocks and a flexion of the thighs at the hips with very slight or no observable reaction in the upper extremities, and 43 percent showed no observable reaction.

A few authors report on the responses of infants when the body is raised or lowered and, as noted above, Schaltenbrand says that any such movement of the body gives a Moro response. As described in the literature, the responses appear to be similar to a Moro response, rather than exactly the same movements that are found on typical Moro stimulation. Schaltenbrand (177) found that when the infants were held about the body and moved downwards quickly, the arms were extended forward and the fingers spread. The corresponding response to lifting was fairly weak and disappeared during the second half year. He notes that decerebrate animals and those without a cerebellum react to dropping in the same way. When the infant is lifted in a sitting position the arms are bent in and the head is bent down; when lifting ceases, the arms are stretched and the head raised. When the infant is lowered in a sitting position he reacts as he does when he is dropped in a horizontal position. Half of the newborn infants showed this reaction, and it appears regularly after the sixth month. He states that this is a readiness to jump reaction with the extremities acting like springs to allow a smooth landing on the ground. Peiper and Isbert (159) did not find the reaction as often as Schaltenbrand reports it. They state that it was missing or weak during the first half year of life and was sometimes entirely missing during the second half year, but usually showed very distinctly in older children.

Irwin (94) made a study of the responses of infants under one month of age to vertical movements. Twenty-one infants were dropped a distance of two feet a total of 85 times. No response occurred in 12 percent of the trials. In 88 percent of the trials there were various patterns of limb movements of which the most definite was an extensor-flexor pattern, present in 53 percent of the trials which gave a response. Crying occurred in only two of the trials. Twelve infants were also accelerated against gravity 45 times. There was no response in 22 percent of the trials; in the others there were again various patterns of limb movements, but the extensor-flexor pattern was not so striking as when the infants were dropped. The responses showed a tonic character. Irwin suggests that responses to vertical acceleration may be a compensatory effect.

Jensen (98) reports that the Moro reflex was released by suddenly dropping an infant a distance of four inches. His observations were made during a study of differential reactions to taste and temperature by recording changes in the feeding curves of the subjects. He believes that the dropping technique, combined with quantitative records of the feeding reaction, lends itself to a differential study of the reflex which is not possible with the usual methods of stimulation.

Landau Reflex.—In 1923, Landau (112) published an article describing the reflex observed when an infant lying prone is lifted into the air by a hand placed under the abdomen. He found that 50 percent of infants between six and eight months of age arched the back, raising the head and legs, and that they retained the lordosis for from half a minute to two minutes. He states that this reaction is seldom seen before the seventh week and is rarely seen after the age of fifteen months, and that it disappears when the higher static faculties develop. It is especially strong in rachitic infants with flabby musculature. Flexion of the head downwards relaxes the contraction of the back muscles. This reaction is known in the literature as the *Landau reflex*. Schaltenbrand (177) states that Landau's reflex is found in infants from six to eighteen months of age, and that indications of it are found in all children between one and two years of age. He gives as the apparent explanation of the reflex, that the head is raised in response to labyrinth stimulation, and the bowing of the body serves to keep the infant's balance, that it is a combination of the labyrinth-righting reflex and some reflexes of the neck and trunk, affecting the extremities. He also notes the fact that if the head is pressed down the infant relaxes and collapses like a jackknife, and that passive lifting of the head does not cause a stretching tonus of the back and legs. He believes that the reflex in its classic form is found in only about 10 percent of young infants. Troemner (197) reports that the Landau reflex was lacking in the decerebrate he studied.

Tonic Neck and Labyrinth Reflexes.—Schaltenbrand, and Peiper and Isbert have classified the reflexes of infants following the Magnus De Kleijn classification of the movement and body-righting reflexes of decerebrate animals. Schaltenbrand (176) states that "it was found that in the development of human motility the well known righting reflexes of four-legged animals were present for a certain period of time, but that later some of them were lost in favor of the special motility of man." His investigations (176, 177) were made on more than 120 children from birth to eight years of age. As all these children were convalescents, he believes that the ages he gives for the presence or disappearance of the different reactions may be a little above those that would be found for perfectly healthy children. These reflexes he divides into two kinds, reflexes of movement which are temporary in character and probably are reactions of the semicircular canals, and reflexes of position which are permanent in character and are partly released by the otoliths and partly by the proprioceptors of muscles and sensory organs of touch of the body surface. The reflexes of position include the righting reflexes which cause the organism to return to the normal position, the postural reflexes which cause it to maintain the normal position, and the compensatory eye-position. Moro's reflex and the preparation-for-jumping reflex he lists as reflexes of movement, and Landau's as a reflex of posture.

The tonic neck reflexes are shown as the tendency to bring the body into a position corresponding to the position of the head. These are found in children during the first two years, but are not found in healthy children after the age of two. The labyrinth-righting reflexes keep the head in the normal position in space or bring it into a normal position. Schaltenbrand states that these are present in all mammals including man. The body-righting reflexes bring about a normal position through deep-pressure sensations in those parts of the body which are against a hard surface.

The symmetrical tonic neck reflex is the stretching of the upper extremities when the neck is bent back, and their bending when the head is bent forward. The asymmetrical is the stretching of the upper extremity on the side toward which the head is bent or turned, and the bending of the extremity on the other side. The asymmetrical reflex was found by Minkowski in five-month-old fetuses. It is often found in young children when the head is turned to the side. One of the symmetric tonic neck reflexes, Brudzinski, which is a symptom of meningitis, is, according to Schaltenbrand, found only in a few infants; in this the legs are drawn up and bent as well as the arms when the neck is bent forward. Brudzinski (21), in a study of 42 meningitis cases, got the response from 97 percent of the cases.

To test the labyrinth-righting reflex of the head, the infant is blindfolded and held around the pelvis, and is then moved slowly into different positions without touching any other support. In the newborn, the head usually hangs down by its own weight, but when the infant is held in a ventral position or on his side, short attempts are often made to bring the plane of the face vertical and the line of the mouth horizontal, which is the normal position of the head. As age increases attempts to bring the head into normal position are more frequent and succeed for a longer time. When the infant is in a dorsal position the head is raised. When he is on his side the face is turned downwards and then lifted. This is first seen distinctly after the second month, and is found in all older infants.

To test the neck-righting reflex the infant is laid flat on his back and his head is turned 90 degrees to either side; the response is a reflex torsion of the spinal column in the same direction as that in which the head is turned. If the pelvis is held, the shoulders and abdomen turn in the same direction as the head. If the thorax is held, the pelvis turns in the opposite direction to the head. When the reflex is strong, the whole body turns. These responses are found regularly in the newborn and fairly regularly up to the ages of three or four years. They are absent after the age of five. Schaltenbrand says that these reflexes are regularly found in animals and persist after decerebration and extirpation of the cerebellum.

The body-righting reflexes show a progressing development with age, and are shown by the child's natural method of getting up from a lying position. When the young infant is laid on his back, the head is turned to the side after a while and then later the whole body. In the second half of the first year, infants begin to roll upon their stomachs, the head is turned first, then the shoulder, then the pelvis. The head is then lifted into the normal position and the infant gets on all fours. He gradually learns to get into a sitting position and thence finally to stand. The skill and speed of this sequence increases. During the second and third years the child rolls from his back to his side and then pushes himself up with both arms on that side. In the fourth or fifth year, the adult method is used, that of raising the body by pushing with the arms evenly on both sides. Schaltenbrand includes the grasping reflex, and the movement of the eyes as the body is moved, among the reflexes of movement and position.

Schaltenbrand states that the body-righting reflexes develop, and all the tonic postural reflexes of the extremities disappear. He compares his results with children with those of Magnus on animals. The postural reflexes are absent in healthy older children and are hard to observe in uninjured higher animals. The righting reflexes are much more strongly suppressed in children than in animals and become more so as age increases. All the righting reflexes are fully developed at birth in many animals; in the human infant only the neck-righting reflexes are fully developed. The symmetric method of getting up from a lying position is distinctively human, developing through the stage of all-fours and appearing as the neck-righting reflexes disappear. Reactions to movement are much stronger in infants than in animals, which show only turning reactions of the head and eyes. In contrast to

animals, human beings have the ability to suppress all righting-
reflexes at will. These differences between the reflexes of man
and those of animals are explicable by man's upright posture and
by the higher development of his nervous system.

Peiper and Isbert (159) made an investigation of 78 healthy
infants and a few pathological cases, along similar lines to that
of Schaltenbrand, and following the Magnus classification of
reflexes. They state that the normal position of the human body,
and of the body of the higher animals, is brought about by the
integrated coöperation of different groups of reflexes, with the
sense organs coöperating in the release of the reflexes. Magnus
was able to classify these reflexes on animals because he cut off
the cerebrum in his subjects, and so eliminated the inhibitory
effect of that organ. Magnus and De Kleijn also observed the
same reflexes in a few hydrocephalic infants. Magnus, however,
could not obtain the reflexes in 26 normal neonates he examined,
according to Peiper and Isbert. They state that it is difficult to
say how much of the results of Magnus's animal experimentation
may be applicable to humans since they cannot be operated on as
his animals were, but that with patience the results they got can
always be obtained. Sick infants do not give the responses, but
with improvement of condition, these responses appear.

Thirty infants were tapped with a percussion hammer on the
chest bone; all gave movements of the arms and legs, stronger in
some than in others; in 6 cases the head was simultaneously
moved backward as far as their positions would allow. Asymmetric
tonic neck reflexes were found most frequently in premature
neonates; in normal infants during the first week they were
present in half the cases; after this they are only occasionally
found and by the second half year they are entirely missing. In
2 cases of tubercular meningitis they were found at one and one-
half and at two and one-half years.

The labyrinth-righting reflexes were also tested for. During the
first week only a few cases reacted when held up by the heels. At
three months bending the head backward was the regular response, and from the seventh month on, the infants tried to raise
themselves by bringing the head forward. The righting reflex of

the head, these authors found, showed much more clearly when the infant was rolled sideways than when the body was moved in an upright position, as the weight of the head then makes it hang down on the body. The neck-righting reflex was found in infants during the first year, and an idiot of two and one-half years showed it. The body-righting reflex was almost always present during the first year. It was sometimes missing in premature infants with little muscle tonus. If the chest was held in a fixed position it was less observable.

These reflexes were also observed in combination. The labyrinth reflex plus the asymmetric tonic neck reflex, was found more frequently than the asymmetric tonic neck reflex alone; it was always present during the first four weeks, gradually fading out, until it entirely disappeared by the second half year. The labyrinth reflex on the head plus the tonic neck reflex, was a'most never found in premature infants during the first quarter year; 50 percent of the infants born at term show it during the first month, if lying on a table. When held in space only one infant showed it as early as the fourth week; from the second to the sixth month about one-third gave the reaction. During the second half year the majority of the infants showed it. All these reflexes operating at once were found in the infants from the sixth month on, though they could always be inhibited. The infants raised their heads, rotated the pelvis, stretched the arm on that side, flexed the other close to the body, stretched the leg on the side of the turning pelvis, and flexed the opposite leg.

They also tested for Brudzinski's reflex and found it sporadically. It was completely missing in premature neonates. To find out whether it was a tonic neck reflex, the infants were tested in the lateral position, but there was no regularity in the reactions in this position. Freudenberg (61) also tested for this reflex. He states that bending the neck is not the only stimulus that will cause the infant to draw up his legs. It can be elicited by spreading the infant's arms and quickly bringing them together over his head. He says therefore it should not be called a neck reflex, as Brudzinski names it. He calls it a symmetric, leg-shortening reflex. Older infants do not show it, but he found it in neonates.

Only 6 of the 70 infants he tested gave a reaction which could be described as more of a grasping response, when their arms were spread and brought together. Freudenberg states that the reaction of young infants, where a stimulation on the legs causes a reaction of the arms and one on the arms a leg response, is similar to the coördination shown in animals, and that it should be profitable to prove this hypothesis.

Marquis (133) made a study of the activity and postures of infants during sleep. The infants were not tested for the presence of the tonic neck reflexes, but spontaneous changes in posture would be expected to elicit the response. The only evidence of their presence which the author reports finding is a greater frequency of asymmetric arm postures at eight, twelve and sixteen weeks of age than at six months of age and beyond.

Tonic Skin Reflexes.—Peiper (133) describes the tonic reflexes elicited to stimulation of the skin with a needle or a wooden rod. These reflexes, he says, are most noticeable during the first month, both in infants born at term and in premature neonates. They are dependent upon the general condition of the infant and increase if the condition is good and decrease if it is poor; they cannot be observed in crying infants. The reactions obtained are in general movements like the tonic neck and labyrinth reflexes. Peiper states that they are in the nature of defense mechanisms or removing the body from the stimulus, and historically may be likened to the automatic fastening of the infant to the mother's hairy skin in the human-ape stage.

When the inside of the knee opposite the patella is stimulated, there is a reaction in the whole leg and sometimes a weak one in the arms; the knee and hip joint bend. Sometimes the reaction is stretching, but this is weaker than the flexion. The reaction lasts as long as it is not disturbed by voluntary movements. To stimulation in the armpit, the reaction is a closing of the arm, on the side stimulated, and a slight inner twist. Stimulation in the hip joint or inner upper leg elicits a bending of the knee and hip joints, usually in both legs. Stimulation of the palm of the hand gives the grasping reflex, and pressure against the sole of the foot near the toes gives a similar grasping movement with the toes, but weaker than that in the hand. The reactions to stimulation of the big toe are variable, differing to each stimulation in the same child. Stimulation of the elbow and of the knee also give irregular reactions. Stimulation of the skin on the back next to the vertebra makes the pelvis turn toward the stimulated side. In another paper Peiper and Isbert (159) report this reflex as present during the first half year in 5 per cent of normal infants and present in the great majority of the premature. After the first half year, it is found only now and then. This is known as *Galant's* reflex. Stimulation of the chest and abdomen makes the infant draw back so that the vertebra form an arc open toward the stimulated side. There is frequently a simultaneous stretching of the knee and hip joint on the side stimulated. The head posture is often influenced, the head turning first toward the stimulated side. Stimulating first one side and then the other causes the head to move from side to side toward the last stimulation. This reaction is also elicited from stimulation of the armpit, and very susceptible children show it if stimulated near the middle line, but the reaction does not occur on stimulation of the upper leg. The most sensitive parts of the chest and abdomen for this reaction are the lateral parts of the abdomen; the reaction diminishes if the stimuli are moved toward the front or back near the middle line. These are the tonic skin reflexes on the vertebra. They do not completely vanish with age, according to Peiper, but are shown in the reactions of children to a tickle stimulus, which makes them withdraw the stimulated side. He says that these reflexes are not due to skin stimulation alone, but that the deeper tissues are involved. The validity of his statement is shown by the recurrence of the reactions in older subjects with pathological conditions such as bone fractures and diseases of the articulations.

Peiper's conclusions are that it is possible to obtain several different tonic reflexes from stimulation of the skin of infants, and that the variations which occur are due to "blocking" of the reflexes. Reflexes, as observed by the investigator, are an abstraction of part of a total reaction of the whole nervous system, which is also influenced by general bodily conditions. The central nervous system is not a sum of reflexes, but an entity, stimulated as an entity and reacting as one. The tracks must be free in order to elicit a definite reflex. That is, if two different reflexes are stimulated at the same time, only one of the stimulations shows a reaction; the other is inhibited by the central nervous system. The younger the infant, the less developed are the inhibitory mechanisms, with the result that the neonate shows spreading of the stimulation over the whole body. With increasing age inhibition increases, which limits the spreading to definite tracts.

THE GRASPING REFLEX

All authors who have invetsigated the grasp of newborn infants are agreed that a reflex grasp is present from birth, when the stimulus touches the palm of the infant's hand. This is often so strong that the infant's entire weight can be supported by his grasp on a small rod or a finger. This reflex disappears during the first year, as coördinated hand movements develop.

Chaney and McGraw (31) investigated the reflex in the 125 infants they tested. In 43.5 percent of the cases the neonates closed their fingers over the rod spontaneously, in 16 percent the infant was raised almost off the table by lifting the rod, in 37 percent he was raised completely, and only 3.5 percent showed no resistance to withdrawal of the rod from their grasp. In 26 percent of the tests the neonates failed to grasp the rod when tested for grasping suspended, the others were completely suspended; little difference was found between the time the grasp was held by each hand, and the range in time was from one to 39 seconds. Four of the partunates supported the body weight when grasping suspended.

Bryan (22) in a study of 66 infants during the first ten days of life, reports that only a few infants could support their own weight by grasping, but that the reflex was very lively in some; one infant was observed to grasp the vulva during delivery and when that hold was broken the cord was grasped. Givler (68) maintains that the grasping reflex is practiced for three or four months of intrauterine life, since the hands develop during the eighth week and are held in a semifixed posture very close to each other, so that maternal movements give a touch stimulus to fingers and palms. In early grasping, the hand resembles a paw; the grasping is enveloping and forceful, and is performed by the fingers. Differentiation of digital function does not occur until after the twentieth week. Thumb opposition begins to function as the grasping reflex disappears. Tenacity of grasp is lost about the one hundred and fiftieth day. Givler believes that grasping is the basis of learning, even in adult life.

Valentine (198), who studied his own son, reports that it was very difficult to say when reflex grasping ended and voluntary grasping began. He noted signs of deliberate movement the tenth week, but even then grasping seemed to require the accidental touching of the object. He found that the reflex was stronger, in one of his daughters, if there was some excitement, such as fear of failure of support, or other disturbing situation. This infant's grasp on a pencil rigged as a dynamometer was very gentle when she was quiet, but when the nurse inserted cotton in her nostril to clean it the grip increased to two pounds. Valentine states that grasping may continue in sleep, or may not. Gesell (65) states that the grasping reflex of the newborn disappears during sleep. Bühler (23) states that the newborn child closes his hand automatically when an object comes in contact with the hand, and that this reflex grasp is to some extent the starting point of the development of hand movements. With the two-month-old child, the reflex is not always present; he will sometimes feel objects with his fingers instead of closing his fist over them. An earlier study of grasping is that by Watson (207) on about 100 infants. He found the reflex present in the great majority of cases, and observed that most of the infants could support the body weight for a longer or shorter time and with either hand, and that the reflex begins to give way about the time eye-hand coördination is formed. Troemner (197) investigated a decerebrate who lived two days. The grasping reflex was strong enough to lift the infant 10 centimeters.

Peiper (153) lists the grasping reflex in his classification of tonic skin reflexes. Stimulation of the palm of the hand gives a tonic hand reflex, which is the regular grasping reaction, and is strong enough so that the infant can be lifted by the thing he is grasping. He finds a similar reflex of the toes when a pencil is pressed against the sole of the foot, under the toes. He states that this is a regular grasping reflex of the toes and that it is weaker than the hand reflex. In his paper written with Isbert, Peiper (139) again describes the reflex. He says that all healthy and premature neonates show the reflex. During the second quarter year it becomes rarer, and disappears toward the end of the first year. In older infants, it is sometimes difficult to distinguish it from voluntary grasping. Sometimes an infant will grasp for as long as one minute. If stimulation is repeated at short intervals, the length of the grasp becomes shorter. The grasp is stronger before feeding. Pylorospasmotic infants have a stronger grip than normal infants. Of 29 neonates he tested, 13 showed a certain relation between head and legs during suspended grasping. If the head hung backward, the legs were drawn up toward the body, with marked flexion at the knees. If the head was moved forward until the chin touched the chest bone, the legs stretched at the hips and knees. He states that these are postural movements tending to maintain equilibrium.

Langworthy (115) says that the grasping and hanging reflex in the newborn appears to be of no value to humans. It is believed to be a survival mechanism observed in many primates, by which the young are able to hold to the hair of the mother, and thus be carried safely.

STEPPING, SWIMMING, CRAWLING AND SITTING REACTIONS

Studies have been made of the presence at birth, or soon after, of reflex movements which can be classified as stepping, swimming, crawling or sitting motions. The literature suggests this as a fertile field for further investigation. It indicates that such reflexes may exist at a primitive or atavistic level at birth, only to disappear in a few weeks, until they emerge later as part of the developmental pattern. Shirley (180) reports that one of the 24 babies she followed through the first two years, who was somewhat spastic at birth, could, during the first four or five days, be lifted to his feet if a hand were placed at the back of his neck and shoulders, and that he could stand thus for a few minutes supported only by a hand at the nape of the neck. Another infant when prone lifted his pelvis from the table and pushed with his toes on the second day, and on the sixth day squirmed along the table a few inches in this way.

Myers (153), a behaviorist, studied the evolution of walking in his own two infants. He observed that during the first three days the infants pushed against pressure exerted on the soles of their feet, and that this reaction grew, until by the twenty-fifth day one infant pushed his feet in unison if the soles of his feet touched anything. He concludes that "Pushing against objects touching the soles of the feet, throwing out the arms when quickly raised or lowered, and the vigorous grasping reaction on the first day of the child's life, all of which parents and nurses must have observed from time immemorial are undoubtedly among the few fundamental original reactions out of which the numerous other reflexes are conditioned and other habits are developed to make up what is called walking." Most authors who have noted the early stepping and crawling reflexes state that they disappear after a short time, and no one as yet seems to have postulated a theory of the relation between such reflexes at birth and their reappearance in a purposeful or coördinated form.

Peiper (156) says that neonates have an intricate reflex system as a protection against damage, and he lists among these reflexes crawling with aid and walking if properly helped. Bauer (6) says that if neonates are placed prone on a table, they make motions as if trying to push themselves along. If the sole of the foot be touched, the infant begins to crawl, by first drawing up the legs and pushing with them and then moving first one arm and then the other. He ends by crawling backward. Bauer considers this, next to sucking, the most complex activity of the newborn, as it involves a whole series of movements. He states that the reactions disappear at about four months after birth even if the infant is given practice. These movements should not be confused with the integrated, associated crawling efforts which take place just before creeping appears. They are always reflex in character, apparently stimulated by bodily contact with a hard surface. They are always in the nature of crawling, that is the belly rests against the support, never like true creeping, when the hands and knees support the whole body weight.

Gesell (65) says that on the first day, a baby placed in a prone position "flexes his legs in a manner which simulates mild crawling movements." Valentine (198) reports that, in his observations of his own son, he found a walking reflex on the second day which disappeared after a few weeks. Taylor-Jones (189) mentions the fact that a day-old baby, if held under the arms so that his toes touch a hard surface, will push against the surface with walking motions, and that when placed prone and with pressure exerted against the soles of the feet, will simulate crawling motions. Bryan (22) in her study of 66 infants reports a number of reactions among these babies that are in the nature of walking, crawling and swimming. On the fifth and sixth days several of the infants crawled a few inches when prone on a hard surface. One baby placed in a warm and cool bath to start respiration, began a rhythmic treading motion with both feet alternately at the rate of 80 motions a minute, which closely resembled swimming. Another child on the ninth day, when his feet touched the table, at once stiffened and bore *all* his weight on his feet. The examiner held him by one arm which was flexed at the elbow; the other arm was stretched straight out in front of the body at the shoulder level. He balanced and maintained the position long enough so that a photographer present took his picture. This is an unusual reaction, as the customary position of the arms during reflex standing or stepping is with the elbows flexed and the arms drawn in against the body and across the chest.

Watson (206) reports an absence of swimming movements when infants are carefully lowered into a small tank a few minutes after birth, when breathing is firmly established. The infants were held in the water lying on their backs and the only motions observed were "violent expressions of fear," crying, checking breath and then hard breathing, and uncoördinated slashing of hands and feet. He does not state how many infants were tested in this way, but presumably more than one. The tests were carried out as a method of getting concrete data on the recapitulation theory. It is possible that had the infants been a little older or had he tested a larger number, he would have observed swimming movements. Bryan's single illustration is the only one found in the literature, but Chaney and McGraw, at the Normal Child Development Clinic, have tested for the swimming reflex in neonates, and the protocols of their work report rhythmic swimming movements in a number of infants.

The most thorough analysis of these postural-movement reactions among the newborn seems to have been made by Chaney and McGraw (31) on 125 infants from birth to ten days of age. This is the only report we have found of testing the sitting reaction of the newborn. The infants were raised from a supine to a sitting position by the support of the examiner's hand between the shoulder blades. Twenty percent of the 25 babies tested during the first twenty minutes of life showed increased muscle tonus of the back and abdominal muscles when brought to a sitting position. Of the 100 tested between the ages of two hours and ten days; 38 percent tended to stiffen their legs and rise to their feet; 55 percent assumed the sitting position; and 42 percent held their heads in the plane with their bodies; 70 percent toppled over, usually forward or to the side; and only 7 percent showed utter flaccidity of the back muscles. The infants were also raised to the standing position by grasping their hands and by support at the shoulders under the arms. Of those over two hours of age, 72 percent were flaccid with finger support, and 36 percent were flaccid with shoulder support; 15 and 27 percent, respectively, supported their own weight by the two methods; 3 and 23 percent, respectively, made stepping movements; and 33 percent, with finger support, held their heads in a plane with their bodies. The greater number of these infants had insufficient muscle tonus to support the body weight even momentarily. When the head was held in a plane with the body, the number increased. These babies were also tested for crawling movements by elevating them by a band around the abdomen, to allow the hands and knees to make contact with a table. Twenty-five percent were unresponsive to this test, 37 percent propelled themselves forward by using both arms and legs, 4 and 6 percent, respectively, by the arms or legs alone; the test was not given to the remaining babies. Mc-Graw (130) describes the walking reflex as follows:

Ordinarily the lower extremities flex and abduct beneath the body. A few partunates and most neonates will occasionally extend their lower extremities and momentarily help support their body weight, . . . or they will make prancing or walking steps. The posture of the infants when making these steps seems to have developmental significance: the spine is held vertical to the substratum. There is an exaggerated flexion at the two major flexion foci of the lower extremeties, namely the hips and knees. Locomotion is of the digital grade and usually of the scissors type, not unlike that of the spastic paraplegia suffering a lesion in the spinal portion of the pyramidal tracts. The upper extremities are ordinarily flexed and adducted, apparently unassociated with the propulsive movements of the lower extremities. Certain types of activities appear to function on a reflex level before they become a part of a controlled muscular pattern. The reflexes tend to disappear before or about the time the controlled neuro-muscular pattern emerges. For example, there is a diminution of the early reflex stepping movements before the controlled process of walking becomes part of the infant's behavior repertoire.

ORAL REFLEXES

The literature on oral reflexes is extensive, and all authors agree that mouth reactions are present from birth. Cameron (26) states that the young baby is a suction apparatus and, if difficulties occur, there is some external trouble such as stoppage of the air passages, low temperature and so on. Gilmer (67) describes the sucking of the newborn infant from his motion-picture records. The tongue is protruded beyond the lips and there are rhythmic motions of the lower jaw, the corners of the mouth are retracted, the lips rounded and protruded, and the chin drawn in. Sucking occurs spontaneously when the infant is hungry and also when anything touches the lips or the face area near the lips. Pratt, Nelson and Sun (164) found the sensory area for the reaction to be the lips, the surface above and below the lips, the cheeks, tongue and inside of the mouth. They also found that thermal, gustatory and olfactory stimulation release sucking reactions, and that even during the first twelve days of life there is evidence that the sensory area is narrowing down to the lips, and that thermal and olfactory stimulation is decreasing in effectiveness. They conclude that with increasing age the stimulation area for sucking becomes more specific. General oral activity is also elicited by the same stimulation that calls out sucking.

Chaney and McGraw (31) distinguish between the reactions found when the cheeks, the chin, the upper lip, and the external buccal membranes are stimulated by stroking, and those occurring when a nipple is placed in the mouth. With external stimulation, 38 percent of the reactions of 100 neonates consisted of general oral activity, 13 percent of opening the mouth and turning the face toward the source of the stimulation, and 41 percent of the tests gave no reaction. All of these babies, except one who was only two hours old, sucked when a nipple was placed in the mouth. Of 25 infants less than half an hour old, 16 percent made definite sucking movements, 32 percent bit down on the finger of the examiner, and 44 percent gave no response; the remainder were not tested. Bühler (23) who classifies the reactions she observed on an interpretive basis, says that sucking is the only reaction of the infant which is surely positive from the beginning, that it is always aimed toward the pleasurable act of taking food and is the chief play activity at first.

Chewing, which is mentioned by a number of authors, is described by Gilmer (67), from his motion-picture records, as an up-and-down movement of the lower jaw with no tongue play or lip reaction as in sucking. The mouth is usually horizontally open, sometimes closed, the face is wrinkled and the eyes are closed. Shirley (180) speaks of the fact that the infants she tested made chewing movements or chewed their fists, as well as sucked.

Jensen (98) made a study, employing a technique which makes a real contribution to method. He used measured responses to the feeding reaction as a method of studying differential reactions of the newborn to taste and temperature. The sucking curve was taken from the infant's performance on a specially constructed nursing bottle. Seventeen subjects were used for the first six weeks of life, and a number of results on sucking and the feeding reaction are presented. The infant often makes excellent sucking responses the first time he is presented with the feed situation, but these last for a brief time only. Eight infants made only from 4 to 7 coördinated sucks, one gave no coördinated sucks, and another continued them for 60 seconds. One infant was able to suck, but was unable to coördinate it with swallowing; the condition disappeared by the sixth day. The most vigorous and continued sucking was done by hungry, awake babies. The feeding reactions in a hungry, crying baby are often disorganized at first, and if he has been crying, apparently from hunger, there is often a pronounced jerk of the head as the bottle is presented. Sucking becomes disorganized as the baby's stomach becomes full. Changes in the sucking curve showed that the infant makes different responses to a full and to an empty stomach, and that food alone is not the complete stimulus. No swallowing occurred when the infants were sucking on air. While these infants were sucking or had just ceased, the hair of their heads was pulled, the great toe pinched, and they were suddenly dropped four inches. All these stimuli brought about resumption of sucking in all cases; this was more prolonged when the infants were sucking on milk than when they were sucking on air. Troemner (197) reports that in the decerebrate he studied, pressure on the lips gave weak tongue and lip movements only.

A few investigators have reported on the presence of certain lip reflexes which are present at birth and which disappear as the child grows older. Lambanyi and Pianetta (111) state that the buccal reflex is found sometimes in certain mental illnesses as well as in infancy, but that it is not found in normal adults. Rolando (172) reports this reflex as positive in 72 of the 80 neonates he tested. Thompson (191), in 1903, published a paper on a lip reflex of the sleeping, newborn infant, which is elicited by gentle taps on the upper lip a little above the angle of the mouth or on the under lip a little below it, and which ceases when the infant wakes. The response is a slight jerk, then the lips close, if they were open, and purse to a pout. If the tapping is continued, the lips become more and more protruded. Thompson says that this reflex is found in the healthy newborn who are sound asleep, and is rare in those who are awake. It is fairly common to the third or fourth year and then becomes less so. He found it in one child twelve years old. It is present to a marked degree in infants taking large doses of chloral, and also in babies in convulsions, who are not taking sedatives. He believes that it is useful "in assisting the infant's first unpractised attempts at sucking." According to Thompson there have been only two other accounts of this reflex, one by Loos and one by Escherich. Rolando (172) reports the orbicular reflex as present in 72 of the 80 neonates he tested. Thompson says that this is not the same as the reflex which he describes; it occurs during waking, in response to a tap on the upper lip, and is a sudden contraction of the orbicularis oris.

DEFENSE REACTIONS

Watson (206) seems to have been the first to classify certain movements of infants after specific stimulation, as defense reactions. The noses of the infants were lightly pinched and the length of time it took the infant's hand to touch the experimenters' fingers was noted. He gives results for only 4 infants from three to twelve days old, but implies that these are typical, characteristic responses of a large number of tests. The infants raised their hands and struck or pushed the experimenter's hand, in from two to eighteen seconds. He also lightly pinched the inside of the infants' knees, and found that the opposite leg was brought up "almost with the regularity seen in the reflex in the frog." Shirley (180) tried this experiment on 25 infants during the first fourteen days of life. She found some reaction in 63.6 percent of the tests, but more than one-third of the babies did not react at all. The majority who did, did so with the same leg. Less than one-fifth reacted in the manner described by Watson, that is, by pushing with the opposite foot. She says that her results may have been due to the fact that she gave only a momentary pinch, whereas Watson apparently prolonged the pinch until the baby responded in the expected way. She also points out that the newborn baby is kicking and waving his hands and feet during most of his waking time and that if a pinch were prolonged, the examiner's hand could hardly escape being hit by one of the baby's limbs. Pratt, Nelson and Sun (164) held the noses of 67 infants. Bringing

the hand to the nose was noted as only one percent of the responses. The typical reactions the authors observed were a
drawing backward of the head, arching of the back, general restlessness and non-specific body movements. Taylor-Jones (189) reports on 75 infants tested the first two days after birth. She
found that some of the babies tried to push the examiner's hand
away with the opposite foot when the knee was pinched, while
others did not.

Watson (206) also says that "Almost any child can from birth
be thrown into a rage if its arms are held tightly to its sides."
Shirley, and Pratt, Nelson and Sun have checked this. Shirley
(180) found that only 18 percent fussed or screamed, there was
no reaction in 77 per cent of the tests, and the remainder of the
reactions were smiling, kicking and grimacing. Pratt and associates (164) found the infants passive to 58 percent of the stimulations, in 26 percent a brief period of activity was followed by
inactivity, in 13 percent the arms immediately flexed again or
there were other signs of activity, and in 3 percent a brief period
of quiet was followed by activity. They noted that passivity increased with age.

Sherman and Sherman (179) tested 96 infants during the first
twelve days after birth for a defense reaction to pressure of the
finger on the infant's chin. They counted the number of movements up to thirty before the infant coördinated, that is until
both hands touched the examiners' fingers with a pushing-away
motion. No infant under twenty-one hours of age succeeded in
doing this within 30 movements. At one hundred and eight hours
of age the reaction was fairly regular and accurate, but the best
infants needed at least four trials.

Shirley (180) reports a defense reaction in all but 3 of the 25
babies. When the doctor placed the stethoscope over the babies'
hearts, they shrugged their shoulders and drew in the left arm
with a rotary movement that often brought the hands or wrist
against the stethoscope.

With the exception of Watson's report, all the authors seem
to be in agreement that definite defense or rage reactions are not
the characteristic response of the newborn to pinching the nose

or the knee, or to holding the arms. Shirley's notes on the reactions to a stethoscope on the chest suggest that further investigation might bring to light new data on defense movements in the newborn.

Bühler (23) did not make any specific tests on the young infants she observed, but she has classified their spontaneous activity and their responses to normal daily care. She interprets most of the reactions of the young infant as "negative expressional movements," but makes a distinction between movements of flight, such as turning away the head when the nose is cleaned, and movements of defense, such as moving the arms and legs against the stimulus. The latter, she says, do not appear until the fourth month, when they are random and impulsive; by the fifth month she noticed real pushing-away movements, and during the sixth month the child was able to hold firmly the hand of a grown-up. This evidence has perhaps little or no bearing on the present discussion because she did not give specific tests and so, with the exception of grasping, failed to note those reactions which disappear shortly after birth. It is possible that the early defense reactions belong in this class and that those Bühler mentions are the later developmental defense reactions which emerge in a purposeful form.

THE PLANTAR REFLEX

The plantar reflex has received such wide attention, in postnatal studies of infants, because it is one of the more easily observed reflexes that change with age. The normal, adult plantar reflex is a flexion of the toes, analogous to closing the fist in the hand, on tickling or cutaneous stimulation of the sole of the foot. Adults suffering from lesions involving the pyramidal tracts show an alteration of this normal response in the form of a fanning of the toes with extension of the great toe. Babinski is given the credit for the first description of the various modifications of the normal adult plantar reflex found in pathological subjects, and since 1896 the reflex showing these modifications has borne his name. The normal, adult plantar reflex is not the usual infant response. Kussmaul in 1859 was the first to note the extension of

the toes upon plantar stimulation in newborn babies, and many
workers have since described the various responses of infants to a
stimulus on the sole of the foot. In many instances, it is more or
less extension of some or all of the toes, sometimes with, and
sometimes without, extension of the great toe. The most careful
workers state that this extension is not the same reaction found
in adults with lesions in the pyramidal tract, but, in the literature,
it is very commonly referred to as a Babinski reflex. There
has been some dissection, especially of fetuses, and considerable speculation, as to the relation between the infant modifications of the adult plantar reflex, which resembles the
Babinski, and the maturity of the pyramidal tract. Some authors
claim that the early plantar responses indicate immaturity in
the pyramidal tracts; others maintain that since a response like
the normal adult plantar can be elicited in the newborn and a
number of other responses are also observed, the development
of the reflex from before birth to the normal, adult plantar cannot be so explained.

Some of the reasons for this confusion in the literature and
for the seemingly contradictory data appear to lie in the methods
used in making observations, and in the tendency to record reactions as a positive Babinski if an infantile dorsiflexion is
found, and as negative for all other responses. Much of the confusion may be avoided by describing every movement due to
plantar stimulation. The data of authors who have done this show
fairly conclusively that a number of responses are normal in newborn babies—one of them being a true plantar digital extension
reflex—and that the so-called infant Babinski is not the same reaction occurring in adults with pyramidal lesions. Other necessary
precautions in producing this response are constant stimuli and
conditions in making the tests. A characteristic position of the toes
in the newborn is a flexion much like that of an adult plantar response. If the toes are in this position when the stimulus is applied, it is obvious that it is impossible to get a plantar response,
and if any response occurs it must be in the nature of an extension. Therefore, it is important to keep the baby's feet warm,
and to see that the toes and legs are relaxed before stimulating.

Newborn babies are so active that if the stimulus is applied for any length of time, almost any reaction may be observed and attributed to the stimulus. Before repeating the stimulations the experimenter should make sure that the toes have relaxed and the foot and leg have resumed the standard position decided upon for the test. In spite of the confusion on the subject of this reflex, there is no doubt that it is one of the reflexes in which the form of the response changes during the first few years after birth.

Minkowski (141) has traced the development of the plantar reflex from the earliest responses, which he observed on operatively removed fetuses at about the third month of fetal life, to the adult form, giving his hypothesis as to the neural mechanisms predominating at each period. As pointed out above, this is the only instance found in the literature where the sequence of a behavior pattern is traced from its first appearance in the fetus to its adult form. The first phase which he gives after birth is the *neonatal* or *cortico-subcortico-spinal* stage, which lasts until a few weeks after birth. During this period flexion is found as often as extension, and both may be observed alternately in the same individual. But a change is taking place in favor of flexion, probably owing to the beginning of myelinization in the motor centers. In the next, or *infantile* stage, the same neural mechanisms are active, but with a predominance of the subcortical elements. During this period the Babinski type of response is more or less constant. The next period is one of transition from the infantile type of reflex to the adult, and is associated with the development of the pyramidal tracts. The last stage lasts from about two years of age to old age. The mechanism is *cortico-subcortico-spinal* with the cortical element predominant, and the response is flexion of the typical plantar type. He states that the transition may have some connection with learning to walk, and cites Solomonson as authority for the statement that in rachitic children who walk late, the Babinski reflex lingers longer. He also cites other authors in support of the statement that the Babinski type of response disappears in older children during deep sleep and during epileptic fits, and states that this is probably due to a weakened cortical activity. If the pyramidal tract is weakened, responses like those of a four to six-month-old fetus appear. He states that the adult pathological Babinski is a slow dorsal movement of the big toe, tonic in character, with the toe maintaining the new position for some time. In the infantile type of Babinski, the big toe is moved quickly, as are the other toes, and the position is not held.

Bersot (10, 11) has published careful studies on the development of the plantar reflex during the first two years of life. He believes that the disagreement and confusion found in the literature regarding the reflex is due to a failure to observe the reaction of the organism as a whole to plantar stimulation. He states that the reactions of infants show clearly that the reflex cannot be understood from the few local reactions of the stimulated extremity, and defines the reflex as the "general response of the organism to any tickling of the sole of the foot." The response may take the most varied forms, from a slight motion of the toes to withdrawal of the leg, accompanied by reactions in the limb on the opposite side, and even by movements of the torso, head and so on. The characteristic response of the baby to all tickling is generalized; he tends neither to localize nor to vary his reactions, neither to differentiate nor to place the tickling. The adult, on the other hand, responds to a particular stimulation with a well-organized reaction which varies if the stimulation varies. The reactions which appear in the baby have not altogether disappeared, however, but may be present in a latent state, and might be elicited with extremely strong stimulation. Bersot states that the plantar reflex evolves through the whole of life, being strongest from the twentieth year to the thirtieth, and decreasing again after that age. He insists that the plantar reaction is part of an ensemble, and that it is only in its relation to the ensemble that the reaction is of value. He emphasizes the marked variability of response in the toes, as well as in other parts of the body, not only in different infants, but in the same subject on repeated stimulation.

Feldman (56) tested the plantar reflex of 500 children from birth to eight years of age, and found that 75 percent of those in their first year gave a plantar flexion of the great toe. He cites the fact that Bertolotti elicited the response in 10 percent of his cases by pinching the skin of the abdomen. Feldman found with his subjects, under eighteen months of age, a considerable area of skin, in some cases as high as the abdomen, stimulation of which produced the plantar reflex in a larger percentage of cases. He found the Babinski reflex more usual during sleep, and that his breast-fed subjects showed it less often than the bottle-fed babies. He states that a Babinski, when it does occur, does not have the pathological significance it has in later life. Two postmortems of infants who gave a Babinski type of response, showed myelinization in the pyramidal tracts. He believes the pyramidal tracts can function at birth, but that circulation disturbances compress them and cause a functional blocking.

De Angelis (2) reports the results of an examination of 88 newborn infants, and is in substantial agreement with Feldman's work. The Shermans (179) tested 96 infants during the first twelve days of life and report that 57.3 percent gave a plantar reaction from the first day, and only 10.4 percent gave a positive Babinski and kept on giving it to rapidly succeeding stimuli. They conclude, therefore, that the lack of myelinization of the pyramidal tracts at birth is not an adequate explanation for the infantile Babinski, and suggest as a possible explanation that the threshold of pyramidal function is very high. Wolff (215) studied 60 normal infants for a sixth-month period and reports that the classic Babinski occurs but rarely during the first six months of life, but that at the seventh month a high percentage of cases showed a characteristic flexion. She found a dorsal extension of all toes, with or without fanning, to be the most frequent response under six months. Wolpert (216) found dorsal flexion in 30 percent of his infant subjects. He states that the dorsal flexion of the big toe in sucklings is not identical with a Babinski reaction; it is more athetoid, like the pseudo-Babinski of double athetosis.

The same interpretation of the dorsal flexion of the toes in infants is upheld by Rabiner and Keschner (165), who maintain that the adult plantar flexion is due to dominance of pyramidal over extrapyramidal systems. Convincing clinical evidence is given to indicate that the dorsiflexed toe on plantar stimulation is due to release or liberation of the older extrapyramidal system from the normal dominance of the newer pyramidal tract.

Galant (63) says the plantar flexion to touch, not stroking is analogous to the grasping reflex of the hand, and questions whether the so-called Babinski response in infants is an identical flexion with that found in pathological conditions. Kherson (100), who investigated the plantar reflex in 500 normal children from five to fifteen years of age, found the characteristic response to be an irregular movement of the toes, an alternating dorsal extension and plantar flexion, and that therefore the *formes frustes* of the Babinski has no diagnostic value.

Juarros (103) reports on the results of plantar stimulation on 400 infants during the first week of life, and 150 backward children in a special school. He states that observations should be made after the infant has had a rest period, is in good physiological condition, with a standard posture, and with the feet warm, as the response is weakened by cold and strengthened by warmth. In 200 cases tested at the end of the first week, he got the same response to repeated stimulations on 112 infants, and variable responses on 88. He states that a physiological Babinski—the occurrence of the reflex without external stimulation—sometimes occurs in neonates and is no indication of a neural lesion and has no relation to the development of erect posture or immaturity of the pyramidal tracts. He concludes that both the physiological Babinski and the Babinski response to stimulation on the sole of the foot are probably due to a disequilibrium between the tonicity of the flexor and extensor muscles, possibly caused by the intrauterine position of the toes.

Stolte (186), in a discussion of the pathological significance of the Babinski reflex, states that by three-quarters of a year of age, and sometimes earlier, children respond to a touch on the sole of the foot (and that stroking is not necessary), with a flight reaction (evidently referring to a plantar type of response). They also prance and push their feet against the support if the soles of the feet are pressed or if they are held in a standing position. They also spread their toes simultaneously as if to grasp the object touching the sole. From these reactions a conditioned reflex necessary for walking develops. Brain lesions will cause these normal reactions to disappear, but the existence of a lesion should not be assumed from their absence, and the Babinski reflex has pathological significance in older children only during the weeks of transition from constant lying to walking and standing, and only if the child was able to stand and run normally before illness. Stolte gives as illustration the case of a healthy boy who gave a Babinski type of response. This was found to be due to the fact that he wore wooden-soled sandals, which he held on by lifting the big toe against the sandal straps with each step, and thus had developed a different type of plantar response than the usual one. This was borne out by the fact that the Babinski type of response disappeared after the child had worn a different type of shoe.

Conclusions at variance with these findings are reported by other workers. Jones (10) found that only 5 of 73 infants tested by her gave a negative response, although 26 of the remainder reacted negatively on continued stimulation. Burr (25) tested the reflexes of 96 infants and reported extension as the most frequent response, but stated that it may be absent a long time and present at one moment and absent the next. Watson (206), reporting before 1920, found a positive reaction almost always from birth up to the age of six months or a year. Hayashi (79) states that the Babinski reflex is always found under six months of age and that the normal upper limit for it is three years. De Bruin (48) investigated the reflexes of 200 children and reports a Babinski reaction in the majority. Gesell (65) lists as one of his normative items, found at the age of two weeks, the Babinski response to tickle with a feather, with the great toe extended and a spreading or fanning reaction of the other toes; in another place he refers to this as simply a "toe extension reflex." Peiper and Isbert say that a Babinski response is normal in the first months, when the infant is on his back with the head turned forward and the legs drawn up, and that later it is found in infants with meningitis.

Several recent studies have described in detail the reactions

observed and, from the conclusions presented, it seems probable
that much of the confusion found in the literature on this subject
is due to a failure thus to present detailed observations, if not at
times to an actual failure to distinguish between a plantar and a
Babinski type of response. Rolando (172) states that the reflexes
of newborn infants present a great variety of behavior, which
makes their systematization difficult, and describes the reactions
obtained from testing 80 neonates under rigidly controlled conditions. He found plantar flexion and retraction in 19 infants,
plantar flexion in 14, plantar flexion and the Babinski reflex in 16,
the Babinski alone in 16, sticking up like fan and retraction of
foot in 12, extension of foot and retraction in 2, and flexion of
foot and retraction in 2. He concludes that, since it is possible
to provoke all the more common and important nervous reflexes
by a definite method, it is the constant absence of certain reflexes
with a deviation in other reflexes, such as marked inequality of
the reflex on the two sides, which will give indications as to the
status of the central nervous system and the probability of the
presence of an organic or functional change.

Other authors have reported on the variability of the response
in the newborn. Bryan (22) in her study of 66 infants for the
first ten days of life, found no Babinski on the first day. All the
infants showed it in some variable form during the ten days. One
child gave a definite plantar on the third day and a Babinski on
the fifth. Some of the infants gave a Babinski when asleep, before
they gave it when awake. Taylor-Jones (189) found a positive
Babinski in 68 of 75 infants on the first or second day, a negative
one in 5, and both a positive and a negative in 28. She does not
describe the reactions which she listed as positive and negative.

Pratt, Nelson and Sun (164) tested 71 infants during the
first seventeen days of life, by means of a device which kept the
pressure on the soles of the feet constant. They say that the usual
plantar reaction is not simple, but involves a complex of reactions
of which the most important are extension of toes, flexion of the
foot, flexion of the toes, and fanning of the toes, with flexion of
the foot and extension of the toes the most numerous. They
found no consistent increase in the percentage of reactions with

increasing age. They noted that, in this reflex at least, there is a spread, in the activity of the effector segments involved, from the toes which are nearest the zone of stimulation to the legs which are most remote from the zone. They take this as contributory evidence to Bersot's theory that the infant's behavior is more or less generalized, rather than highly specific.

Waggoner and Ferguson (204) investigated 155 babies from birth to ten days of age, and 52 from six months to one year of age. Their work indicates careful study, and they emphasize the importance of keeping the strength of the stimulus constant, the foot of the infant warm, and the muscles relaxed. Their conclusions are worth quoting:

The plantar reactions are variable during the first few days, but with the proper stimulus are predominantly pure extension. Extension of the great toe with flexion of the others is much more frequent than pure flexion.

Extension of the great toe with flexion of the others is predominant at six months, while at this period pure flexion and pure extension about equal each other (the non-Babinski group).

At one year the reaction has become almost entirely that of adult flexion.

Studies of children at various ages indicate that the change from one type of reaction to another is gradual.

Chaney and McGraw (31) investigated the reflex on 125 newborn infants. They state that:

Practically all infants (99.8 per cent of the neonates and 92 per cent of the partunates) made some response to plantar stimulation, although the responses varied as to type. The most characteristic response was a dorsiflexion of the toes. Ninety-six per cent of the total number of plantar responses made by the neonates involved dorsiflexion of the toes, either alone or as part of a more complex pattern. Ordinarily this pattern was an integral part of a complicated reaction. It was frequently associated with withdrawal of the lower extremity. The soles of the feet of newborn infants are more sensitive to cutaneous stimulation than are the dorsal surfaces of the feet or the lateral aspects of the legs and thighs. . . . There is nothing in this investigation to substantiate the contention that certain reflex patterns, such as the Babinski (considered of pathological significance when present in adults) is in infants a normal reflex reaction attributed to an immature nervous system. Reflex reactions of normal newborn infants are different from the characteristic reflexes of normal adults; they are, however, also different from the classical pathological reflex patterns.

Troemner (197) reports a lively, clear plantar reflex in a decerebrate, and concludes that in development there are two plantar reflexes, the *paleo-plantar* and the *neo-plantar*, the former being more primitive than the Babinski and preceding it developmentally, the latter succeeding the Babinski.

PSYCHOGALVANIC REFLEXES

Emotional responses in adults have been tested by some investigators by means of a galvanic current, the electrodes for which are in contact with the skin of the subject. Electrical resistance in the body is localized in the skin. Emotional stimuli of sufficient strength bring about visceral changes, which cause a change in resistance. These are termed *psychogalvanic* reflexes. A few studies have been made of these reflexes in young infants, and differences noted between adult and infantile reactions.

Peiper (158) states that psychogalvanic reflexes are not found in infants under one year of age, except for one or two doubtful single reactions. Older children give a reaction just as adults do, but it is not found in infants or children during deep sleep nor if the child has been quieted with chlora[1] hydrate. He concludes from his experiments that either the central or centrifugal part of the reflex arc is not yet functional, and that in sleep the connection is broken at some point. Jones (101) got results at variance with those of Peiper. He used bandage electrodes attached to the sole of the right foot and the calf of the left leg. Responses were obtained from infants three months of age and over. The most effective stimulus was electrotactual, on an arm or the left leg, just strong enough not to make the child cry. The next best stimuli were loud sounds. Other stimuli used were removal of bottle while nursing, and withdrawal of support. There was no reaction from visual stimuli unless by conditioning, none from relief from tension, and none from pleasant stimuli. The resistance curves obtained were like those of adults. He found no change in resistance during sleep. The intensity threshold was higher in the infants than in adults. He also observed frequently an inverse relation between the reaction and the infants' overt movements. He concluded that children's emotions have a "surface" character, without a persisting visceral reinforcement, and that their emotional behavior may be related to the development of the mechanisms that determine the proportion of somatic and visceral discharge.

Richter (170) investigated the electrical resistance of the skin of newborn infants in 50 neonates. He applied electrodes to the palms and backs of the hands. Palmar resistance in adults has been found to increase with depth of sleep, and dorsal resistance with relaxation. As he expected from this, Richter found a much higher resistance in the infants than the average for adults, although the variability in the infant was very high. The average dorsal resistance of 50 adults was 181,300 ohms, while only 7 of the infants had a resistance below 1,000,000 ohms and the average for the 50 was 4,197,100. The average palmar resistance of the adults was 23,600 ohms, and of the infants 273,000 ohms. Restless, crying babies showed a great fall in resistance. High palmar resistance indicates low activity of the sympathetic nervous system, but Richter is uncertain whether to consider this a characteristic of infancy or of sleepiness.

MODIFICATIONS IN BEHAVIOR DUE TO ENVIRONMENTAL INFLUENCES

A few studies have been made on those behavior modifications which can definitely be traced to environmental influences, in the newborn infant. A few authors have made comments on the subject or drawn conclusions from the results of their investigations. The only direct evidence is that found in two studies, using the conditioned reflex with newborn infants. In both instances the reflex was established during the first few days of life. The general remarks fall into the category of speculation, since it is very difficult to distinguish by observation between increasing skill due to changes within the organism and modifications in behavior that can be attributed to active adaptation of the individual to his environment.

Aldrich (1) reports on establishing a conditioned reflex in a newborn girl, as a method of testing for hearing. The infant showed none of the usual reactions to sound. In order to find out if she were deaf, a bell which the infant could not see was rung every half hour and at the same time the sole of her right foot was scratched with a pin, hard enough to cause pain. The child drew up her leg and cried at the scratch. This procedure was carried out through one night and into the morning. By mid-morning the infant cried and drew up her leg when the bell was rung although she was not scratched. Aldrich suggests using conditioned reflexes to test all senses in the newborn.

Marquis (132) worked with 8 neonates from birth to the tenth day of life, at the Ohio State University Hospital. A buzzer was rung each time the babies were fed, 6 times a day. Seven of the 8 infants established the conditioned response; the eighth was in poor physiological condition. Changes in behavior on hearing the buzzer began to be observable about the fourth day. Marquis concludes from this experiment that an alert state of mind favors the response, and that individual differences in learning ability are evident, even during the first ten days after birth. She comments on the fact that Pavlov's school claims that conditioned response is impossible in the newborn because the cerebral cortex functions imperfectly, and suggests that the midbrain may perform the function of "pace-setter" at this age, since it is myelinated at birth.

Ripin (171) studied the feeding reactions of 272 babies from one day to six months of age, and reports increased skill during the first week. The responses increased with each feeding during this time, but there were no active adjustments and the infants hindered their own feeding by shutting the mouth, sucking the finger, turning the head away, stopping sucking and going to sleep. Shirley (180) also reports that the development of specific capacities and abilities could be observed during the first two weeks but that it was extremely difficult to record in objective terms, and that, in general, development was less apparent in specific capacities than in general activity and conduct. Sherman and Sherman (179) found that the coördination in defense reactions increased with age during the first ten days. Taylor-

Jones (189) concludes from her study of 75 infants during the first two days of life, that babies "learn" even on the first day and that habit and character formation begin then. She says that if on the first day the foot is pinched, the infant cries but does not draw away, but that on the second day all but ten of the infants drew the foot away when pinched. None of these data, however, can be advanced as true evidence of modification of behavior patterns from environmental influences. The most that can be said is that the experimenters observed modifications in behavior which appeared to them to be traceable to environmental influences.

Summary

In general it may be said that, although the literature to date is inconclusive as to many forms of specific response which are present at birth or shortly thereafter, especially as to the degree to which these responses are developed, certain general conclusions as to the nature of the behavioral life of neonates and its development during the first few days can be made. Individual differences are marked in the newborn, there are practically no reports which state that any one reaction was elicited in every subject tested, or was elicited to every stimulation, and a number of investigators comment on the fact that responses can be elicited at some times and not at others. These differences appear to be greater than can be accounted for by the possible differences in ages of the fetus at the time of birth, since work with premature infants shows that most of the responses observed in infants born at term can be elicited from those who are born prematurely.

The change from the restricted activity and the limited stimuli which are possible in the uterus, to conditions in a larger and more varied environment, brings, from the moment of birth, a great increase in the behavior of the infant, but the change progresses and increases during the first few days after birth, so that, in an infant a few days' old, behavior is observably different and more varied than it is at birth. This change is difficult to describe in objective terms, since it appears to be shown by increasing organization and growing specificity in general activity, rather than by definite changes or increased coördination in specific reactions, or by the emergence of new skills. There is evidence even in this short period that development is proceeding in a cephalo-caudal direction. Testing for specific responses in the newborn gives total body movements with a more pronounced reaction in the stimulated area, and movements spreading throughout the body which become less as the distance from the stimulated segment increases. All the mass movements of infants at this period are uncoördinated, even such small segments as the eye and the lid or the different fingers moving quite independently of one another. All the special senses appear to function very shortly after birth in forms which are unlike the responses of adults, but appear to suggest that the different sensory tracts are in the process of development. There are a few reports which seem to show that it is possible to establish conditioned reflexes in infants just born.

Some of the obvious needs for future investigations which are indicated by a survey of the literature of the neonatal period, are the following: the exact period covered by the term *neonatal life* should be agreed upon. At Ohio State University this period covers the first twelve days of life. Shirley uses it to cover the hospital period, in her study this was to the tenth or the fourteenth day. The Normal Child Development Clinic uses the term for the first ten days of life, and the term *partunate* for the first half hour of life. The authors who define the length of the period are in general agreement that it lasts from birth until the umbilicus is healed, that is, until about the tenth or fourteenth day. But the reports of a large number of investigations fail to state the age of the infants, simply designating the period as "neonatal," the "first few days of life," the "first weeks," "under one month," "young infants," and so on. A more careful description of the conditions under which the tests are given or the observations made, is also needed. This is illustrated by the literature on the plantar and Babinski reflexes. There is a very general failure to describe the body and leg position of the infants when the stimuli are applied, and to state the length of a stimulus, and in many instances the responses are simply given as positive or negative, instead of listing all the movements made by the subject. Among the workers who give the conditions and responses in detail there is agreement that, owing to the constant generalized movements of the newborn normal infant, the recording of a specific response as the result of a specific stimulus is a delicate matter. Pratt, Nelson and Sun (164) comment on this point as follows:

When one finds, for instance, that a specific movement always follows upon a specific stimulus,. one is disposed to conclude that the response is in some way identified with the stimulus. When, however, it is found that the given reaction occurs about as frequently without any external stimulation, and that this seems to be merely a day in which "fanning of the toes" is occurring a great deal, one loses some of his assurance as to the specificity of this stimulus-response category. . . . Any stimulus that is made strong enough will release a reaction, but then these reactions are to terminal forms of stimulation and so do not reveal the specific character of the reaction; nothing is gained.

Careful analysis of the spontaneous activities of infants seems to be a necessary prelude to a final classification of the stimulus-response categories that are present at birth. Sherman (178) made a study of the ability of students of psychology, medicine and nursing to judge the responses of infants under twelve days of age, when they did not see the stimuli. The response was crying. The characteristic cries of hunger, pain and fear are quite easily distinguished in older babies, but Sherman found his observers unable to judge the cause of crying in newborn infants when they did not see the stimuli. While not strictly applicable to our discussion, this is cited as another example of the special complications and difficulties which confront investigators of the behavior of newborn infants.

The literature is in general agreement that the behavior of the newborn infant is on the whole diversified, involves total body responses, and is uncoördinated, and that organization of this generalized behavior into purposeful behavior patterns begins soon after birth. Although this organization is perhaps impossible to measure quantitatively, it can be roughly described. Shirley (180) says that the first two weeks of life showed marked changes in general behavior; there was development of specific abilities, but it was extremely difficult to record in objective terms. The baby's eyes were closed and he seemed to sleep most of the time for the first twenty-four to forty-eight hours, the period of reduced activity due to the shock of birth. This period gave way to one of greater random activity and longer periods of wakefulness. The babies, born limp, gradually developed muscle tonus, and those spastic at birth gradually became less so. Crying increased during the second week and reached its peak on the fourteenth day. She states that the babies ceased to be passive animals and became active ones sometime during the first two weeks. She uses the term *active* simply as a contrast to a quiescent state, not in the sense that the infants gained control of their functions. Development was less apparent in specific capacities than in general activity and conduct. Even during this early period, she found that the cephalo-caudal direction of development was observable.

Gesell (65) says, "Although birth does represent a drastic alteration, it carries with it no marked developmental transmutation." The newborn infant presents a picture of intense diversified activity. He states that the process of organization and growth is going on rapidly during the first week of life and that the rate at this period is probably far greater than that during any comparable interval in later infancy. Langworthy (115) says:

Even the new-born infant responds to stimuli with widespread motor responses which spread and increase in intensity with the strength of the stimulus. It is only later, as differentiation from the response of the organism as whole, that refinement and delicacy of activity evolve.

Chaney and McGraw (31) conclude that individual differences are apparent from birth, and that the more complex the reaction, the more marked is the individual variation. They also found an apparent change in behavior at about the seventy-fifth hour. This was in the nature of either increased or lessened activity. Grasping, convergence and sitting were the only reflexes that showed a definite relation to age in hours. Although they found great variability in the reflexes among newborn infants, they state that the absence of reaction to reflex stimulation is so unusual that it can be taken as evidence of the probable presence of some abnormal or pathological condition. Pratt, Nelson and Sun (164) also found evidence of behavioral growth during the first twelve days of life. They observed a restriction of the generalized reactions, as shown by a decrease in the number of effector segments involved and an increase in specificity of responses to stimuli.

We have seen that the transition from uterine life to life in the normal environment does not bring any marked and immediate changes in the behavioral life of the individual. The reactions which are found, with the possible exception of some of the special senses, have been developing in utero and are possible even at that time, when conditions are suitable. Thus there is no sharp developmental break between fetal and neonatal life. Our picture of the behavior of infants during this period gains enormously from even the very partial picture of fetal behavior that is available today. It follows that the break between the neonatal period and the development which occurs thereafter is a purely arbitrary one, made for purposes of convenience. This distinction is justified since none of the responses which develop after birth appear during this period. This period is also linked to the fetal period as indicated by the fact that the umbilicus is still not healed. However, until studies of behavior include this period as part of the development of behavior to a much greater extent than has been done in the past, we cannot get an accurate picture of the entire sequence of some behavior patterns. The grasping reflex and the early stepping, swimming and crawling movements, although they disappear temporarily or undergo marked alterations later, are clearly so like the same reactions in their fully developed form, as far as their mechanical execution goes, that there must be some genetic relation between the two stages. We have seen that regression, or a period of latency, is an accepted principle in the development of neural structures. It seems quite possible that these patterns may, when understood, represent a behavioral period which corresponds to some period of regression or latency in their controlling mechanisms. We have also seen that, at the time of birth, myelinization in the cortex is just beginning, indicating, at least in all probability, that this mechanism is at the threshold only of playing a specific rôle in behavior. Thus again the question is raised as to whether all types of behavior are controlled during all of their different growth stages by the same mechanisms. Is it possible, for instance, that the grasping reflex, which is so often compared to the grasping reflex of monkeys, is, during fetal and early life, controlled at a spinal or subcortical level, and that the transition from it to the beginnings of the development of the adult form of prehension occurs at the time when the cortical fibers controlling the muscles involved, begin to mature and introduce their control? The labyrinth reflexes would then fall under some such general explanations of developing behavior, with the probability that the regressing mechanism, in their case, is submerged under some higher cortical control, enabling us to control the posture of our members in relation to the position of our bodies on a purposive or voluntary level. The original patterns would then reëmerge only in pathological conditions which again made them dominant. The early stepping movements might then be linked to the development of walking by a period of latency in which the transition from a subcortical to a cortical level begins only when the organism is physiologically ready to begin purposive walking.

PART IV

BEHAVIOR DURING INFANCY

IV

BEHAVIOR DURING INFANCY

THE END of the neonatal period does not mark a break in development or a time of emergence of new skills. The literature shows that growth in behavior is a very slow process during the first three months of life, at least so far as the number of new reactions which appear are concerned. In general it takes the form of an increasing organization of general behavior similar to that which is observable during the first two weeks of life, a growing co-ordination in movement, and an increasing localization and specificity in responses to external stimulation, especially auditory and occular. We have already reviewed the literature which deals with the development, regressions or changes in specific reflexes, and are here concerned with the development of the behavior patterns which bring about adaptation to the environment on an adult level. The literature on these different patterns is uneven, and, in general, there is little which traces a pattern from the beginning to its adult form or to the developmental stage reached at the end of the second year. We are dependent for most of our information on studies of the state of specific abilities at certain ages and on the reports of the age at which reactions appear. For instance, the literature on the beginning of language is voluminous, yet most of the work is confined to studies as to the age at which the first words are spoken, the size of the vocabulary and the ages at which different parts of speech begin to be used. The progressive development, after the neonatal period, of smell and taste, which have been the subject of so much controversy for the earlier period, have apparently never been studied. The literature on early postural control is meager compared with that on hand activities and language and even on walking proper; yet it is clear that before we can have a complete picture of the development of adult postural and bodily control, the successive stages in early life and their relation to other skills must be mapped out.

All that is known of behavior during the first two years, then, does not give us an adequate picture of developmental progression from which other than the most tentative suggestions as to the total growth processes which underly it can be drawn. Since most of the studies have been made for definite reactions and for certain age levels, we also lack an adequate picture of the total behavioral organization of infants, such as is furnished in outline by the studies of mass activity and the general descriptions given for the neonatal period. This is especially true of the literature on the second year, for which there is little save the items in the test scales and the studies of language development, and from which it is impossible to assemble a general picture of the total development that takes place or even of the total behavioral level of a child at any one stage during the year. Another lack in the literature is in studies of the relation of bodily growth to growth in behavior. Bone growth and changes in bodily proportion which take place during the first year must clearly have some definite relation to the development of such skills as erect posture and locomotion, but aside from the general assumption that growth takes place in both fields in a cephalo-caudal direction, nothing on the subject was found.

The literature has been assembled under the different behavior patterns and we have attempted to present what is known about each pattern in such a way that, as far as possible, a general picture of the progressive development of the different stages involved will emerge. Some of the literature emphasizes the emotional and intellectual interpretation of behavior to a greater extent than such an arrangement of the material can bring out. Since we are here concerned with the development of objective behavior and the theories of the processes governing it, we have not attempted to bring out the interpretations involved in attempts to classify the affective and intellectual elements in responses and adjustments.

The Development of Locomotion

HOLDING UP THE HEAD

We have seen that the newborn infant is able to turn his head from side to side when lying on his back, and when prone he can turn the head to free the nose for breathing and lift his head momentarily. Shirley (180) reports that during the first two weeks some of her 24 subjects also lifted the chest while lifting the head in the prone position. Chaney and McGraw (31), in testing 100 infants during the first ten days for a reflex sitting posture, found that a small number held their heads in a plane with the body when lifted to the sitting posture. The literature makes it clear, however, that these earliest head reactions are reflex in character and different from the reactions which occur later, after the infant begins to gain postural control of his head. Reports on the development of behavior after the neonatal period indicate that head posture is the first bodily control gained by infants. This control of the neck muscles is listed by a number of authors as the first step in the developmental sequence leading to erect posture and walking.

The literature distinguishes between lifting the head when prone, holding it erect when in a sitting posture, and lifting it when lying on the back. During the third week 88 percent of the infants tested by Shirley (180) turned their heads when prone. This reaction decreased in frequency after this age, because the infants began to lift the head from the table more and more; by seven weeks three-quarters of the infants had acquired this skill, and at or before nine weeks half the babies could lift the head and chin and hold the position for one minute. This chest-lifting was of two sorts, the infant supported his weight on the elbows and forearms, or he raised himself up further and supported his weight on his hands. Shirley says that for many weeks the infants made no progress beyond this, except that they supported themselves for longer periods and sometimes waved or pushed with their legs while in this position. She considers gaining this control over the neck and shoulder muscles when prone as the first step in progress toward creeping. Gesell (65) lists lifting the head when prone as a developmental item established at four months of age, and lifting the head and chest as established at six months. Rasmussen (168) says that one of his daughters lifted the head when prone at sixty-eight days of age and held it up a long time, and at four months she lifted the head, neck and shoulders. Linfert and Hierholzer (122) have found age norms for some of the Gesell normative items by testing, according to a procedure worked out by themselves, 300 infants, 50 each at one, two, four, six, nine and twelve months of age. At one and two months, 78 percent of the infants raised the head at least an inch or two when prone; at four months 96 percent did so. Bühler (23) says that at two months of age an infant can lift his head when prone, and at three months he lifts the head and chest; at five months he can support himself in this position on his hands, and at eight months, on one hand. Hetzer and Wolf (84) have used Bühler's scale, with slight modifications developed under Bühler's direction, on 35 infants at each month from two to twelve months of age. They place these reactions at the same age levels as Bühler, except that they do not use support on both or on one hand as test items. Since their work follows Bühler's so closely, it will not be referred to again.

Shirley does not give the age at which her subjects held their heads in a plane with the body when held in the sitting posture with support. She lists tensing the muscles for being lifted as established by the median baby at fifteen weeks and by three-quarters of the infants at eighteen weeks. The illustrations of this reaction indicate that at this time the infants had good control of the neck muscles. She gives this as the first reaction leading to an upright posture. She says:

At birth the baby has no control over his head and neck muscles. . . . In a short time he achieves control of the head and neck muscles, and the nurse's hands need only be placed at the nape of the neck.

Jones (102) includes head support in her attempt to devise a scale for the reactions of young infants, but gave it up as too difficult to judge objectively. She says, however, that half of the 54 infants tested while sitting on a table with support under the arms, could support their heads for two seconds or longer by the ninetieth day. Gesell (65) gives as one of his normative items for four months, resistance with the neck muscles when the head is bent to the side or forwards or back, and he states that a normal four-month-old infant can maintain a fairly continuous erect posture of the head if not too fatigued. Linfert and Hierholzer (122) found that at one month 30 percent of the infants they tested held their heads erect and firm, at two months 34 percent, and at three months 46 percent. Bühler (23) gives holding the head erect as a second-month test. Her technique probably explains the earlier age for this reaction. The infant is lifted with complete support into the vertical position, and the support removed from the head only; if the head is then held erect for "several" seconds the test is passed. Simon (182) in his tests for the first two years lists erect head at three months, and good head posture and control at six months. Hazlitt (80) lists as the first step in progress toward walking, sitting with support and holding the head erect at four months. Kuhlmann (109) gives as a sixth-month test holding up the head when the infant is held by the examiner in a vertical position; the test is passed if the head is balanced.

Lifting the head, or head and shoulders, when in the dorsal position develops a little later than the other head reactions. Shirley (180) gives it as established by the median baby at twenty weeks. Sometimes it was accompanied by stretching out the arms to be lifted. Bühler (23) gives five months as the age at which babies begin to raise the head and shoulders when in a dorsal position. Gesell (65) gives four months as the age at which all infants normally make an effort to sit up when on their backs; this of course involves lifting the head and shoulders. Simon (182) places raising the head from the pillows at five months. Rasmussen (168) says that at six months one of his daughters began to grasp the quilt on her crib and pull herself up from the dorsal position, the other one pulled herself up to a sitting posture at eighty days of age.

SITTING

Gaining control of the head and neck muscles so that the head can be freely moved and maintained in a plane with the body, appears to be the first observable step in a developmental sequence toward the assumption of the sitting posture. Shirley and other authors believe that the progressive development of the ability to sit alone, and to get into and out of a sitting posture, are steps in the development of erect posture and locomotion. Most authors state that the first motor control gained by the infant is that of the head, and that control moves from the head and neck to the chest and shoulder muscles and gradually down the trunk, corresponding to the cephalo-caudal direction of embryological development. There is a tendency to include the legs and feet in this developmental course, in discussing infant growth, although, of course they are not part of a cephalo-caudal pattern, but must be considered as appendages like the arms. Studies of fetal growth and behavior show that the limb buds appear very early in embryonic life and that development progresses distally at the same time that it is progressing caudad. Therefore to include the legs and feet as part of the developmental pattern for the head, trunk and tail is clearly a confusion of terms, which serves only to retard the organization of a picture of total bodily development. The literature also indicates that at the same time that the infant is learning to sit up, development of other motor patterns is going on; these appear to be specifically arm and hand motions, such as reaching, grasping and fine prehension, and progress toward creeping.

Shirley (180) has divided all the motor reactions into five orders of skills, as divided by fairly marked gaps in time between the different orders. The first order is passive, postural control developed by the median baby (of those she tested) before twenty weeks of age, and including lifting the chin and chest when prone, making stepping movements, tensing the muscles for being lifted, straightening the knees and sitting on the lap. The second order is postural control of entire trunk and undirected activity, developing at the median ages of twenty-five to thirty-one weeks, and including sitting alone momentarily, knee push or swim, and standing well with help. The third order consists of active efforts at locomotion, which overlapped with the second and fourth orders in age of appearance, and includes progress when on stomach and scooting backward. The fourth order consists of locomotion by creeping, developing at median ages between forty and fifty weeks, and including standing with the help of furniture, creeping, walking when led, and pulling to a standing position with the help of furniture. The fifth order consists of postural control and coördination for walking, developing at median ages of sixty-two to sixty-four weeks, and including standing alone and walking.

Shirley concludes that the development of motor skills is not haphazard, but follows an orderly plan: first, postural control of upper trunk region; second, postural control moving downward to include the entire trunk region, and exhibiting random activity little directed toward locomotion; third, activity and vigorous efforts at locomotion, but poorly coördinated movements; fourth, postural control of the entire body and locomotion by two or three methods; fifth, postural control and coördination combined, the infant reaching the goal of walking, toward which all of his development has been tending. Shirley found that this pattern was inflexible in its broad aspects, but was modified in its details by the different capacities of the individual infants. She also states that the ages for walking with help and for creeping forecast precocity or retardation in walking, and that fair prediction of a baby's age at walking may be made by doubling his age at sitting alone, or by reckoning walking age as once and a half of the age at creeping. She found no direct relation between any anatomical or physiological traits and motor development, but did find that muscular strength, as measured by muscle tone, appears to be an important factor in motor development. In general, thin, muscular babies and small-boned babies walked earlier than short, rotund babies and exceedingly heavy ones. Shirley concludes that locomotor capacity, such as walking at an early age, cannot be used as a criterion for superior intelligence and, conversely, that retarded motor development should not be taken as an indication of inferior intelligence unless it is so marked as to be a clear sign of a pathological condition.

Gesell (65) gives the earliest date found in the literature, four months, as the time when all babies begin to try to sit up by lifting the head and shoulders when in a dorsal position. Shirley and Bühler give five months as the age for this reaction. Shirley (180) gives the steps in sitting up as tensing neck muscles for being lifted, median infant, fifteen weeks; sitting on the lap during a ten-minute test, with support at the lower ribs and with complete head control as established at a median age of eighteen and one-half weeks. Shortly before six months of age the babies were able to sit in a high chair for periods of from fifteen to thirty minutes. The median age at which the infants could sit alone for one minute was thirty-one weeks. All could sit alone momentarily before they could sit for a whole minute, and by the time they could sit one minute, sitting was so well established that they could sit indefinitely. Shirley says that the entire trunk must be under control for the baby to be able to sit alone. The baby who is almost, but not quite, able to sit alone gives away in the lower part of his trunk, not in the upper. Leaning forward, which she found characteristic of this period, is a way of getting support for the trunk.

McGraw (120) describes the development of sitting as follows:

With progressive development increments in this resistance to gravity is quite evident (first in the region of the head and neck and then the trunk) until finally the baby is able to support himself a little while in an open-jack-knife position. Still later he can support himself in an upright sitting position though he is unable to get into that position without help. Finally he can not only resist gravity sufficiently to maintain a sitting posture, but he can carry the superior portion of his body counter to the force of gravity in order to attain a sitting position.

Hazlitt (80) gives four months as the age at which an infant can sit with support and hold the head erect. Brainard (20) reports that his daughter sat with very slight support at four months and eight days of age. Gesell (65) includes sitting with slight support of pillows or blankets, for only 20 per cent of

infants at four months. At six months over half can sit in this
way and about 20 percent can sit alone for some seconds. By
nine months sitting alone should be established by practically
all normal children according to his norms. Linfert and Heirholzer (122) found that 36 percent of the infants they tested
could maintain a sitting position at ease at six months, and 100
percent after six months. Bühler (23) says that at six months
an infant sits with assistance. At eight months he sits alone and
can get into and out of a sitting position with help, and at
nine months he can perform these movements alone. Jones (102)
tested 365 babies. The infants were placed in a sitting position
on a table, the legs were straightened and separated at an angle
of about 50 degrees. If the infant maintained his balance for five
seconds, he was considered to have passed the test. The youngest
infant to pass was one hundred and fifty days old (five months),
25 percent passed at two hundred and five days, 50 percent at
two hundred and seventeen days, 75 percent at two hundred and
fifty days, and 100 percent at two hundred and eighty days.
Simon (182) gives five months as the age at which infants begin
to raise their heads from their pillows, eight months for sitting
with pillows, and ten months for sitting alone. Figurin and Denisova (58) have developed a scale from tests on 200 children up
to one year of age. Sitting with and without help are two of their
tests. They state that the ability to sit alone develops just before
the child is able to raise himself up, and that it is especially hard
at first to make a child get into a sitting position. Some children
do so by turning themselves to the prone position and then pushing themselves back with their arms and turning the body over;
others push themselves from the side using the elbow. They
give the steps in sitting up as holding head erect, sitting with help,
sitting without help, sitting down alone.

Kuhlmann (109) gives as a sixth-month test sitting indefinitely
when supported with pillows at the back, and sitting for five or
ten seconds without support. Sitting unsupported for two or three
minutes, he places as a twelfth-month test. This reaction was
standardized on 83 infants in their twelfth month, it is probable
that if his tests had been continuous from the sixth to the twelfth

month he would have found this ability earlier, but he gives no tests for the months between.

Schaltenbrand (176, 177) traces the development of erect posture from a study of 120 infants. He uses the terminology and classification of reflexes made by Magnus. When a young infant is placed on his back, the head is soon turned to the side, and later the whole body. In the second half of the first year, the infant begins to roll on his stomach; the head is turned first, then the pelvis. The head is then lifted into the normal position and the infant gets on all fours. He gradually learns to get into a sitting position from this position. This is the only description we have found of the development of the pattern of getting into a sitting position from the all-fours position.

SWIMMING

Search of the literature has revealed no reports on the swimming ability of babies. Mention has already been made of the brief reports of the presence or absence of reflex swimming movements in newborn infants. The protocols of the work done at the Normal Child Development Clinic, where a number of infants were tested in a small tank, indicate that young babies make rhythmic swimming movements when lowered prone into water, and that they also tend to turn over on their backs. Shirley (180) in the tests made of progress toward creeping, reports what she terms a "swimming stage." The babies were placed on their stomachs on a flat surface and from the thirteenth week on, a bell was rung and placed just out of their reach in front of them. The swimming stage she describes as "drawing up legs frog-like and in kicking them out suddenly as if swimming." There was frequently a great straining and reaching with the arms at the same time, particularly if the infants were headed for the bell. The abdomen was not lifted off the floor and the hands and feet often worked at cross purposes. If there was progress, it was usually backwards. Although she calls this "swimming," it is not the same as actual alternate swimming movements. These reactions were the first marked progress in motor development noted, after lifting the head and chin, and were established in the median infant at twenty-five weeks of age. She puts this swimming stage between lifting the head and chest and rolling over, with some overlapping with the latter in the progress towards creeping. In 14 of 19 infants, the swim preceded rolling over, and in one infant the two reactions appeared simultaneously. Shirley calls the swimming stage one of the second order of motor skills—postural control of the entire trunk and undirected activity which are developed between the twenty-fifth and thirty-first week. At this time the postural control of the trunk was complete and was gradually moving downward to the pelvic and upper-leg regions, and the other skills which were developing were sitting alone momentarily, rolling, standing with help, and sitting alone one minute.

ROLLING OVER

Rolling over is the next gross motor reaction to develop in infants. Like the other reactions, it does not appear suddenly, in the sense that no observable movements have been made which may be considered as leading up to or preparing for the skill. Shirley (180) reports, as mentioned above, that some of the 24 infants she tested, especially the weak or premature ones, did some rolling from the stomach to the side during the hospital period. She believes that this rolling was due to the fact that, when prone, neonates tend to assume the fetal position, which is so unstable that a stretching out of one leg and a slight push with the toes will turn the baby completely onto his side. The literature also mentions the kicks, squirms and wriggles that normally take place when a two- or three-month-old baby is placed on his stomach.

Shirley regards rolling as a step toward creeping, and classifies it in the second-order motor skills, as noted above. The median infant in her series rolled from back to stomach at twenty-nine weeks; an easy roll from the back was achieved by flexing the hips and stretching out the legs at right angles to the trunk. Rolling by twisting the pelvis was seldom noted at this age. Shirley's next recorded step toward creeping is the ability to make some progress when on the stomach. In two of her 17 cases with records on these reactions, the order of these two skills was reversed and "making some progress" appeared before rolling.

Gesell (65) states that practically all infants at four months of age can roll onto their backs when placed on their sides, and that less than 20 percent can roll completely over from back to stomach or from stomach to back at this age, but that by six months from 50 to 84 percent can do so. Linfert and Hierholzer (122) found that 6 percent of the infants they tested could roll onto the side at one month, 10 percent at two months and 58 percent at four months; the percentages for rolling from the side to the back for these months were 36, 78 and 94. This is undoubtedly the same sort of accidental or uncontrolled rolling described by Shirley (180) as occasionally found shortly after birth. Rolling from the stomach to the back was developed in 76 per cent of the infants at six months, and in 100 percent after six months; rolling from the back to the stomach was present at this age in practically the same proportion of infants.

Bühler (23) places rolling from back to side at five months, and from the prone to the dorsal position and from side to side at six months. Brainard (20) reports that his daughter turned completely over by squirming and throwing her legs at four months and fourteen days of age. Schaltenbrand (176) states that not until the second half of the first year do infants begin to roll onto the stomach by turning the head, then the shoulders and then the pelvis. This is one of the very few instances in the literature in which the movements involved in a response pattern are exactly described. The differences in ages for which different investigators report the appearance of a response are largely explained by the failure to give such descriptions. For example, one author may not list rolling over as established until it occurs in a mature coördinated form of the kind described by Schaltenbrand, while another may list it when it occurs in the accidental manner Shirley describes as occurring occasionally in the neonatal period.

CRAWLING AND CREEPING

Progress toward true creeping, that is the ability to support the body weight on the hands and knees and to make progress by moving the different members alternately, is going on at the same time that the ability to sit up is developing, and apparently appears at about the same time as the ability to make a complete voluntary roll of the body from the back to the stomach or from the stomach to the back. Shirley (180) gives the most complete description of the developmental steps leading up to and including creeping. She states that the 24 babies she tested went through almost the same series of reactions in approximately the same order. This series she gives as follows—(all reactions are for infants in the prone position): chin up, median, three weeks; chest up, median, nine weeks; knee push or swim, median, twenty-five weeks; rolling, twenty-nine weeks; rock or pivot and make some progress, thirty-seven weeks; scoot backward, thirty-nine and one-half weeks; creep, forty-four and one-half weeks. No stage was listed as a characteristic part of creeping until it was observed in from 16 to 22 babies. There were no exceptions to chin lifting preceding chest lifting, or to chest lifting preceding the knee push or swim. In 14 out of 19, swimming preceded rolling; in one infant the two reactions appeared simultaneously. In 15 of the infants rolling preceded "making some progress"; in two this order was reversed. In every case "making some progress" preceded "scooting backward," which preceded "creeping" in all but two cases, where the two appeared simultaneously.

Shirley reports that some of the babies showed interesting variations in the sequence. One of the infants, at twenty weeks, hitched the length of a long table by arching her back and inching along on the crown of her head and the soles of her feet; another drew up the knees, lifted the buttocks and pivoted along on the shoulders. At thirty-seven weeks of age, the median baby was making some progress backwards or sidewise when prone on the floor; frequently the stomach served as the pivot. Eight babies, the median at thirty-eight weeks, made suspension bridges of their bodies by rising on their toes and hands, and held their weight thus for a moment or more. Most of these infants crept about two weeks after this. The final stage before creeping was scooting backward, which appeared in the median at thirty-nine and one-half weeks, and was done by propping on the hands and moving them back toward the knees, thus shoving the body backwards.

One infant attempted to reach the lures by backing up to them and progressing in this way. All of the infants did not creep in the exact sense of the word; four hitched in a sitting posture before going on all fours, one swam across the floor, one used his folded forearms to pull himself along on his stomach, one walked by alternating both hands and one foot with this leg bent at the knee. Shirley says that all these methods were usually abandoned for regular creeping after a few weeks and that creeping was observed to be a purposive reaction, in that the babies crept after the lures, to get away from things they did not like and to get attention. When walking began, creeping was given up as a means of locomotion, though it was still used in play.

According to Shirley, the babies proceeded through these stages toward creeping regardless of the speed of development, and from this she believes that it is safe to conclude that development of creeping proceeds in an orderly and fairly fixed way. She believes that there are other stages in the development of creeping which her test methods did not reveal. In her classification of orders of motor skills, creeping, walking when led, standing by furniture, and pulling to a standing position by furniture are called fourth-order skills. This group of reactions developed at median ages of forty to fifty weeks. There was a correlation of 84 ± 0.05 between the ages of walking alone and of creeping; and the ratios figured for her different steps in motor development indicated that when a baby creeps he has covered about two-thirds of the way toward walking.

Burnside (24) has made an analysis of motion pictures of 9 infants taken in a study of coördination of limbs, body postures and sequences of movements involved in the development of human progression, especially those movements preceding walking. For comparative purposes, pictures were also taken of the movements of an adult, of a twelve-year-old girl, of a dog and of a cat. She found great variation in methods of locomotion. In the early stages, the child makes manifold motions of all limbs in an effort to reach the lure. As growth proceeds, these movements are coördinated in such a way that locomotion results. There is an overproduction of movements in the early efforts. In the

crawling stage which precedes creeping, the abdomen is in contact with floor or table, the body is pulled along by the arms
alone, acting nearly simultaneously, the legs dragging. There are
many asymmetric movements. Then the arms begin to move
alternately, and the legs come into use, moving simultaneously or
with one dragging. When paired members are used together, there
is a hopping motion, and lateral movements of the spine are
accentuated at this stage. She also found that hitching, rolling
or some other method may be used to achieve the first progression. Two of the subjects did not go through a crawling stage.
The creeping posture is with the weight on the hands and knees
and the trunk carried free of the floor. Perfect coördination of
the four extremities and precise adjustment of the body develop
gradually. At first the movements are frequently arhythmic as
cross-coördination begins. As cross-coördination becomes complete, one limb at a time is moved with rhythmic movements.
Later, diagonal limbs move together for part of the time. The
ages of the infants during the study extended from seven months
and twenty-five days to seventeen months and twenty-nine days.
Burnside reports that although great individual differences were
found, there was no evidence to indicate that a child may go from
the sitting position to walking without any of the intervening
types of locomotion.

Schaltenbrand (176) gives a brief description of the development of the creeping posture, as he observed it in his studies
of the changes and development of the tonic neck and labyrinth
reflexes, which he believes are the mechanisms bringing about
erect posture and locomotion in man. In the second half of the
first year, infants begin to roll onto their stomachs, the head is
turned first, then the shoulders, then the pelvis. The head is then
lifted into the normal position and the infant gets on all fours.
It is from this position, according to Schaltenbrand, that the infant learns to get into a sitting position.

Brainard (20), in a study of his daughter, reports that at eight
months the child could pull herself up to a standing position
easily, and that she stood on her hands and knees but did not
creep, although she was crawling at this time. Eight days later,

however, she crept. Bühler (23) lists attempts to push the body sidewise and forward as occurring at four months. In the sixth month, the infant draws his body forward and sidewise, and in the eighth month these attempts are successful. These reactions and those of the head and of sitting and rolling, she lists as reactions to changes in position. In her test series, "locomotion," that is turning from the back to the stomach or the stomach to the back or moving sidewise "in some other manner," is a seventh-month test. "Crawling," by which she undoubtedly means what the literature in English calls creeping, is an eighth-month test. She states that this reaction usually occurs without a special stimulus, and that the child moves about forward or sidewise by "crawling." Gesell (65) in his developmental items states that if the infant is placed prone on a hard surface, "some kind of squirming, wriggling progression is all but universal at four months"; this he calls crawling. Creeping, according to his scale, shows a definite progression in the age at which the majority of children achieve it. At six months about 20 percent creep, at nine months three-quarters of all infants creep, and at thirteen months all infants can. He states that "since retardation in walking is one of the outstanding symptoms of developmental defect, it is well to have a perception of all these earlier locomotor responses which antedate walking." Linfert and Hierholzer (122) in their scale, give lifting the head and limbs when prone as present in 10 percent of the infants at six months, in 97 percent at nine months, and in 100 percent at twelve months. Propelling the body when prone was present in 42 percent at six months, and in 100 percent by nine months. Creeping was present in 19 percent at six months, in 71 percent at nine months, and in 88 percent at twelve months. Figurin and Denisova (58) in their test series, give the ability to rise on the hands when prone as an important step in the development of creeping, and state that the child can usually use his elbows for support earlier than he can his hands. They test for creeping by using a lure a little less than a meter away from the child. At six and one-half months a child should be able to creep slowly on straight arms to this lure. There is variation, however, with individual children.

Warden (205) in a brief note on the development of a boy, says that the first means of propulsion was sitting and placing the hands behind the back to move backwards. This occurred first on the two hundred and sixty-seventh day and a few days later the child moved forward in the same way. On the two hundred and thirty-sixth day he crept on hands and knees, but still reverted to the earlier method, and only gradually shifted to creeping entirely. Rasmussen (168) says that one of his daughters first moved herself along by lying down from the sitting position and making a half roll, then sitting up again and repeating the process. She began to creep at eleven months of age.

Variot (199) studied 80 infants, in a French children's home, for the development of walking. Of these infants, 42 began to walk without going through a creeping stage, and 38 went through various stages of prewalking locomotion. Three crept on their hands and feet without putting the knees to the floor; 22 crept on their hands and knees, and 13 first propelled themselves by sitting and pushing or hitching themselves along in some manner. He describes the creeping in some detail: the infant progresses by alternately advancing the hands which are placed flat on the floor, with the fingers and thumbs spread out, and the hips flexed on the pelvis with the knees on the ground. Sometimes the feet are dragged on the ground, but more often the toes are flexed to push the body along. Some infants creep on one knee only and push with the toes of the opposite foot. There is a tendency to contract the neck muscles and bend the head back so as to look ahead.

The literature on locomotor development up to this point is disappointing; that on the development of walking proper is somewhat fuller. With the exception of Shirley's account of the developmental stages made from observations on a comparatively small number of babies, in simple test situations, and Burnside's analysis of crawling and creeping movements from motion-picture records, there seem to have been no studies of postural and movement control and growth leading up to erect posture and locomotion. Practically all the rest of the literature which mentions the earlier motor skills is based on scales or normative items for checking the normal progress of the individual infant. Although these scales were made from norms obtained on fair-sized groups of infants, the description of the movements to be observed are often so sketchy and even vague that it would be very difficult to rate an infant accurately from the printed directions and explanations. These scales also, of course, fail to give a picture of progressive development. Without actual experience in investigation of infants or without first having read Shirley's account of the development of the skills, it is hard to see how the student could form any picture from these scales of the development of postural control. Further work on the motor phases of growth in the earlier months is clearly needed. That there has not been more of it is curious when one reviews the vast amount of work that has been done on such items as prehension and eye reactions.

ERECT POSTURE AND WALKING

The studies of the development of erect posture and locomotion in all its stages are surprisingly few. Shirley (180) gives a complete account of the development as she observed it in less than 25 babies from birth to two years of age. Schaltenbrand has made a very careful analysis of the changes and development of all the reflexes which he believes contribute to mechanisms of erect posture. Bühler (23) gives a brief listing of reactions which can be assumed to contribute to this development during the first year, but which she calls posture reactions and reactions to changes in posture. Burnside (24) has made motion-picture records of the development of the motions in creeping and in walking from seven to seventeen months. Other reports and the test scales for young infants give ages for the appearance of walking, or take up some one phase of the subject, or trace the presence of actual stepping motions at different ages. There is also a body of literature on the strictly physiological and anatomical aspects of walking, some of it dealing with growth.

Davenport (47) says of the genetics of walking:

The mutations that have led to the human foot are the end of a series of mutations that have been going on for a long time in the Primate series, and which have been found advantageous for survival. The human foot has permitted the upright position and that has freed the hand from locomotion and permitted its higher uses and this has favored the evolution of a brain adapted to meet the needs of the hands.

Lucas and Pryor (125) conclude from measurements of 1,000 children, from two weeks to seven years of age, made to develop indices for judging skeletal differences, that large heavy frameworks require larger muscles to move them and can also carry a larger mass of fat and subcutaneous tissue than smaller ones. No literature was found, however, which presented a scientific account of the relation of the mechanics of the infant body to the development of walking. Investigation along these lines might throw light upon the soundness of some of the theories of the development of behavior. Certainly the relative length and skeletal development of the lower extremities and the condition of the joints must undoubtedly play some part in the emergence of walking. In most discussions of the maturation theory, maturation of the nervous system is the only type of growth considered, and yet it is obvious that muscular and skeletal development also play an important part in development of motor skills.

Since Shirley's (180) account is the most complete one found of progressive behavior toward and including walking, it will be given first. This account also serves to present a summary of the phases of gross motor development which have been presented above. It should be remembered, however, that Shirley's observations were made on a small number of children, and that although she employed an objective method of recording reactions, her study was made without the aid of motion-picture records or other exact apparatus for recording or controlling the test situations and reactions. The tests were made in the homes of the infants, with apparatus that could be transported easily; observation lasted for only about an hour at each examination, and the examinations were made only once in two weeks from the end of the hospital period to the end of the first year, and during the second year at four-week intervals. Thus, although Shirley has worked out the sequence of reactions in motor patterns more consecutively than any other author found, she may not have observed all the detailed stages in any one pattern, and certain reactions may have escaped her. Our picture of the behavioral development of erect posture and locomotion would be much more complete were there a study like Burnside's which covered some such sequence as that worked out by Shirley.

The steps which Shirley gives in the development of erect posture are adjustment of the muscles for lifting, sitting on the lap, lifting the head and shoulder from the floor when in the dorsal position, sitting alone momentarily, sitting alone one minute, standing holding to furniture, and pulling to a stand by holding on to something. Her median subject stood holding to furniture for one minute at forty-two weeks. As he perfected the skill, he leaned less and less heavily on the chair and frequently let go for an instant. Several infants were able to lower themselves carefully to a sitting position about two weeks after they could stand holding to a chair. Pulling to the standing position was established for the median baby at forty-seven weeks. Standing alone was not observed in most of the infants until they were able to walk alone. Shirley points out that the reactions she has listed as leading to an upright posture, begin at the head and proceed down the neck and trunk with increasing age.

Variot (199), in a study of the prewalking progression of 80 infants, states that the child begins to pull himself up to a stand when he feels sufficient strength in his lower extremities. At first he maintains his balance by holding to the walls or furniture. This reaction usually occurs in the ninth or tenth month; and before the infant walks alone, he walks by holding to furniture or by pushing a chair in front of him.

Bühler (23) gives the ages at which some of the reactions appeared in the infants she observed. It must be remembered, however, that the criteria for judging the presence or absence of the reactions differ with the investigator. She says that rising to the standing position with help (what kind of help or from what position is not specified), appears in the tenth month, and rising to a standing position without help was present in 60 percent of the infants at one year, and that standing alone appears in the eleventh month. She also lists kneeling with support as appearing in the ninth month. The normative items which Gesell

(65) lists under postural control are resisting head pressure at four months; holding the head erect at from four to six months; lifting the head or head and chest when prone at from four to six months; postural tonus of the back while handled at four months; trying to sit up, beginning at four months, with the ability to do so fully developed in all children by nine months; standing with help, appearing in a few children at nine months and well developed by twelve months; and standing alone, beginning at twelve months, and fully developed by eighteen months. Linfert and Hierholzer (122) in their scale, say that at six months 10 percent of the infants could stand with help, at nine months 92 percent, and at twelve months 100 percent. The percentages for standing alone are zero at six months, 37 at nine months and 84 at twelve months.

Figurin and Denisova (58) include a number of postural tests in their series, but unfortunately the only access to their work which we have had is an unpublished translation from which the age of the appearance of the different reactions is missing. The items listed by these authors, which may be assembled under the development of erect posture, are: standing holding to a rail, which they state depends upon the coördination of the muscles of the hand and arm; pulling to a standing position; standing supported by one hand; and standing without help, which they say comes late, usually when the baby begins to walk. Simon (182) in his scale, puts postural control very late, erect head at three months, lifting the head from the pillows at five months, lifting the body when in the crib at seven months, sitting with cushions at eight months, sitting alone at ten months, and maintaining balance a few seconds when standing at eleven months. Brainard (20) in his report of observations of his own daughter, says that during the seventh month she succeeded in pulling herself to a stand and in getting down again, and that during the eighth month she could do this easily. Kuhlmann (109) gives as a twelfth-month test standing alone on the floor for 5 seconds or longer.

Rasmussen (168) states that there is sure ground for assuming that the child's interest in his surroundings and his curiosity play an essential part in his efforts to stand up and walk, acting as a driving force. One of his daughters at ten months and three weeks of age pulled herself to a stand on her mother's lap, the mother supporting her under her arms after she stood up; at eleven months she pulled herself to a stand in her crib, holding on by the edge. When she stood up in this way, she planted the outer edges of her feet against the supporting surface, "just like the anthropoid apes," and the weight of her body was then shifted to rest on the soles of the feet.

Schaltenbrand (176) believes that the body-righting reflexes bring about a normal position of the body through deep-pressure sensations in those parts of the body which are against a hard surface. The development of the labyrinth-righting reflexes plays a part in the development of erect posture. At birth the infant, when his body is turned or bent, will make brief attempts to bring the head into the normal position, with the plane of the face vertical and the line of the mouth horizontal. As age increases, the attempts become successful. When the infant is in a dorsal position the head is raised. When he is on his side the face is turned downwards, then lifted. The neck-righting reflexes disappear as the ability to assume an erect posture symmetrically, appears; or they develop into the distinctively human forms at this age. In the infant these reflexes are shown as a torsion of the spine in the same direction the head is turned. If the pelvis is held, the shoulders and abdomen turn in the same direction as the head. If the thorax is held, the pelvis turns in the opposite direction to the head. We have already given the early postural reactions leading to sitting up, which Schaltenbrand, in his sequence of the assumption of an erect posture, attributes to the body-righting reflexes. After the infant has learned to get on all fours, he gradually learns to get into a sitting posture from this position, and finally to stand. During the second and third years, in getting up from the dorsal position, the child rolls from his back to his side and then pushes himself up with both hands on the side toward which he rolled. Not until the fourth or fifth year is use made of the adult method of getting up without torsion of the spine and by pushing with a hand held on each side of the body.

WALKING

That stepping reactions are sometimes present at birth at the reflex level, has been shown by the work of Chaney and McGraw (31), already reviewed. The literature contains a number of accounts of the stepping reactions made by older infants before they are able to support their own weight. Shirley (180) obtained stepping records of 20 babies from seventeen to seventy-eight weeks, and on 17 of these to one hundred and four weeks of age. Until the thirty-second week, the examiner supported the infant under his armpits, holding him so that his feet touched the record paper. Infants over thirty-two weeks of age were supported by grasping their wrists and holding the fingers along their arms for support; this was continued until the infant could walk alone. In the early weeks of the test, many babies danced and patted with only their toes touching the paper; no heel marks were made. Stepping motions, without supporting any weight or straightening the knees, began at seventeen weeks and lasted about eleven weeks, with great variation in the age at which this period ended—from the fifteenth to thirty-third week. Shirley calls this stage the early period of stepping. The next period was standing with support. In this, the babies stood bearing most of their weight on their feet and tensing the muscles of their outstretched arms to keep from losing their balance. A few of the infants had reached this stage when their records were begun at twenty-one weeks old. The period lasted from eight to twenty-three weeks, and 11 infants passed through it; 3, however, did not stand at all, but made some progress from the start. The median length of the period was four weeks, extending from the twenty-eighth to the forty-second week. Shirley considers this an important stage toward walking; the sooner it is reached, the earlier the infant walks; and the later, the more walking is retarded. The rank order correlation between age of walking alone and this stage is 80 ± 0.06. During the next period the babies walked when led by the hands. The most precocious infant began it at twenty-three weeks, the most retarded at seventy-two weeks, with a median age of forty-two weeks. The median length of the period was twenty-two weeks, and during this time there was rapid progress in the speed of walking, growing uniformity in the length of step, increase in the width of step, and great variability in the size of the stepping angle. The correlation of age at this stage with age of walking alone was 91 ± 0.03. Shirley's next stage was walking alone. For 21 babies this period began at ages from fifty to seventy-six weeks. Improvement in walking was for the median from the sixtieth to ninety-fourth week; at the end of this time perfection in walking skills was reached, as far as the items she measured are concerned. Improvement was shown by a very rapid increase in speed of walking, increase in the length of the step, gradually decreasing width of step, and a decreasing angle of step. From the ninetieth week to the end of the tests, the infants were on a plateau as far as walking skill went. During this period it was the infant's attitude that was measured rather than his skill, and the babies began to lose interest in the test after they became proficient walkers. Shirley sums up her records as showing that there are four stages in progress toward walking: (1) early period of stepping, in which slight forward progress is made; (2) period of standing with help; (3) period of walking when led; (4) walking alone. The speed of walking increases slowly when the babies are led and at an accelerated rate when they are walking alone. The length of the step increases gradually during the two walking stages. The width of step increases until the babies walk alone and then decreases slightly. The width of the standing base and stepping angles show great irregularity in the early stages, but the angles gradually decrease and approach zero degrees after walking alone starts. Dancing or walking on the toes only is common in the early stages; in the later stages the full footprint is made. A large percentage of steps are out of sequence in the early stages; after walking alone is established, the feet follow each other in sequence. Most of the infants toed out in the early stages, but the steps became straighter with proficiency; pigeon-toeing was characteristic of only 2 infants. There were many individual characteristics in many of the details of the pattern.

Burnside (24) describes the movements involved in early walking, as analysed from motion-picture records. The records stop at seventeen months and twenty-nine days of age. She found that the rate of development of progression is different for different individuals, and concludes that it goes on as the increasing integration of the nervous system permits. As walking begins, stability depends upon the basis of support. The position of the center of gravity and the weight of the body are determined by the coordination of the muscles for the restoration of equilibrium. These functions being immature at first, the infant falls. He counterbalances this by placing the feet far apart, by a slight flexion at the hips and knees which lowers the center of gravity, and by raising the arms to help balance himself. As ease in walking increases, the arms are flexed at the elbows only, and the forearms are held forward. In the early steps, the feet are raised relatively high. The walking showed a rhythmic alternation of the limbs, as each in turn supported the body weight. Throughout the entire series of pictures, the head was carried sufficiently erect for the child to survey the field in front of him. In this connection, however, it should be noted that she used a lure held in front of the child to induce him to advance. There was an increase in harmonious coördination and rapidity of movement, with increase in age. The length of the steps increased with age, and the width and variability of the steps decreased. The children commonly turned their toes out, but the individual differences in the different patterns were great.

The age at which walking alone appears is given in all the different test scales. Bühler (23) says that at nine months many children walk with assistance, and at one year most, but not all, do. Her tests for the first two months of the second year give standing and walking with support while holding a toy in one hand. Tests for the third through the fifth month of the second year, are walking to the examiner without support when called, and picking up an object from the floor while standing alone without falling down or holding onto anything for support. From the sixth through the eighth month of this year, the tests are holding something in the hand while walking alone without dropping it, and climbing upon a box or low stool while holding to a support, when the examiner holds out a lure. During the last three months of the second year, the child is tested for climbing upon a chair and standing on it to reach a lure.

Gesell (65) also includes a series of normative items which precede walking alone. At four months, if the infant is held under the arms and suspended so that his feet just touch the floor, he will make pushing movements in response to the stimulation of the hard surface against the soles. At nine months about 75 percent of infants will make rhythmic stepping motions if held in this way. Gesell says that this reaction may be merely a playful one, comparable to patting the table or to splashing, or that it may be genetically related to walking. Standing is tested by holding the infant in the same way. Less than half stand with help at nine months, and practically all children at twelve months. Less than half stand alone at twelve months and practically all at eighteen months. At nine months less than 20 percent walk with help when supported, and about three-quarters at twelve months. At twelve months less than half walk alone, and at eighteen months practically all do. In this connection Gesell says that although the age of walking has some broad relation to the development of intelligence, the examiner should know how to make clinical discounts for individual cases, and so on. Linfert and Hierholzer (122) say that 6 percent of the infants they tested made stepping-movements at six months, 75 percent at nine months, and 100 percent at twelve months. At six months none of the children walked with help, at nine months 37 percent did, and at twelve months 94 percent. Walking alone did not appear until the twelfth month, when 30 percent were able to do so. Figurin and Denisova (58) give a number of tests for walking with help, and state that the youngest of the 200 infants they tested walked alone at ten months of age, and that if the child walked much later than this a cause was always found.

Brainard (20) states that his daughter made stepping movements when held suspended under the arms and walked holding to the furniture at ten months, and took a few steps alone at eleven months. After her first birthday, she easily walked short distances alone. The primary responses in the development of walking which he observed, were pushing against pressure exerted on the soles of the feet, and alternate leg movements and balancing by reverse movements when losing support. Rasmussen (168) describes the first walking of his daughter, which occurred at thirteen and one-half months, as a highly uncertain performance. The child walked with stiff legs and twisted the body about on a vertical axis, throwing the right side of the body forward in an arc when the right leg was advanced and repeating the body movement on the other side as the left leg was advanced. The soles of the feet were turned in.

Myers (143) has published an account of the development of walking in his own child, in which he includes the reactions from birth which he believes lead up to walking itself. Since this is one of the very few studies of the sort found, it is given consecutively here instead of in parts under the different patterns involved. He finds the genesis of walking in the newborn infant's tendency to push against pressure on the soles of the feet, a reaction which grew in his child until on the forty-ninth day, he pushed his feet in unison against anything touching their soles. On the fiftieth day he rolled over when lying on his side, and on the eighty-seventh day he pulled himself to a sitting position by holding the hands of an adult who held the arms taut. On the one hundred and twelfth day he sat on an adult's lap without support. On the one hundred and forty-third day, while being lifted he straightened and stiffened his legs and gave a strong push with the legs. On the one hundred and fifty-second day he raised himself from a dorsal position to a sitting position, while his feet were held firm by an adult, and then fell forward, and on the next day he sat fifteen minutes in his carriage with the support of the front strap. On the one hundred and eightieth day he got on his forearms and knees in trying to reach for a toy, but his hands and feet failed to coördinate. On the one hundred and eighty-fourth day he made dancing steps when held upright with his feet touching the floor. On the one hundred and ninety-second day he pulled himself to the sitting position by grasping the side of his carriage, and on the two hundredth day for the first time put out his hands to protect himself as he started to fall forward, while sitting. On the two hundred and tenth day the child could sit on the floor unsupported, and ride in his carriage standing up supported only by the strap. On the two hundred and twenty-fifth day he got on his hands and feet, but did not move forward; later he could move backwards by pulling with his hands and pushing with his feet, and on the two hundred and ninety-second day he moved forward in this way. After this he crept, and on the three hundred and fifth day began to move his arms and legs alternately, on the three hundred and thirteenth day he crept with his weight on his hands and toes, and on the three hundred and twentieth day he crept "as an adult would." On the three hundred and nineteenth day he rode for several blocks in his carriage standing up, and on the three hundred and twenty-first day he walked when held by the hand, and walked along a couch alone, holding on. On the three hundred twenty-fifth day he crept holding an object in one hand. On the three hundred and thirty-first day he pulled up to a stand by a table. On the three hundred and forty-fifth day he stood unsupported for several minutes, and on the three hundred and fifty-seventh day he took three steps alone. The distances walked increased slowly, and on the three hundred and seventieth day he walked five and a half feet alone and squatted on his haunches. On the three hundred and seventy-sixth day he stood alone for some time and walked ten feet, and carried an object while walking. On the four hundred and twenty-seventh day he began running, and on the four hundred and forty-seventh day began flexing his knees in walking or running instead of holding them stiff. From this time on improvement took the form of walking backwards, turning his head to look about while walking, getting up and sitting down while walking, stepping up and down curbstones alone, and jumping on a spring bed without losing his balance. The records stops at the six hundred and ninety-sixth day.

Dudley, Duncan and Sears (53) have published observations of the locomotor activities on one infant in a nursery school, at the end of her creeping period and during the early weeks of walking. This child took her first steps alone during the fifty-

seventh week. During the fifty-fourth week the child crept, sometimes on her hands and knees, and sometimes on her hands and
feet; she crept with things in her hands, and pulled herself to
a stand, first with both hands and then with one. The next week
she walked along a table by holding to the edge, but refused to
walk when helped by one of the observers. She continued to creep
on her hands and feet and developed considerable speed until
she walked alone. In the fifty-seventh week she walked about
twenty steps, holding to a doll carriage, but fell down after three
steps when the observer, who was holding her from the rear, let
go; she also stood up for a second unsupported. The next week
she walked further with support and stood alone several times
for a few seconds. During the fifty-seventh and fifty-eighth weeks
she walked alone and could pull herself to a stand with ease, and
usually entirely with one hand, but she still crept as the method
of getting to a desired spot. In walking she held her arms in front
of her, the steps were uneven, the feet far apart and lifted quite
high, and her eyes fixed on the goal. She fell and got up frequently
and also staggered and regained her balance. In the fifty-ninth
week she began to hold one arm at her side instead of in front
of her and gained speed in walking, but still fell down frequently;
she also balanced on one foot by holding to the wall and digging
her toes into the table. During the next weeks, up to the sixty-
eighth, when the observations ceased, she made steady progress
in walking skill; she began to run, to carry things in her hands,
and to practice turning corners and walking in a circle. The feet
were not lifted so high and were held closer together. In the
sixty-sixth week she climbed up onto a chair, but fell off when
she stood on the seat.

Smith, Lecker, Dunlop and Cureton (183) have made a study
of the effects of race, sex and environment on the age at which
children walk. They used the questionnaire method, getting from
the mothers the ages at which 725 babies took the first step.
These children were all born in the Hawaiian Islands, but repre-
sented seven races. The median age of walking for these children
was 12.71 months and the average age 13.25 months. These results were combined with those given in three other studies, one

by the same authors on 109 children, most of whom were born in Iowa, one of 50 children in and near New York, and Terman's study of 565 gifted children in California. They failed to find significant racial differences. The median age of walking of the 1,449 children was 12.8 months. Their conclusions are that girls walk approximately two weeks earlier on the average than boys; that children in warmer climates walk earlier than those in colder climates (the difference between the children in Hawaii and those in Iowa was approximately six weeks); that children of lower intellectual and social levels walk at later ages than those of higher levels; and that the number of children who walk younger than the average age is greater than the number who walk later. They point out that there are necessary errors in all studies of the age of walking which are made by such methods as they employed.

Variot, and Variot and Gotcu have published the results of their studies of walking on French infants. Variot (200), from a study of two over-sized brothers, concludes that the appearance of walking depends more on age than on height. One, who was breast-fed, walked two months earlier than his bottle-fed brother, both were considerably taller than the average height at beginning to walk, and both were 80 cm tall at the time of beginning to walk alone. Variot and Gotcu (201, 202) studied the age of walking in 500 infants, in relation to age, height, birth weight, weight at walking, dentition, feeding and sex. They state that walking does not appear until the muscles are strong enough, and until the neural mechanisms are sufficiently developed to bring about the simultaneous coördination of movements of the trunk and of the lower members, necessary to insure equilibrium in an erect posture. Children can often walk with support before the motor coördination for equilibrium is sufficiently established to enable them to walk alone. They state that the age of walking has hereditary characteristics, that in general the members of some families walk early, while those of others walk late. The percentages for the age of first walking of the 500 children are as follows:

MONTHS	PERCENT WALKING
9	1.25
10	5.50
11	10.35
12	21.0
13	22.0
14	14.25
15	10.0
16	5.0
17	2.70
18	5.20
19	1.35
20	0.45
21	0.70
22	0.25

These figures show the skewing at the lower ages mentioned by Smith *et al.* The height of these infants at the beginning of walking varied from 66 to 83 cm, the average height being 72 to 75 cm. There was no consistent relation between height and age at walking. They conclude, therefore, that the maturation of the neural mechanisms for walking go on independently of height, and subject to age. There was no relation between age of walking and weight at birth when allowances were made for birth at term. Weights at walking varied from 8,700 gm to 10,200 gm, with the average at 9,600 gm, and there seemed to be no definite relation between weight and age. The majority of the children had four to eight teeth when they began to walk, and 67 percent had as many as from six to eight. The authors found a small relation between method of feeding and age at walking, in favor of the babies who had been entirely breast-fed. The girls were slightly younger than the boys, at walking.

Wolff (214) has studied the walking of 50 children, eighteen months to four years of age, by means of footprint records. She does not give the ages at which the changes she observed take place, but says that during early walking and often up to twenty months the footprints show that there are no distinct impulsion points. With increasing age until the fourth year, when the adult method of walking is usually established, the points of impulsion increase in number and change in position. The first point of impulse is at the heel; the points move forward and toward the outer edge of the foot as they appear, and they indicate that the foot comes to be rolled forward in walking.

McGraw (120) from work with newborn infants and from unpublished work with older babies, points out the need of further investigation of the sequence of motor development toward erect posture and walking. Although the standardized tests and scales for measuring infant development make use of a number of reactions which are steps in the development of erect posture and locomotion, there is still no satisfactory method of correlating the responses into a satisfactory picture of individual behavior growth, which explains why one normal infant walks at nine months and another not until he is eighteen or twenty months of age. McGraw believes that much of the difficulty is due to the fact that attention has been centered on the age at which such reactions as sitting alone, stepping movements, standing with help, and so on, appear, without sufficient analysis of the process or means whereby these reactions are acquired. Data, reviewed here in the section on the newborn infant, show that at birth the infant is able, with help, to support his weight on his feet, to hold the head in a plane with the body momentarily, and to make stepping movements. These early reactions are qualitatively very different from the same reactions when they appear later as parts of integrated behavior patterns, yet they are present. The tests and scales give an incomplete picture of development, since, by ignoring the early reactions, they make it appear as though the reactions tested for were entirely new patterns emerging for the first time at the age periods for which they are listed. McGraw says:

It would seem that the infant's inability to walk at birth is due more to an undeveloped equilibratory apparatus than to the absence of a walking mechanism. A primitive or vestigial mechanism is there, but appears to be segmental and not integrated with related functions essential to upright ambulation.

In order to walk upright an individual must be able to support his weight, maintain his balance, and propel himself forward. The flexion and extension of the lower extremities at the two major flexion foci functions at birth and the big task ahead of the infant is to develop a resistance to and a control over the force of gravity.

McGraw's conclusions from her analysis of a longitudinal study of a good-sized group of infants, in their progress toward walking, are worth giving in full since, with the exception of Shirley's account of development, it is the only one found in the literature which traces patterns from their early beginnings to their complex form, when integrated into controlled and purposive behavior. Shirley's (180) account omits the reflex movements of the lower extremities, which are present at birth. Bühler's (23) account of development places the emphasis upon the integration of the personality and the emergence of psychic qualities, and interprets the physical behavior observed largely in these terms. Therefore, no clear pictures of development of physical behavior patterns are formed from a perusal of her careful and detailed work. McGraw's conclusions are:

(1) Certain types of activities appear to function on a reflex level before they become part of a controlled muscular pattern. The reflexes tend to disappear before or about the time the controlled neuro-muscular pattern emerges. For example, there is a diminution of the early reflex stepping movements before the controlled process of walking becomes a part of the infant's behavior repertoire. (2) There is no evidence of a sudden emergence of a new totally integrated pattern. That is to say, the infant does not use one distinct pattern of response and cast it off for the use of another pattern when a new phase in his development has become evident. Rather the new pattern unfolds, bit by bit, and dovetails with the old pattern and gradually the new pattern becomes more and more dominant until finally it is superimposed upon the old pattern though in times of stress and strain the infant will revert to the less mature response. (3) Growth in the assumption of an erect posture and walking is extraordinarily gradual. Although the acquisition of the power of walking erect is obviously dependent upon a degree of maturation or ripening of the nervous system, it nevertheless has the essential elements involved in a learning process. . . . For the infant, behavior development is not so much a question of eliminating false responses and selecting satisfying ones as it is an increase in the degree and precision of response, the initial pattern of which

is desirable. Infants tend to make a partial response rather than a false one and "learning" consists of a completion of the reaction pattern rather than selection and elimination of responses. (4) Standardized tests and scales for measuring infant development can be of little practical value until these phases on the development of a single trait have been minutely analyzed and determined.

HAND AND ARM REACTIONS

The literature on the development of the use of the arms and hands is much fuller than that on other aspects of motor development. Largely owing to the influence of Gesell's work there have been a number of detailed controlled investigations of the development of reaching and prehension. The standardized tests and scales also lay emphasis on hand activities. It is not possible to isolate many of the later responses involving the use of the arms and hands from other complex reactions involving a variety of behavior reactions. At an early age, the coördination of eye and hand movements appears to play a large rôle in the development of accuracy in reaching, and to a certain extent in grasping. As age increases, the hands become a more and more important tool for a great variety of activities, and, especially in the second year, their use becomes coördinated with intellectual behavior so that it is no longer possible to say that the reactions are purely motor responses. The first attempt of a child to use pencil and paper is a very complex response, involving many neural mechanisms besides those governing the coördination of arm, hand and eye patterns. Activities of this nature are, however, classified here under hand responses, for purposes of convenience. We are presenting a review of the literature in objective behavioral terms, and the categories which we have adopted permit us to avoid the necessity of making interpretations of the nature of the responses reported upon. The section on adjustment for solution of problems will review the material in the literature that seems unequivocally to be in the nature of adaptation to an immediate problem; aside from this we have purposely shunned labeling any reactions as intellectual, or as the results of learning, in the ordinary sense of the word.

There is no doubt, however, that development in the use of

the hands is closely linked with the kind of development which in older children is called learning, and with growth of purposive behavior. Givler (68), a behaviorist, goes so far as to state that grasping is that by which we learn. He traces the grasping reflex back to about the eighth week of fetal life, at which time, he says, the hands develop and assume a semiflexed posture, and believes that the reflex has been practiced for three or four months before birth. The reflex, he states, is a true spinal one not involving the cerebrum, and as long as it lasts, it shows "attention," that is, the sense organs of the palms are kept so adjusted as to receive the stimulus most effectively. Tenacity is lost about the one hundred and fiftieth day, but deftness and flexibility are gained with increasing growth. He states that adults learn, fight, gain possession of and maintain authority, and use tools, by means of the grasping reflex, and cites a long list of words having hand or grasp ideas as roots. He believes that there is slight trace of hand motion as these words are used.

Halverson (77), who has made the most complete and careful studies of the development of reaching and prehension found in the literature, presents a more objective statement of the importance of the arm and hand in learning and adaptation to the environment. He points out that "At least seven distinct senses, the muscular, tendinous, articular, warmth, cold, pressure, and pain, have their sense-organs generously distributed throughout this limb, particularly in the hand." The hand, especially the palm, is the most important tactile sense organ of the body. In it, the kinesthetic and cutaneous senses coöperate to teach the primary concepts of the qualities of objects. These senses then coöperate with vision and audition in enabling them to make correct judgments of qualities. Halverson also points out the mechanical perfection of the hand for varied action: its suspension at the end of the arm, its freedom of operation owing to the three arm joints, the manipulatory and exploratory qualifications of the three-jointed long fingers, the sensitivity of the finger tips, and the value of thumb opposition. He gives the following list of physiological and psychological conditions that are likely to be instated in a total act of prehension:

maintenance of bodily equilibrium, involving bracing by legs and heels; hip flexion, to bring the shoulders and head of the infant nearer the object; lowering of the head medially; rotation of the body above the hips to swing forward the favored side; extension of the lateral angle of the scapula, bringing forward the arm from the shoulder joint; extension and flexion of the elbow; wrist movements; hand-rotation; digital extension, flexion and abduction; and thumb-opposition. Beside these conditions, there are direction of the approach, length and form of approach, its vertical profile, time elapsing between the presentation of the object and the start of the approach, time required to contact with the object, time required for grasp, kind of grasp, amount of displacement of the object before it is grasped, and other conditions too numerous to mention at this time.

The early development of behavior in the arms and hands can properly be classed under motor reactions which are of primary importance to the organism, that is reactions fundamental in the course of development to the growth of every individual, and part of universal normal human patterns. Probably before the end of the first year, however, individual differentiation, or learning, has already begun to give a specialized turn to some hand responses, so that after the end of this period, the course of development is an individual matter closely linked with intellectual faculties and with each child's peculiar environment. The scales, especially Gesell's (64) normative items, give tests for older ages for skills which are dependent upon the use of the hands. These tests probably give a generalized picture of activities that in their broad outlines are common to the majority of such homogeneous groups as have been used for obtaining the norms. It is obvious, however, that such tests as copying pictures and drawing a man involve so many intellectual and environmental factors that the responses can no longer accurately be classed as part of a general behavior pattern that is common to all normal human development. Halverson (76) says of acquisition of skill, for instance, that,

Rapid increase in the development of motor skill by the hand is absolutely essential to normal growth as it is only by such development that the infant can acquire adequate knowledge of his environment. Backwardness in development of skill in the use of this prehensile organ must necessarily result in retardation of mental development.

Made in these general terms, this statement is undoubtedly true. But it appears to be equally true that there is no such simple and easily applied criterion for judging where the normal essential increase in skill leaves off and individual differences begin, as there is in the case of walking. The hands are used for so many activities, even by a young infant, that it seems impossible to select certain ones as better illustrations of necessary normal growth than others. The studies which have been made of the sequence of the development of the use of the hand, give an analysis of the movements at different ages, and of the changes which take place in them. So far as these pictures are complete, we have an outline of normal development in reaching and prehension. As soon, however, as the emphasis is shifted to the activities themselves, that is to what the hand does, not how it does it, as the test series do, we have lost the developmental pattern and are dealing with individual reactions.

REACHING

It is difficult to state exactly when definite reaching begins. The young infant constantly makes waving motions, with one or with both hands, and the object to be reached for must be held before the child long enough for him to see it. If accidental contact with the object is made during this time, it is grasped and, even after real reaching begins, the movements are uncoördinated and there are many misses. Shirley (180) says that tentative reaching or waving in the direction of a stationary object was observed in a few of the babies she tested from the seventh week on; the median age for this reaction when lying on the back was thirteen weeks, and fourteen weeks for the sitting posture. Halverson (76) in a quantitative study of reaching made on eight infants at intervals from twelve to sixty weeks of age, found that at twelve weeks the infants did not get very near the small pellet which was used as the lure, and that for most of them the hands were actually further away from the pellet at the termination of the reaching movements than at their beginning. Valentine (198), in a longitudinal study of his son, says that he observed signs of deliberate movements in the tenth week. None of the large number of infants tested by Jones (102) succeeded in grasping a bright toy moved slowly toward them, until the fourth month, and at this age Gesell (65) considers his test with the dangling ring passed if the infant "regards" the ring or makes incipient arm or hand movements. Less than half the infants bring their hands together in a "closing in" movement, which brings the ring within their grasp. He states that definite reaching is not expected of four-month-old subjects. Bühler (23) describes the reaching that results with her four-month-old test. Up to this time the hands move toward an object without looking at it. At four months the eyes begin to help the hands move toward the object. The object must be near, and the arm movements are uncertain, the hands clenched into fists, and the reaching is with both hands to grasp between the fists; the hands usually miss and pass over the object. Bailey (7), whose test series is largely based on Gesell's, credits any reaching movements, even if uncoördinated, toward a red ring suspended within easy reaching distance, at three months; and at four months credit is given if, in reaching, the infant manages to close in on the ring with both hands.

The next stage in the development of arm-and-hand reactions, as observed by Shirley (180), was that of reaching, touching and momentarily grasping the object. The median age for this reaction was fifteen weeks. The babies frequently made passes at the object, only to catch their own hands, and grasping was not a sure process. Reaching for a dangling object came somewhat later; the median age was nineteen weeks. Shirley states that the reaching responses could be measured only in descriptive terms, but they were active, with grasping as the goal. There were variations in the quality of the early reactions. Sometimes the reaching seemed to be purely random, sometimes the baby reached and missed repeatedly, and sometimes he seized the toy immediately. Shirley's developmental tests from the third to the sixth month, which were repeated at the ninth month, consisted almost entirely of reaching tests. During this period the reaching function was established practically to completion, both in the lying and sitting postures, and for stationary and moving objects. The initial skill was greater in the lying than in the sitting posture, but progress was more rapid in the sitting posture, though a plateau in the skill was not reached as early as it was in the lying posture. Shirley concludes from the results of the tests she gave that during this period reaching and grasping reactions developed and became perfected almost to the exclusion of development in other channels; with progress in the skill, attention, reaching and grasping became almost simultaneous. The steps in the development of the reactions to the reaching tests during this period were reaching and missing, reaching and touching, grasping and not holding, grasping and retaining, holding and manipulating, and holding and manipulating with one hand. Shirley says that although progress in the reaching function may be fundamentally gradual, on the surface it appeared to be sudden; the sudden sharp rise in the curves between the nineteenth and twenty-first weeks bears this out. The number of infants showing no reactions to the tests decreased from the thirteenth to the twenty-third week, reaching zero at the twenty-second week. The percentage curves show that the ups and downs were slight, and that progress toward the goal of reaching took a fairly steady upward course. The curves start fairly high, showing that some of the babies had developed the responses before the testing started at thirteen weeks.

Bühler (23) says that in the fifth month, the infant begins to reach out and grasp with one hand, and in the second half year he begins to reach toward things that are out of reach and to move the body toward them. From the sixth to the ninth month, the legs assist in reaching and grasping. One of her seventh-month tests is moving toward a desired object by changing the position of the body as well as reaching, and she places reaching for a toy through the bars of a crib, and getting it, at eight months. Gesell (65) states that variations in promptness, directness and accuracy in reaching undoubtedly correlate with the developmental status of the child, and gives as normative items up to twelve months the reactions to be expected to the dangling ring test. At six months the child is seated in the mother's lap for the test, and the ring is dangled about a foot above and in front of him. About three-quarters of the infants seize the ring when it is lowered in front of them, and about half when it is above them. At nine months the reaction is more mature and the child tries to pull the ring down; at twelve months many infants begin to notice the string and to reach for it too. Marked persistence in reaching for the ring occurs in about half the subjects at six months, and in over three-quarters at nine months. Bayley (7) places reaching for the dangling ring as a fourth-month test, and credits any reaching movement of the arms, even though very slightly coördinated. At five months the child is given credit if he reaches for a one-inch cube on a table close to him, and also if the eyes coöperate in the reaching, making it directed. At six months credit is given if the infant recovers his rattle when in a dorsal position. At seven months the cube is placed just out of the subject's reach, and credit given if he reaches for it persistently, and credit is also given if reaching or manipulation tends to be unilateral at this age. Gesell (65) includes a test of reactions to an 8-mm white pellet placed on a table within easy reach. At six months a little over half react by looking at the pellet or reaching for it. Bayley, and Linfert and Hierholzer also use a small pellet. Bayley (7) gives credit at six months if the infant looks at the pellet, apparently without any attempt to reach it. Linfert and Hierholzer (122) found that only 39 percent of their subjects perceived the pellet at six months, but at nine months and after, all did. Kuhlmann (109) gives a sixth-month reaching test in which a bright object, a colored ball or a hand bell is held out to the child, and the test is passed "if he readily reaches."

Figurin and Denisova (58) include tests of reaching in their scale, and say that when an object is held in front of an infant the earliest reaction is general excitement, next he puts his hands out and touches it, and later he holds the object and manipulates it. Brainard (20) reports that during the fifth month the reaching and grasping of his daughter improved, but that she would not begin to reach until the object touched her hand; if the back of the hand was touched, she would turn it over. The eyes followed, but did not direct, the hands. He believes that eye-hand coördination develops by the accidental meeting of eye and hand stimulations. Jones (102) reports on the ability of 365 infants to reach and grasp a bright-colored toy in ten seconds, when it was moved slowly toward them in a line between the eyes. The infants were lying on their backs unless they insisted upon sitting up. She does not distinguish between reaching and grasping, but calls the test one of reaching. The youngest child to succeed was 116 days old. At one hundred and thirty-five days of age 25 percent succeeded, at one hundred and fifty-two days, 50 percent; at one hundred and seventy-three days, 75 percent; and at two hundred and sixty-nine days, 100 percent. Heubner (85) says that reaching for things that are beyond the reach develops in the second quarter of the first year.

Halverson (76) has made a systematic study from motion-picture records of the development of the movements in reaching, from the twelfth to the sixtieth week, in 8 infants. The tests were made at monthly intervals, with the infant seated at a table. The object to be reached for was a pellet 7 mm in diameter and 3 mm in height, placed six and one-half inches from the near edge of the table in front of the child. If the pellet was not secured in nine seconds, it was moved to a point three and one-fourth inches from the near edge of the table, and the subject was allowed another ten seconds to get it. At twelve weeks of age, a one-inch cube was substituted for the pellet, as none of the infants reached for the pellet and only 6 gave any signs of perceiving it. Since his studies were the only ones found which analyze reaching movements, some of his conclusions are quoted in full.

Reaching at 12 to 20 weeks consists of discontinuous lateral arm movements in which the hand slides on the table top, revolves clockwise above the table, or combines both of these activities. Later the movements become more continuous, the lateral deviations decrease as forward projection increases, and the sliding and circular motions diminish. At 60 weeks the infant's capacity in the perception of visual space and his ability in the coordination of trunk and arm movements are so highly correlated that reaching is accomplished by a smooth continuous movement of the hand with little or no spatial error.

At sixty weeks of age skill compares favorably with that of an adult. During the first stage of acquiring skill, the movements are simple sensorimotor responses, with abductor-adductor movements of the shoulder most prominent. The second stage is one of slowly acquired voluntary movements ranging from crude groping to direct reaching, and finally the movements become largely automatic. The skills required for accurate reaching are perception of visual space, and synergic control of the muscles functioning in sitting equilibrium, in inclination and twisting of the trunk, and in flexion and extension of the joints of the arm and hand.

Lateral deviations of the hand in reaching increase in amount up to 24 weeks and then diminish until 40 weeks, after which time the lateral error is uniformly small.

The amount of digression inward, toward the median plane of the body, becomes greater up to 20 weeks and then decreases, while the amount of digression in the opposite direction increases up to 24 weeks and then gradually decreases. After 44 weeks no median digressions occur. Lateral digressions, however, occur normally at all ages.

The increase in the amount of median and lateral errors from 12 to 24 weeks signifies an advance in arm mobility and not an actual loss in cortical control over arm movements.

Progress in advancing the hand toward the pellet takes place slowly from 12 to 20 weeks. From 20 to 24 weeks a remarkable gain occurs in which the hand almost attains the distance of the pellet. At 28 weeks all infants can reach forward to the pellet.

From 16 weeks on, the elbow and digits participate in reaching movements with increasing effectiveness until at 40 weeks they closely approximate the shoulder in usefulness in reaching.

The trunk and wrist are functionally retarded. They display little effectiveness until after 32 weeks when they improve rapidly in usefulness in reaching. At 40 weeks the trunk and wrist participate as effectively in the reaching movements as do the other anatomical parts.

Arm movements which result in under-reaching the pellet are common in the first half year of life.

Ulnar flexion of the wrist in pointing, which is an adult characteristic, begins to function after the sixth month.

The time consumed in reaching is in no way a measure of the speed of accuracy of arm movement. However, infants of 40 to 60 weeks accomplish the reaching in one-half the time (1.0 to 1.5 seconds) required by younger infants.

Halverson (77) states that "Development of motor skill in reaching movements, then, in addition to being contingent largely upon anatomical and physiological maturation, depends on constant modifications in central correlation of exteroceptive impulses from the retina of the eye and proprioceptive impulses from the moving parts of the trunk and arms as they undergo changes in posture." The unnecessary movements which carry the hand away from the object are gradually eliminated and those which contribute to quick accurate reaching are retained. "The coördination of these essential components into a smoothly continuous act constitutes perfection in the reaching movements."

In another study, Halverson (77) gives a more generalized picture of the reaching motions made in grasping a cube. He observes three types of approach: a backward sweep, and a very circuitous approach employed by infants from sixteen to twenty-eight weeks of age; from thirty-two to thirty-six weeks a less circuitous approach is used; and after forty weeks a direct approach is usually used. The backhand and circuitous approaches straighten out into a direct approach. Until twenty-four weeks of age, the hand was usually pointed so that the whole hand came to rest on the cube; after twenty-eight weeks of age, the hand was directed so that the forefinger passed over the middle top of the cube. In the earlier stages the thumb hung down, and its position during the approach indicated the type of grasp to take place. Accuracy in reaching improved gradually and steadily in most cases from sixteen to fifty-two weeks. At sixteen weeks of age no infants are likely to touch the cube; at twenty weeks one third grasp the cube crudely; at twenty-four weeks one-half grasp or touch the cube; and at and after twenty-four weeks all infants can grasp the cube if they desire it. A lateral view also shows three methods of approach, and combinations of these methods: a slide which is used by many up to thirty-two weeks of age, a loop which also was used in early reaching, and a planning approach which was characteristic after thirty-six weeks. Up to twenty-four weeks both hands are frequently used in reaching, and up to twenty-eight weeks the hand is raised relatively high in reaching. After this, until fifty-two weeks (the end of the study), the height of the approach gradually lessens. The infants who reached the cube up to twenty-eight weeks, pointed the forearm directly above the cube at the final stage of approach, and after this time this method was usually replaced by an aim which takes the hand to a point above the side of the cube nearest the reaching hand. The age of twenty-eight weeks seemed to be a critical period in the development of reaching and prehension, the infants looked at the cube longest and oftenest at this age, the hand was just beginning to free itself from the forearm in reaching, direct reaching was just beginning and also the pointing of the hand so that only the grasping fingers passed over the cube. The first reaches are directed by the shoulder and upper arm, with little or no flexion of the elbow and wrist; the hand usually passes beyond the cube and attempts to scoop it toward the chest with a whole arm motion.

PREHENSION

At birth the reflex grasp is fully developed. If the palm of the hand is stimulated, the whole fist closes tightly, and in many infants this grasp is strong enough to support the body weight suspended. There is no thumb opposition at this age, and the whole hand is used in a pawlike manner without differentiation of the fingers. This grasp gradually disappears and voluntary reaching and grasping develop; some authors believe the ability to support body weight suspended lasts through the first year. Halverson (78) quotes Watson as saying that the reflex grasp disappeared as early as the eightieth day in one infant and functioned much later than five months in others, and Adie and Critchley as setting four or five months as the age at which reflex grasping shows signs of weakening. Bühler (23) says that in the first quarter year of life, grasping, like all reactions at this period, occurs only through direct stimulation of the organ. The grasping reflex is sometimes restrained under certain circumstances in a two-month-old child; for example, the hands come in contact with the bars of the crib, if the contact is accidental, the reflex grasp usually occurs, but at times the infant moves his hands "exploringly" over the bars instead of closing the fist. At this time the infant reaches toward objects he touches without participation of the eyes. Bühler describes this as active grasping. The four-month-old child begins to move his hands toward objects with the help of his eyes. At this time grasping is with uncertain movements of the arms and toward objects in the immediate neighborhood of the infant. The hands are clenched into fists and both reach beyond the object and grasp it between the fists. At five months grasping is done with one hand and objects are gripped in both hands. Before thumb opposition begins, the palm of the hand, rather than the fingers, is used in grasping. Thus in the fourth and fifth months grasping becomes independent of a direct stimulus, and at the same time hand and eye coördination is established. At the beginning of the second half year children begin to reach toward objects which are out of reach and to grasp all objects which they see. At this period change in body posture, to assist reaching and grasping, also begins, and attempts to assist grasping by head and mouth movements are inhibited.

Halverson (78) says of grasping before six months of age, that lack of voluntary control in reaching results in gross displacements of the hand upon the object, so that absurdities in grasping take place, such as missing the object, a radial grasp, and a cramped digital hold. For the first six months the infant closes the hand on the object so that it is forced against the palm, with the point of pressure moving forward on the palm toward the fingers, with increasing age. Voluntary control over the digits appears between the sixteenth and twenty-fourth week. Differentiation of digital function does not appear until after the twentieth week. The ulnar digits function strongly in reflex grasping, while in skilled prehension the index finger and thumb function principally. Thumb opposition, therefore, begins as reflex grasping disappears. Halverson states that the palm grasp of early infancy is a *holding* grasp and that the digital grasp of the one-year-old child is a *feeling* grasp. Older infants resort to palmar grasping when difficult reaching interferes with prompt grasping, or in rough play such as banging an object on a table.

Early grasping is immediate, unadjustable, forceful and tenacious. At one year grasping is deliberate, adaptable with respect to size, form or weight of the object and only as strong and tenacious as the occasion requires.

Shirley's (180) developmental tests, given between the ages of three and six months to the 24 babies she followed throughout the first year, were almost entirely tests of reaching and grasping. The reaching and grasping tests used were holding a pair of bow calipers in front of the baby for two minutes, holding a dangling metal tape within reach for thirty seconds, and offering the baby a sheet of thin yellow paper while he was lying on his back. The infant was then seated on the recorder's lap and the tests were repeated, and a small hand bell was held just out of range for one minute and then brought within eight inches of the baby's face and held there for one minute. The metal tape, closed, was placed before the baby on a rimless tray and he was allowed to reach for it for one minute. As noted above, reaching, touching and momentarily grasping occurred at a median age of fifteen weeks, two weeks after the median age for tentative waving or reaching in the direction of an object. Grasping was not a sure process at this age. Retention of a stationary object and thumb opposition appeared simultaneously in both the lying and the sitting position at eighteen weeks. Reaching, grasping and retaining a dangling object appeared later; reaching, at a median age of nineteen weeks, grasping, at twenty-one weeks; and at twenty-three weeks accidental ringing of the bell occurred, and about three weeks later purposive ringing. There was about a five-weeks range in the ages of the infants at the appearance of these reactions. The tests for reaching and grasping were not given to infants over twenty-three weeks of age, but were repeated once at thirty-eight weeks of age; by this time the grasping of moving objects was established, although it was only beginning at twenty-three weeks. Shirley points out that grasping in itself is not a new response for the infants as the reflex grasp occurs at birth, but that grasping an object not placed against the palm of the hand requires a coördination of arm and hand reactions that is not present in the reflex. Thumb opposition was the first reaction in which the digits acted separately, and it was established at a median age of twenty-three weeks. Shirley found that, in general, skill with the arm is achieved at about the same time that a baby can sit on the lap. Some tests which involved prehension were given at later ages. The median age for transferring an object from hand to hand was twenty-five weeks; for holding a cup to the mouth as if to drink, twenty-seven weeks; for taking the tape out of a wooden slide box, forty-one weeks; marking with a pencil, sixty weeks; putting an object in a round box, sixty-two weeks; pulling out the tape line, seventy weeks; unscrewing the lid of a jar, eighty-four weeks. In general, Shirley reports somewhat earlier ages for the establishment of the various hand reactions than most other investigators.

The test scales for infants all include a number of hand activities and reaching and grasping for rings, toys and other objects. They do not furnish a consecutive picture of the development of skill with the hands, but the progressive complexity of the required responses at different ages gives a rough picture of increasing skill in prehension. The summaries of the prehension tests in the scales are presented separately for each scale, excepting where the tests appear, from the directions, to be practically identical in the different scales.

Gesell (65) in his normative items, places resistance to withdrawal of a small red rod placed in the palm of the infant's hand as practically universal in normal infants at four months of age. Linfert and Hierholzer (122) give the percentages of resistance to withdrawal of a rod in the infants they tested as: one month, 60 percent; two months, 82 percent; four months, 90 percent. Reflex closure on a red one-inch cube and retention for a few minutes or longer are also practically universal at four months, according to Gesell. At four months, less than 20 percent will pick up the same cube when it is placed on a table before them within easy reach, and even this number of infants require that their attention be called to the cube before they will pick it up; at six months, over three-quarters of the infants will pick up the cube without having their attention called to it. Bayley gives credit for looking at the cube at four months, even without attempts to pick it up; reaching for the cube is a fifth-month test. Picking it up, partial thumb opposition, and simultaneous finger flexion and thumb opposition, are sixth-month tests, and picking it up deftly and directly, a seventh-month test. Complete thumb opposition is placed at eight months. Gesell (65) places one of the cubes in each of the infant's hands at six months of age, and if he retains both he passes the test. About three-quarters will pass at six months, and at nine months all normal infants will. Bayley (7) gives this as a sixth-month test, and also reaching for and picking up a second cube when the infant is holding one in his hand. Gesell then presents a third cube to the subject. At six months about half will drop one cube to accept the third, and at nine months, three-quarters. At nine months less than half will take the third cube without dropping either of the others, and at twelve months three-quarters will; at eighteen months the same proportion of children is able to accept a fourth cube. Bayley gives credit at nine months if the subject picks up and holds cubes presented one after the other. Gesell is in agreement with other investigators in saying that the ability to release hold of an object is a later development than the ability to hold or to pick one up. At nine months less than 20 percent will put a cube in a cup when told to, even if shown how; at twelve months practically all children will. Gesell says: "Reluctance or motor difficulty in releasing hold of the cube is frequent at the one-year level."

Gesell, Bayley, and Linfert and Hierholzer, all use the dangling-ring test at successive age levels. According to Gesell (65), at four months, less than half the infants will close in on the ring with both hands; at six months about three-quarters seize it while seated on the mother's lap with the ring hanging in front of their faces, and a little over half when it is held above their heads. Bayley (7) gives credit if the infants manage to close in on the ring with both hands at four months. In Gesell's (65) items, three-quarters of infants should try to pull down the string holding the ring at nine months, and at twelve months the same proportion should reach for and try to grasp the string itself. Linfert and Hierholzer (122) give the percentages for the babies who reached beyond the ring for the string, or for whom similar attempts with a window-shade cord are reported, as six months, 12 percent; nine months, 98 percent; twelve months, 100 percent. Bayley gives credit at eight months if the infant scoops or pulls the string toward him and so secures the ring when it has been dangled before him and then laid on the table with only the string within reach; and at ten months she gives credit if the string is pulled adaptively to secure the ring.

A small white pellet placed on a table in front of the child and within easy reach is used by Gesell (65) to observe the development of prehension as well as of reaching and observing reactions. At six months nearly half the subjects will scoop up the pellet with a whole-hand motion, and less than 20 percent will pick it up with the thumb and finger; by nine months over half will pick it up with a precise pincer prehension. Gesell says:

The six-months infant ordinarily disregards or does not perceive the pellet; and if he secures the pellet it is by a coarse infra-human kind of palmar scoop. Although this test establishes a cleavage between the six, and the nine-months levels, there is a gradation of responses between the simian scoop and the precise pincer prehension.

Bayley, and Linfert and Hierholzer record perceiving or regarding the pellet. Bayley (7) gives credit if the child looks at the pellet at six months, and Linfert and Hierholzer (122) found that only 39 percent of their subjects perceived it at six months and that 100 percent did at nine months and thereafter. Bayley gives credit if the infant secures the pellet with a raking or scooping palmar prehension at seven months, with partial finger prehension at eight months, and with the precise thumb and forefinger prehension at ten months.

Gesell (65) places ringing a small hand bell in a purposive manner as a reaction which is beginning at nine months, at which time less than half of infants succeed, while at twelve months about three-quarters do. Bayley (7) places manipulative interest in a hand bell as an eighth-month test, interest in sound production, including ringing the bell, at the same age level, and purposive ringing as a tenth-month test. The younger age given by Shirley (180) is undoubtedly due to the manner of scoring the test, as she apparently did not require a proposive ringing of the bell, but simply recorded the reaction as present if the baby grasped the bell handle and shook the bell in such a way that it rang.

Linfert and Hierholzer (122) include in their scale two tests of prehension which are not comparable to any of Gesell's normative items. The examiner places her thumb inside the infant's closed fist and if the thumb is held tightly, the test is passed. Their figures for the infants passing this test are: one month, 88 percent; two months, 94 percent; four months, 98 percent. A one and one-quarter inch cube is placed at the tip of the infant's fingers. The test is passed if the cube is grasped; at one month 10 percent of the subjects passed, at two months, 16 percent; and at six months, 66 percent.

Bühler (23), in her tests for the first year of life, includes a number of tests of grasping. At four months a rattle is moved near the child, and to pass the test he should move both hands toward it to grasp it between the fists, and an object is placed so that the child's hand comes in contact with it; to pass the test, he should grasp the object. At five months the baby should be able to grasp an object in one hand, clutching it with his fingers, and should show some sort of resistance to the withdrawal of a toy from his hand. At six months the infant, seated on the lap and near a table edge, passes the test if he grasps the table edge. At seven months the infant should make some effort to pull a toy from the examiner's hand when the toy is held within reach, and should accept and hold a second rattle when he is already holding one. At eight months he should be able to reach through the bars of his crib and seize a toy placed within reach, and should make some attempt to imitate the examiner's movements in squeezing a rubber doll. At nine months he should be able to pick up and hold two objects without losing his balance while sitting alone. Attempting to imitate the ringing of a bell is a tenth-month test. At eleven months the child should be able to grasp a string attached to a toy and pull the toy to him, and handle blocks from a nest of blocks with "all the signs of attention and care."

Simon (182) traces the development of prehension roughly in his test series. At one day of age the infant makes uncoördinated movements of the arms. At three months he shows accidental grasping and carries the object to the mouth. At six months he makes repeated efforts to grasp, and grasps on contact. At eight months he tries to grasp small objects, such as a thread. At nine months he holds on to his support, and at ten months shows accuracy in grasping. At twelve months he picks up objects with the thumb and index finger. On Kuhlmann's (109) scale the infant passes the sixth-month grasping test if he holds a small object placed in his hand "longer than usual reflex clasp." At the same age the infant should hold an inch cube placed in the hand with thumb opposition, or when a pencil is pressed lengthwise in his palm, the thumb should press against the forefinger to grasp the pencil.

Lippman (123) tested 178 infants aged from four to eighteen months for the acceptance of one object, and of a second and a third. The Gesell cubes were used as objects and Gesell's methods were used in giving the tests. At four and one-half months of age, 58.8 percent accepted one cube, at five months 85 percent, and at six months, 91.6 percent. The percentages for the acceptance of a second object are as follows: four and one-half months, 35.3; six months, 74.9; eight months, 77.3; nine months, 85. For the acceptance of a third object, they were: six months, 33.3 percent; eight months, 46.9 percent; eleven and one-half months, 80 percent; twelve to thirteen months, 90 percent. Loss of interest in the test was most marked from six to twelve months of age. At four and one-half months of age the right and left hands were used with the same frequency; after this age there was an increasing tendency to use the right hand. Shirley (180) recorded the hand used in her caliper-reaching test and reports less definite results on handedness than Lippman. In the lying posture very little preference was shown for either hand in touching, grasping or retaining, and both hands were usually used. In the sitting posture the use of both hands was also observed in the greater number of cases, but when one hand only was used there seemed to be a slight preference for the right hand. Shirley concludes that when skill in the use of the hands is just beginning, infants are ambidextrous and that specialization begins only after some degree of skill is acquired by both hands.

Jones (102) tested for thumb opposition by placing a cube, a ball and a pencil in each hand of the 365 subjects she tested. The youngest child to show thumb opposition was one hundred and eight days old. At one hundred and twenty-nine days of age,

25 percent of the infants showed it; at one hundred and forty-eight days, 50 percent; at one hundred and eighty-one days, 75 percent; and at two hundred and twenty-six days, 100 percent.

Halverson (77) has made a detailed study of prehension in infants by means of motion-picture records of a standardized situation. The subjects were 12 or more normal infants at each of the age levels, sixteen, twenty, twenty-four, twenty-eight, thirty-two, thirty-six, forty, and fifty-two weeks. The Gesell cubes were used. One cube was moved along the back edge of the table and down the middle line of the table to within six inches of the front edge. It was left for nine seconds and if, during this time, the infant made no move toward it, it was then moved three inches nearer the subject and left for nine seconds, or for a total of fourteen if motions were made toward it. While the infant was holding the first cube in his left hand, a second cube was presented in the same way as the first, and a third was then presented while the baby held a cube in each hand. Halverson's analysis of the development of reaching for the cubes has already been summarized. He distinguishes four steps in prehension: visual location of the object, the approach by the hand, the grasp, and the disposal of the object. The time spent in looking at the cube increased from four and three-quarters seconds at sixteen weeks of age to eighteen seconds at twenty-eight weeks, and then gradually decreased to ten and three-quarters seconds at fifty-two weeks, at which age a number of the infants grasped the cube without looking at it. The glances were not steady in the younger babies, but shifted from the cube to other objects and then back to the cube and in the older ones there was great variety in the manner of looking at the cube. There was little, if any, significant difference in the time spent in looking at the three successive cubes. At all ages the infants looked at the cube more than they looked at any other object. After twenty-four weeks of age, the infants almost always succeeded in grasping the cube. The speed of reaching increased up to thirty-two weeks and then decreased. Bilateral reaches were common for the first cube at twenty-four, twenty-eight and thirty-two weeks of age. The manner in which the infants held the thumb in reaching, indicated roughly the kind of grasp which was to follow. When the thumb hung down or curled under the palm a primitive kind of grasp occurred; if the thumb pointed inward, the thumb and fingers were opposed in grasping. The plane of the angle formed by the forefinger and thumb just preceding the grasp was vertical in the younger infants; with increasing age the plane of the angle rotated toward the horizontal plane. At sixteen weeks the infants were not likely to touch the cube, at twenty weeks one-fourth touched it, and one-third grasped it crudely. By twenty-eight weeks of age and thereafter all the infants could grasp the cube if they really desired it.

Halverson lists ten types of grasp which appear more or less in sequence with increasing age: (1) *no contact*; (2) *contact appearing at twenty weeks*; (3) a *primitive squeeze*, the hand passing beyond the object and drawing it in against the body or the other hand, appearing to some extent at twenty weeks; (4) a *squeeze grasp*, with a lateral palmar approach and the fingers closing on the cube and pressing it strongly against the palm, no infants succeeded in lifting the cube from the table with this grasp, which occurred most frequently at twenty-eight weeks; (5) a *hand grasp* in which the infant brings the whole hand down fully upon the cube and all the fingers appear to act equally in pressing it against the heel of the palm, occurring frequently at twenty-four weeks, and also at twenty-eight, thirty-two and thirty-six weeks; (6) the *palm grasp* is much like the hand grasp, except that the thumb is now opposed to the fingers in forcing the cube against the palm. Halverson says:

This new feature in the thumb repertoire of functions and the simultaneous budding into prominence of the forefinger are mainly responsible for the higher types of grasp which follow. Up to this point all digits function in holding the cube in the middle of the palm. From now on only the first three digits function prominently in grasping so that we find the cube no longer in the middle of the palm but shifted to the radial edge of the hand.

(7) The *superior palm grasp*, where the infant sets the radial side of the palm down on the cube with the first two fingers curled down on the far side of the cube and the thumb opposing

them on the near side, functions very commonly at twenty-eight and thirty-two weeks. (8) The *inferior-forefinger* grasp is common at thirty-six and forty weeks, and is much like the preceding stage, except that the digits at the end of the approach are pointed more horizontally than downward, as before, and the cube is not pressed against the palm. This marks the step from palmar grasping to finger grasping. (9) The *forefinger grasp* is the first stage in which the fingers are pretty well extended instead of being curled around the cube. The cube is held well out to the tips of the first three or four digits. Halverson found this type fairly common at thirty-six and forty weeks, and found that it was the predominating type at fifty-two weeks. (10) The *superior finger* grasp is just like the preceding stage except that the infant no longer has to place any portion of his hand on the table to aid in placing the fingers on the cube, or to get leverage for lifting it. This type was found only once in the study which ceased at fifty-two weeks, but in other studies of infants at fifty-six weeks and older it was frequently observed.

It was noted that when the infant had displaced the cube so that it was nearly out of reach, he usually reverted to an earlier type of grasp than the one employed when the cube was within easy reach. There was a progressive decrease in time before grasping, in number of adjustments, in looking at the cube and in displacing it with increasing age. None of the results indicated that at any of the age levels one hand was preferred above the other for grasping. At twenty-eight weeks the hand is beginning to free itself from forearm control in reaching, and to lose its pawlike behavior, its exclusively palmar grip and equality of all the digits. Only three of the older infants picked up a cube when they were already holding one in the same hand. There were two common methods of lifting the cube from the table, one, elbow flexion, the other, a hand-elbow action, with the hand, after grasping, rotating on its ulnar edge before flexion began. Halverson concludes that development of prehension progresses in definite patterns from very crude forms of reaching, grasping and manipulation, to highly refined and integrated sequential acts and that, "The increase in the number of higher types of grasp and the increase in the amount and variety of digital manipulation of the cube in infants from 16 to 52 weeks of age are due in part to anatomical growth of the digits of the hand, in part to maturation of neuromusculature, in part to training, and in part, perhaps, to increase in cutaneous sensibility of the finger-tips."

In another paper (78), Halverson reports on the results from presenting a ball, a crayon, a cube, a cup, a hand bell, a pellet, a rattle, a rod, a spoon, and a string to the infants, by a procedure very similar to the one used in his study with cubes. There were seven subjects and the test extended from four to sixty weeks of age, the rattle and the rod being used from four to twenty-eight and twenty weeks of age, and the ball and crayon in their place after that age. The rod, spoon, cup and bell were grasped according to the classification presented above for the cube; while the grasps of the ball, pellet and string required special classification. Halverson says that there was no difficulty in eliciting the reaching and grasping responses, as the presence of an object within visual and reaching distance seldom fails to release the prehensive mechanism. The size of the ball and the absence of opposed surfaces made palmar contact with the ball necessary at all the age levels. At all ages the tips of the fingers dug into the surface of the ball. The amount of exposed surface of the ball which subtended the angle of the thumb and index finger, increased steadily with age, with a great range in the size of the surface for each age. "From 16 weeks to 56 weeks the ball moves in successive stages from mid-palm to radial palm, and from 36 weeks to 56 weeks the thumb appears in active opposition in holding." The small size of the pellet and the string required fine digital adjustments, resulting in grasps different in type from the general classification. In the hand-grasping stage, the palm was brought down on the pellet and the closure of the fingers against the palm so raised the hand from the table that the pellet was seldom picked up. In the second type, palm grasping, the infant brings the radial portion of the palm down on the pellet and then flexes the fingers and adducts the thumb, usually forcing the pellet into the closed palm with the thumb firmly pressed against the radial edge of the index finger. The next stage was a scissors grasp, in which the pellet lies under the index finger or between the thumb and index finger. The infant then closes the three ulnar digits and then the index finger, and adducts the thumb so that the pellet is pinched between the thumb and index or medius finger. In vertical pincer grasping, the hand rests on the fingers, with the two radial digits extended so that the pellet lies under the index finger; the thumb is then adducted and the index finger curled so that the pellet is secured between the volar surface of these two fingers. In oblique pincer grasping, the ulnar edge of the palm rests on the table so that the index finger and thumb point outward as well as downward, and the pellet is pinched between these two digits. This grasp did not occur with the hand held above the table, not resting on it, though Halverson says that at fifty-six and sixty weeks voluntary control of arm movements has reached the point where this type of grasp would be possible to the infant. The last two stages are the typical adult form of prehension. Halverson states that thumb opposition appears late in grasping small objects, because the lack of height of the object requires the infant to hold his palm so close to the table that it interferes with or prevents oppositional movements of the thumb. The pellet was not grasped often until twenty-eight weeks of age, and after that age improvement was gradual but steady. Grasping the string occurred at the same age as the pellet, and development took a similar course.

Halverson now simplifies his classification into three general stages, first the stage of palmar grasping; second, a period of adjustment and refinement of crude, whole-hand grasping into adaptive, digital grasping; third, the stage which begins definitely at thirty-six weeks and continues throughout life, that of digital grasping. During the first half year babies close their hands on objects with a force all out of proportion to that necessary to retain the object, but by the end of the first year they can hold them with just the amount of pressure necessary to retain them. In early grasping, all joints of the fingers are flexed so as to curl them about the object. As grasping loses its excess force, the fingers which do the actual holding flex less and less until, at sixty weeks, flexion occurs largely at the metacarpo-phalangeal joints.

In grasping a large object such as a ball, however, flexion of all joints occurs at all ages.

Castner (30) used the Gesell method for a study of fine prehension in 59 infants from twenty to fifty-two weeks of age. The object was the usual white pellet, 7 mm in diameter, and presented according to the method used by Gesell and by Halverson. Motion-picture records were made and analysed by Halverson's method of dividing grasping into the regard, the approach and the closure of the hand. His conclusions are in agreement with Halverson's. He states in addition, however, that prolonged looking at the pellet usually occurred in connection with repeated efforts to secure it, and that by fifty-two weeks of age, looking at the pellet has become part of a smooth, well-coördinated prehension. At twenty weeks there was a 30-percent accuracy in making contact with the pellet, which increased to 100 percent at thirty-two weeks. By fifty-two weeks of age, the adult pincer type of prehension was the prevailing one. There was considerable difficulty in holding the pellet after it was secured, at all the age levels below fifty-two weeks. At thirty-two weeks no infant held it for any length of time, and at forty-four weeks it was almost invariably dropped.

MANIPULATION AND OTHER HAND ACTIVITIES

The literature reports a number of other arm and hand activities which are not so easily classified as the direct acts of reaching and grasping, such as hand play and arm movements, and the manipulation or disposal of objects after they are grasped. As behavior becomes increasingly complex with increasing age, and as more and more parts of the body are coördinated for the accomplishment of a single act, it becomes increasingly difficult to draw the line between manipulation or hand activities and adaptive behavior involving the whole organism. If, for instance, Bühler's interpretation of early behavior were adopted here, practically all hand activities would have to be classified as adaptive, and Gesell lists some of his normative items which we have included under reaching or prehension as norms of adaptive behavior. In order, as far as possible, to avoid interpretations of behavior and to have a convenient criterion for placing the responses described in the literature, we have classed, under arm and hand reactions, all activities which are on the border line between manipulation and adaptation as well as those which require an interpretation in psychic terms in order to be called adaptive. And we have confined adaptive behavior strictly to those reactions which clearly involve a relationship between two separate acts. Even in such a classification, overlapping cannot be avoided. For example, movement or adjustment of the body to assist in reaching is clearly a form of adaptive behavior, and at the same time it is a definite step in development toward adult reaching and grasping. Putting a cube in a cup when told to do so by the examiner, probably should be called adaptive behavior; at the same time it is from the description of such reactions as this that we know that voluntary release of an object is a later development than voluntary prehension. In classifying the items given in the test scales, we have followed the plan of listing those responses which are the result of a command from the examiner, or of direct imitation of the examiner's performance, under the heading of the mechanism chiefly involved. Those responses in which the infant appears to be trying for the solution of a problem which is immediate to him, we have called adjustment for the solution of a problem. For example, if the subject is given a covered box and succeeds in getting the cover off, we call this manipulation; but when he is given a glass jar with a doll inside and attempts to get the doll, he is making adjustments to solve a problem. In other words, we have classified as adjustive behavior only those reactions which occur in the infants' attempts to solve problems which can be recognized, even by the layman, as problems to the infant.

Shirley (180) observed the hand reactions of the infants she tested during the first two years, in a large number of standardized situations and with a great variety of articles. Reaching and grasping were well established by six months of age. Up to this age, manipulation consisted in little more than holding the objects. Playing with the hands appeared at the same age as grasping an object, when in the dorsal position, the median age being fifteen weeks. During this stage, an infant who appeared to be making every effort to reach the lure would often stop reaching if his hands accidentally touched each other, and become absorbed in grasping one hand with the other. Scratching on a tray top appeared at a median age of eighteen weeks, and was, according to Shirley, a reaction which appeared to give the infants great pleasure. She suggests that the interest in this activity lies in the fact that scratching presents a large number of stimuli in several sensory fields. Putting the object into the mouth, and often chewing it, appeared at the median age of twenty-one weeks. After twenty-nine weeks of age, there was a lull in the appearance of new hand activities. But before this lull occurred, the babies had begun to ring the bell, at thirty-two weeks; to play with the toes, at twenty-four weeks; to transfer an object from hand to hand, at twenty-five weeks; to put the cup to the mouth as if to drink, at twenty-seven weeks; and to pat an object, at twenty-nine weeks. Nothing new appeared until thirty-seven weeks; Shirley explains this lull either by the inadequacy of the tests she used to show the new reactions which were developing, or as due to an actual temporary interruption in fine motor development. The latter explanation is possibly supported by the fact that during this period the infants were making rapid progress in the gross motor activities of sitting and creeping. At thirty-seven weeks the median baby began to try to drink from the bell, and at forty-two weeks he began to point with his index finger and to use this finger to touch objects and pry into holes.

Before the skill to exploit objects in appropriate ways developed, manipulation consisted in patting, scratching, fingering, banging and chewing objects. This Shirley calls random play. Random play showed a very high frequency of occurrence during the first year and a marked decline in the second year. Passive holding showed a more rapid decline than random play, but at from six to twelve months objects were often held in one hand and fingered or banged with the other. There was an increase in the frequency of chewing objects up to nine months. By twelve months the chewing of objects had been eliminated by three-quarters of the infants, and by eighteen months by all of them.

The trend shown by chewing was so similar to that in other forms of random play that Shirley concludes that it should be classed as a manipulative, not an emotional, reaction. The length of time an object was held by both hands at once increased up to thirty-one weeks, and the amount of time each hand was doing a different thing increased up to thirty weeks and then remained constant, as did the time given to attention to the object. Appropriate manipulation appeared very rarely up to one year of age. Shirley found little evidence that development in handedness occurred. In the early weeks there was slightly more reaching, swinging, banging and fingering of objects with the left hand, and somewhat more holding with the right hand. She states, however, that her results do not rule out the possibility that handedness is a developmental trait during this period; several of the infants later proved to be left-handed, and also it was clear that the position of the object determined which hand was reached with, the hand nearest the object always being used.

In the last quarter of the first year and in the second year, manipulation of objects played an important rôle in the tests given by Shirley. The difficulties she mentions in testing for appropriateness of manipulation are making the subjects comprehend the task, interesting them enough to make them attempt the problem, and maintaining interest until they have carried the task through. In the tests given up to fifty-four weeks of age, the correct manipulation of the object was not demonstrated, and the success which occurred appeared to be largely accidental, with the exception of such items as drinking from the cup and ringing the bell. There was, however, an increase in exploratory manipulation with the decrease in passive holding, random play and chewing.

At fifty-four weeks of age and afterwards the correct manipulation of the objects presented was demonstrated. Attention to the demonstration was good at this age and showed no improvement thereafter with age. Up to seventy-four weeks of age, two boxes were used. The infants often tried to repeat an accidental successful opening of the boxes. There were also unsuccessful attempts to open and close them at all ages; the successful attempts increased with age, however. Closing the boxes was a much harder reaction than opening them, and occurred less frequently. There was no shortening in the time taken for a successful opening during these months. Throwing a ball with good aim was accomplished by 50 percent of the children at fifty-four weeks of age, and by 85 percent at seventy-four weeks. Piling up six one-inch cubes to form a tower was demonstrated. Between 50 and 60 percent of the babies at each test pushed over the tower which the examiner had built. Passive holding and random play decreased slightly with increasing age. Taking the tower down one block at a time was also a common reaction at all ages. At fifty-four weeks no baby succeeded in piling more than two blocks, and at the later ages the majority still piled only two. At seventy-four weeks 2 babies piled a six-block tower. Shirley states that the infants' interest in this test was not great and that giving up in discouragement, pushing the blocks away, or giving them to the examiner were frequent reactions.

A pencil-and-paper test was also given, in which the examiner wrote the child's name on the paper, as a scribbling suggestion, and then gave the paper and pencil to him. There was much manipulation of the paper and marking with the wrong end of the pencil. The number of infants who accidentally marked the paper and who drew lines did not change with increasing age, but the number who made several marks without lifting the pencil from the paper decreased with age. The Gesell form board, with the circle only, was presented without demonstration at each of the tests during the second year. Random play with the board or the block decreased from 88 percent at fifty-four weeks to 37 percent at seventy weeks. Up to seventy-eight weeks there were from 40 to 50 percent successes; at eighty-two weeks 80 percent succeeded.

The tests were again changed for the second half of the second year. In nesting four boxes with large differences in their sizes, one-half the infants tried to put a larger box into a smaller one at seventy-eight weeks, and one-third at two years. After ninety-four weeks the babies began to take the larger box out after they had tried to put it into a smaller one. There was an increase with age in the number succeeding in nesting the boxes, but the infants made a better score at ninety-eight weeks than at one hundred and two weeks. Those who succeeded made fewer movements than those who failed. A six-peg peg board was used. All the babies achieved success with all six pegs at seventy-eight weeks, in less than two minutes. The majority of the time scores in the later weeks of this test were under forty seconds. Piling one-inch cubes into a tower was continued from the previous six months, but the demonstration was made with eight instead of six blocks. The number of infants who took the tower down, one block at a time, decreased with age. The number who piled four or more blocks increased up to the one-hundred-and-second week, and no child succeeded in piling eight blocks until the ninety-fourth week. Building a three-block pyramid was also demonstrated. There were only four successes during the entire period, and Shirley states that the difficulty seemed to be one rather of understanding the direction, "make one like this," than lack of manual skill. The pencil-and-paper test was continued, with a demonstration of drawing a line. By the one-hundred-and-second week the number of infants who simply held or manipulated the paper had decreased to about 15 percent, and the wrong end of the pencil was used only once during the period. There was an increase in the number drawing lines, and heavy lines became more frequent than light ones.

A choice test was also given, which afforded the babies an opportunity for the correct manipulation of a number of toys. The use of the object was quietly demonstrated during the test. The rattle and the bell, which had been favorite toys in earlier tests, had little interest for the infants, so the number of successful manipulations has no significance. A toy accordian was correctly manipulated in 60 percent of the cases in which it was chosen, and it was the first favorite. A toy tractor increased in popularity and in correct manipulation with the age of the infant. A toy egg beater was too difficult for the children, and did not interest them. The steel tape measure was used, and only a few infants learned how to push the button to make it roll up. About 60 percent were successful, at each test, in throwing, bouncing or rolling a ball. A toy double boiler was correctly put together by about two-thirds of the infants at each test. The toy telephone was correctly manipulated by from 50 to 75 percent at each test. The individual differences were great in this test, and the fact that it was a choice test affected the effort in manipulation.

Bühler (23) states that the first manipulation performed by an infant is of stationary objects; this takes the form of touching, holding, knocking, and rubbing, before four months of age. Scratching is difficult and appears later. At six months he begins to use objects as extensions of his own hand. At seven months he begins to play with two objects, moving them separately and rubbing or knocking them together, and also begins pressing, stretching and tearing objects. Concepts of form and shape are beginning at this time. At eight months he begins to stick things together, and at eleven months to lay things neatly side by side and to stand them up. She also traces the development of lifting and throwing objects. At four months the grasped object is simply lifted and lowered with the arm, at six months it is permitted to fall, and at nine months lifted and permitted to fall. At ten months it is lifted with one hand, grasped with the other and allowed to fall, and at eleven months it is lifted up and thrown forward. Bühler states that the development of manipulation of moving objects goes hand in hand with the development of grasping. One of Bühler's second-month tests is passing the flat hand or clenched fist several times over a piece of cardboard. The first test, which she calls manipulatory, is given at four months. A rattle is placed in the child's hand and he holds it firmly and moves it about. At six months the child is given one object and another is held near him, and he should hit at the second object with the one in his hand; this she calls the first use of an object as a tool. At seven months he should be able to imitate knocking movements made by the examiner of a rattle against the crib, to crush, roll or tear, or change the form of a piece of paper which is put into his hand, and to hold two objects and move them about. At eight months the examiner squeezes a rubber doll to make it squeak and the child passes the test if he makes any attempts to imitate the movements. At nine months the child passes the manipulatory tests if he takes a toy out of the examiner's pocket, having seen her put it there, imitates the opening and shutting of a picture book, and tries to knock down a tower of blocks. The tenth-month tests are throwing objects after first lifting them up, and opening a cardboard box with a loosely fitting cover. At eleven months the child should be able to imitate beating two spoons together, to set a block down with "all the signs of attention and care," to fit the smaller of a nest of blocks into the larger and to open a box with a snugly fitting cover. In the first and second months of the second year, the tests involving manipulation are imitation of squeezing a ball out of which a chicken pops, rubbing or knocking two sticks together, and taking a nest of blocks apart and putting them together again. The tests for the third to fifth months of the second year are imitating drumming on a drum with two sticks, and putting four or more of six blocks into a box. The ninth-to-eleventh-month tests are imitating the turning of the handle of a music box, fitting two hollow sticks into each other, and piling at least two blocks on top of each other in 5 minutes, without demonstration.

Gesell's (65) normative items include a number of tests of manipulation and other hand activities. At four months playing with the hands is established, about three-quarters of infants can scratch, over half will play with objects, and less than half will splash with the hands in the bath, a reaction which is established at six months of age. The hand-to-mouth reaction is established at four months, is very dominant at six months, on the wane at nine months, and relatively inhibited at twelve months. At four months about three-quarters of the infants react to the edge of a table when near it, or when their hands are placed on it by fingering, by simple manipulation, by mild exploratory movements, by patting or banging; and at six months these reactions are established. At six months over half will pat a table, and at nine months all will. Linfert and Hierholzer (122) give the percentages of infants patting a table as 56 at six, and 98 at nine and twelve months respectively. Bayley (7) uses a table test and gives credit at four months if the subject manipulates the table edge with his hands, and at five months if this manipulation is "active."

Purposive throwing or brushing away of objects because of interest in hearing them fall, Gesell considers an advanced form of play at six months, frequent at nine months, and established by twelve months. Crumpling a piece of paper occurs in about three-quarters of the infants at six months, according to Gesell's norms, while the remaining infants will take it by the edge, which he considers a somewhat higher grade of response, found in three-quarters of the infants by nine months. Bayley gives credit at six months if the baby accepts a piece of paper and plays with it exploitively, crumpling and rattling it, and so on. Gesell (65) and Bayley both invert a cup over a cube, at six months, and Gesell states that about three-quarters will take the cup off, and at twelve months practically all children will remove the cup and get the cube. Bayley gives credit at ten months when the cup is picked up by the handle. Gesell states that at six months less than half tend to reach or manipulate with one hand, and that there is a progressive tendency to reach and manipulate with one hand so that it occurs in about three-quarters of the infants by twelve months.

At nine months of age, Gesell (65) finds that less than half will imitate the rattling of a spoon in a cup or the ringing of a bell, and at twelve months about three-quarters will. Linfert and Hierholzer's (122) percentages for rattling the spoon are six months, none; nine months, 35; and twelve months, 31. Less than 20 percent of the infants at nine months will unwrap a cube in a paper after seeing it wrapped, and at eighteen months all infants will. Linfert and Hierholzer's figures for this are zero at six months, 68 percent at nine months, and 59 percent at twelve months. According to Gesell (65), less than 20 percent at nine months will scribble on paper with a large crayon when shown the movement, and at twelve months about three-quarters will. At twelve months less than half will scribble spontaneously. At eighteen months three-quarters will scribble spontaneously and make a stroke in imitation, and less than half can differentiate the stroke as being a line or a circle, or a line and scribbling. From the eighteenth to the twenty-fourth month, the ability to imitate a vertical line, a circle or a cross begins to appear, but it is not established in all children until thirty-six months. Bayley (7) gives credit if the baby attends to the examiner's scribbling at nine months; if he attempts to scribble at eleven months, and if he holds the crayon adaptively at twelve months.

In Gesell's (65) norms, about half of the infants should be able, at twelve months, to put a cube in a cup when asked to and shown how. Bayley (7) gives credit for this test at eleven months. At twelve months Gesell expects three-quarters of the babies to be able to pile one block on top of another, about 60 percent to pile three blocks, and less than half to pile four. At eighteen months all children can pile three blocks, and less than half of them, four. At twenty-four months three-quarters can build a tower of four or more blocks, and can build a three-block pyramid in imitation. At twelve months less than half can fold a letter-size sheet of paper once transversely in imitation, and at twenty-four months three-quarters can. Three-quarters can drop a rod in its hole in a box at twelve months, when asked to, and less than half can put a square block through its hole. Less than half can put the circle in a simplified form board at twelve months, but, if shown how, three-quarters of the infants can, and at eighteen months this number can, whether shown or not. Gesell says,

The circle is unquestionably the easiest of these three forms. The selective interest of the circle combined with the priority of the ability to use it adaptively is a pretty example of the specificity and orderliness of development.

Bayley gives credit at nine months if the round block is brought into "exploitive relation to the board," and also if the child explores the holes with his hand; and at thirteen months, if the block is fitted into the round hole. Gesell states that at twelve months most children are beginning to try to put on their shoes, and that at twenty-four months less than half can put one on. Linfert and Hierholzer (122) give 4 percent as the number that took off their shoes at nine months, and 50 percent as the number at twelve months. Use of a fork and spoon is beginning at twelve months, according to Gesell, and is established at twenty-four months. Linfert and Hierholzer's figures for use of a spoon are 8 percent at nine months, and 44 per cent at twelve months.

Gesell (65) gives tossing a ball into the open end of a box as a normative item for eighteen months of age, at which time about three-quarters of the infants succeed. At eighteen months less than half can put the circle in the form board, when it is turned so that the square hole is in front of them; and at twenty-four months about three-quarters can solve the three-form form board, within the time limit of one minute each for three trials.

Kuhlmann (109) includes a number of tests of manipulation and hand activities in his test scale. At three months the infant should carry his hand or an object to the mouth with sufficient motor coördination to "carry hand more or less at will, not random, chance movements." At twelve months the tests are shaking a rattle two feet in front of the child and then giving it to him to imitate the movement; and marking with a pencil, when shown how, with a definite purposive reaction which is not merely imitation. At eighteen months the child is given a bowl of food and fed half a teaspoonful; the spoon is then put in the child's hand, and he passes the test if any effort at self-feeding is successful. At twenty-four months the child should be able to imitate roughly three of four arm-and-hand movements by the examiner: raising the hands above the head, clapping the hands, placing palms on top of head, and making a large circle by turning the hands around each other. At the same age, the child passes tests if he is able to make with a pencil on paper any rough approximation of a circle, after watching the examiner draw circles and having his own hand held while the pencil is moved in a circle, and if he unwraps a piece of sugar or candy to eat it after seeing the examiner wrap it up.

Halverson (77) describes the disposition of the cube made by the infants after they picked it up, and the other hand activities which took place during the test. Up to thirty-two weeks of age the chief uses of the cube were carrying it to the mouth, holding it with a strong palm grasp, putting it down and occasionally picking it up again. From thirty-six to fifty-two weeks of age there was a decrease in carrying it to the mouth and in dropping it, and the chief activities were holding the cube with the fingers and moving it about in the hand, inspecting it, changing it from hand to hand, bringing both hands to bear on it, putting it down and picking it up, fingering it, banging the table with it, and at the older ages matching it with the other cubes. The hand activities which occurred independently of the cubes were raising and lowering the fingers on the table, a movement which resembled playing the piano and which occurred most frequently at twenty weeks; rubbing and scratching the table, which occurred from sixteen to twenty-eight weeks; and banging the table, which occurred from twenty to fifty-two weeks, with a peak at forty weeks.

Armstrong and Wagoner (5) made a study of the motor control of children in dressing themselves. Some of their subjects were as young as two years, and they report that these infants were more or less disinterested and indifferent to the activity of buttoning up jackets and seemed not to have the motor control required to manipulate the buttons.

In a study of infants' activity and posture during sleep, Marquis (32) presents some findings which she evidently believes have bearing on the development of handedness. At monthly intervals from eight weeks to one year of age, 9 infants were observed and their movements recorded during sleep. Marquis states that left-arm movements exceeded right-arm movements from twelve to thirty-two weeks of age, and after that movements of the right arm were most numerous, but that simultaneous movements of both arms exceeded movements of a single arm at almost all ages. Hand movements showed the same trend as arm movements except that the dominance of left-hand movements was never as great as that of left-arm movements and ceased at twenty-eight weeks, after which age the dominance of right-hand movements was marked. Simultaneous movements of both hands occurred only rarely after the beginning of right-hand dominance.

EYE REACTIONS AND VISUAL ACUITY

The literature on the eye reactions and visual acuity of infants after the neonatal period is more in agreement as to the course of development than is that on the eye reactions and vision which are present at birth. The phase of the subject which is most controversial and uncertain is color vision. The number of investigations of all phases of vision which have been carried on under exact scientific conditions and with measured stimuli is small. Most of our present knowledge comes from observations of reactions to simple and only partially standardized situations. No studies were found of the distance young infants can see, the general procedure being to present the early stimuli very close to the infant's eyes. Beasley's (8) study of vision in neonates suggests that determination of the optimum distances for the presentation of stimuli, and the rôle of individual differences in these distances, might be a fruitful field for investigation. The eye reactions of young infants have been studied largely by testing for eye movements, visual pursuit and "perception" of objects. Studies have been made with lights and by moving objects in front of the subjects' eyes, and the test scales all contain a number of tests of visual acuity in the sense of ability to see and recognize objects, or at least to react to them so that it is quite apparent that they have been seen. The lack of bodily control and specificity of response in young infants makes it difficult to develop substitutes for the ability to talk, which is commonly used as the method of judging results in vision tests with subjects old enough to follow directions and speak.

Koffka (106) believes that progressive enlargement of the field of vision is a matter of functional capacity of certain parts of the nervous system to form fixed configurations, a maturation depending on use and need. He states, "Biological importance attaches at first only to what is near at hand; and to be able to see at great distances is for most living beings of no importance whatever." The infant's field of vision is very limited; objects at the side, or above or below the center or at a distance, are not seen. Koffka believes that although absolute distance has not been determined for young infants, the radius of vision is not constant, but depends on the kind of object, bright objects being perceived at greater distances from the center than dark objects. A number of authors give their theories as to what the young infant perceives, that is, what the objects in his range of vision look like to him. The general opinion seems to be that he probably first sees indistinct masses of light and dark, and has some visual perception of movement. The details ᵤf the theories are worked out in terms of the general theory of development held by the particular author. Koffka, for instance, believes that these light spots are perceived against a relatively even background, while Bühler (23) believes that such perception could function only with a fully developed consciousness, and that the child lives in a condition of semiconsciousness in which "the child lacks every consciousness of the surrounding world, and only through strong stimuli is he snatched out of slumbering and jostled into an activity of sensory organs." Not until the third month, according to Bühler, does the child make any positive movements involving two organs at once, and the earlier reactions involve only a single condition or experience and are the result of very strong or sudden stimuli, and therefore may be called a sort of negative observation. It seems probable that if studies of vision like that made by McGinnis (129) on neonates were continued with older babies, it might be possible to accumulate data which would indicate with some degree of objectivity what the vision of young infants may be like.

EYE-BLINK

We have seen that the neonate reacts with a blink of the lids when the lid or skin around the eyes is touched, but not to a sudden approach of an object, as adults do. Shirley (180) says that in the 24 babies she tested, blinking at the whole hand moving quickly toward the eyes progressed rapidly with age, but did not occur in every case, even at thirty-eight weeks of age. Progress toward blinking at a pencil threat was slower than that at blinking at the whole hand, with almost none from thirteen to twenty-three weeks, but at thirty-eight weeks the infant blinked at one as readily as at the other. Jones (102) tested for the eye-blink on 365 infants. The examiner stood behind the child and passed the hand suddenly downward before the child's eyes, six inches away. The blink was not considered present unless the child blinked twice in ten trials. The youngest child to blink was forty-six days old; 25 percent blinked by sixty days of age, 50 percent by seventy-six days, 75 percent by ninety-two days, and all by one hundred twenty-four days. Jones believes that this development is by substitution for the reflex blink on contact, present at birth. Warden (205) states, in his notes on a male infant, that the blink was not well established in his boy until about the beginning of the eighth month, and that into the fourth month blinking occurred on contact only. Gesell (65) in his normative items states that at four months 100 percent of the infants blinked when an enamel saucer was hit with a spoon at about four inches from the eyes, 84 percent blinked twice in several repeated trials when a feint was made with the hand within a few inches of the eyes, and less than 20 percent when the feint was made with a pencil. At six months about 75 percent blinked to the pencil threats. He says that it may be that winking at a pencil represents a somewhat more advanced neuromuscular organization than winking at the hand. Bayley (7) gives credit at four months, in her test series, if the child blinks at least twice in ten trials when the examiner passes her hand rapidly downward and back parallel to the child's body and about three inches above his eyes. Figurin and Denisova (58) make the threat at a greater distance from the eyes than the other experimenters, warning against the possibility of a current of air striking the eyes and causing the blink. Their procedure is to secure a fixation on the object at half a meter from the eyes and then move it suddenly a few centimeters toward the eyes. They state that at the beginning of the second month the blink is hard to elicit, "but it can be seen in an undeveloped form." In the third and fourth month the child blinks when the object starts to move. Kuhlmann (109) gives as a third-month test winking at a large object moved suddenly toward the eyes.

The variations in the methods of making what ought to be a simple and easily standardized test for the presence of blinking at a threat, and the range of ages for which the reaction is reported, furnish an excellent example of the state of most of the investigation of infant behavior. It is quite clear that sometime after the third month the baby begins blinking at a threat, as well as on contact, and that, at least at first, a large object may elicit a blink when a small one will not; but aside from this, the different investigations have not established anything very definite. Figurin and Denisova's (58) caution against letting a current of air hit the subject's eyes might account partly for the wide age range, but it is curious that they made the test twenty inches away from the eyes, while the usual method is to make it only a few inches away, and yet report the reaction at an earlier age than any of the other studies, except possibly Jones's.

Two studies of blinking occurring normally say that infants show few true blinks. Blount (17) states that the young child shows "half-blinks" associated with head movements about every five seconds, but few true blinks. Ponder and Kennedy (160) state that a bright light causes a screwing up of the eyes, not a blink, in infants. At about six months of age infrequent true blinks occur, associated with voluntary movements or perception of unexpected stimuli. They say that blinking is associated with the higher mental functions and the paths of the basal ganglia.

VISION

As stated above, the extent and kind of vision of the young infant can be inferred only indirectly from the results of tests of fixation, eye movements and appearance of eye-and-hand, and eye-and-auditory coördination. McGinnis's (129) careful study from motion-picture records of ocular pursuit and optic nystagmus was made on only 7 subjects, but continued until the babies were six weeks of age. His findings indicate that within a few minutes of birth, the ability to make pursuit eye movements is present, and that movements of the visual field have a definite effect on the eye movements of the infant. He states, however, that the movements which occur are not a successful visual pursuit, but only a tendency toward pursuit. He believes the discrepancies in the literature on the age at which visual pursuit occurs are not due so much to differences in experimental conditions, as to the fact that some writers call the type of response which he calls a tendency to pursuit, successful pursuit, while others consider successful pursuit to mean the ability to follow a moving object in adult fashion. He found, during the first two weeks, no cases of ocular pursuit in the latter sense. The number of eye movements in the direction of movement of the apparatus, increased regularly week by week, more than doubling between the second and sixth weeks, and the number of movements in the opposite direction had decreased at the sixth week to one-tenth their number at the second week. The total number of eye movements in both directions also increased gradually during this period. The number of head movements, corresponding in direction with the direction of the apparatus, also increased with age, being more than four times as numerous at six as at two weeks. He found a definite relation between the speed of the moving object and the number of correct eye movements, the number being greater at the medium than at the fast speed, from the second to the sixth week. However, the percentage of eye movements which are in the direction of the moving object is greatest at the fast speed, next at the medium speed, and lowest at the slow speed. McGinnis's general conclusions on ocular pursuit in relation to age during the first six weeks are, that true ocular pursuit first occurs in the third or fourth week, and that by six weeks all his subjects responded to his apparatus with a pursuit that had many of the characteristics of adult pursuit, and was practically free from gross ocular movements which did not correspond with the movements of the stimulus. In the analysis of the pictures taken during the tests for optic nystagmus, it was found that coordinated compensatory eye movements occurred occasionally, from birth on. McGinnis points out that the newborn infant makes so comparatively few head movements that situations calling for such movements are relatively rare. During the last week of his tests, there was a marked increase in head movements, in two of the subjects especially, and a corresponding increase in the number of coördinated compensatory eye movements. The records on optic nystagmus indicated that the number of eye movements occurring during it, was influenced by the number and speed of the bars on the visual field, and to a less degree by the age and experience of the subjects. In comparing McGinnis's results with those of other investigators, it should be noted that his experimental conditions were rigidly controlled and the apparatus used was so arranged that the moving object filled the entire field of vision. Thus if the infant's eyes were open and he was looking at all, it was necessary for him to look at the moving field. His results are therefore probably more accurate as to the eye movements which are within the capacity of infants during the first six weeks of life than those made under ordinary conditions, where the eyes can so easily slip from the experimental stimulus to any part of a usual environment; but the results are also perhaps less typical of the movements which occur normally and spontaneously.

Shirley's (180) subjects were tested for eye reactions when lying on their backs, from birth to thirteen weeks of age, and in a sitting posture after that age. Fleeting attempts to follow a slowly moving light were noted in most babies during the first week; in 18 of 20 babies this was the first eye reaction to appear. The next reactions were watching a person or object other than the light, which was firmly established at about four and one-half weeks, at which age 50 percent were able also to follow a steel tape moved in a horizontal direction before the eyes. The social smile appeared next, which Shirley states is not strictly an eye reaction but has a large visual element. Following the tape when swung vertically, appeared at a median age of nine weeks and when swung in a circle, at ten weeks, with an almost perfect coordination for each direction at eleven weeks. Skill in the lying posture did not carry over to the sitting posture. At thirteen weeks not more than 15 percent of the babies made an effort to follow the object with eyes or head when sitting, but progress was rapid and by the twenty-third week 75 percent showed coordinated following, and the skill was perfected at thirty-eight weeks. The commonest distraction was looking around, but this disappeared suddenly at nineteen weeks. Shirley concludes that the development of eye coördination proceeds from fleeting pursuit movements to fixation on an object, and from focusing on an object to consistent following of a moving object, and that the complexity of eye movements varies according to the direction in which the object is moving.

According to Shirley, the watching of persons appeared before the third week. Letting the eyes rove around was prevalent at this age, but declined as the watching of persons rapidly increased. At thirteen weeks, when the tests in the sitting posture were started, there was a marked increase in looking around. This reaction fell off as the babies became accustomed to sitting, and it fell to insignificance after the fifty-fourth week. After the fifth month persons more often distracted the babies from their toys than did the ordinary room sights. During the second year the distraction of looking at persons declined steadily. At forty-two weeks of age, picture and mirror tests were begun. There was considerable development between forty-two and fifty weeks, though the infants were interested in the mirror and not in the magazine pictures. At fifty-four weeks the babies were shown a picture book and pictures of women, one of them being in each case the mother of the baby. The correct response to the picture book was naming an object, and to the women's pictures was pointing to or naming the mother. These tests were continued throughout the second year and development was steady during the period. The number of correct responses to the book rose sharply from the fiftieth to the seventy-fourth week. Records were kept of the apparent interest in the different pictures after the seventy-fourth week, and Shirley concludes that the babies preferred pictures of human beings and animals to those of inanimate objects.

Shirley concludes that visual development falls roughly into four stages. Beginning with vague reactions to a moving light or a bright object, the infant soon achieves skill in focusing on persons and objects. He next explores the visual environment nearest at hand. For the first three months, his attention is largely confined to the faces and hands of those about him, to such toys as are dangled before him or put into his crib, and to his own fingers. The second stage commences when the baby begins to sit up. His visual range then widens to include the whole room. During this stage eye-hand coördination is perfected and auditory stimuli begin to cause ocular search for the source of the sound. The third stage finds the baby's attention fixed on the remote and the minute. The fourth stage is the ability to see the shadowy, the obscure, the transparent and pictured images. This stage appears to be established by the end of the second year, at which. time, according to Shirley, the child can see with his naked eye anything that the adult can see with his.

Shirley says it is not strange that vision approximates the adult level by two years of age. She points out that in general the sense organs are more mature at birth than are the motor organs, and cites Hymes's measurements as authority for the statements that the cornea reaches approximately the adult diameter between six and twelve months of age, that the lid fissure makes its most rapid growth between birth and two years, though it continues growing slowly until the age of sixteen, and that differentiation of structure within the retina is complete by the end of the first year. She states that her observations indicate that visual development goes hand in hand with the structural development of the eye, and that both are fairly mature by two years of age.

Jones (102) tested 365 infants for eye coördination. She used a small flash light moved a foot in two seconds at the level of the eyes, when the infants were sitting. The light was moved from side to side, up and down and in a counterclockwise circle, five times for each type of stimulation, if necessary. The youngest infant to follow the light when moved horizontally was thirty-three days old, by the ninetieth day all the infants showed horizontal pursuit. The youngest age for vertical pursuit was fifty-one days; by one hundred ten days all showed it. Circular pursuit was observed in 15 percent of the cases between the sixtieth and sixty-ninth days and in all the subjects from the one hundred twentieth to the one hundred twenty-ninth days. The social smile developed in all the infants between the nineteenth and ninetieth days.

Gesell's (65) normative items do not contain so many tests for eye reactions as for reaching and manipulation. Following with the eyes a gross visual stimulus, such as a moving person, is a test which should be passed by practically all infants at four months of age. He states that lateral following occurs earlier than vertical, but that at four months about 75 percent of infants should be able to follow a white enamel saucer moved either horizontally or vertically at a distance of about two feet from the eyes. At this same age over half of the infants will look at a spoon placed on the edge of a table in front of them, and less than half will look at a cube, even when the objects are moved or hit against the table to attract attention to them. Bayley (7) gives credit for looking at the cube at four months. Gesell and Bayley place perceiving a small pellet on a table and directly in front of the child as a sixth-month test, Gesell stating that slightly over half the subjects will pass the test at this age. Linfert and Hierholzer (122) give the percentages for perceiving the pellet as 59 at six months, and 100 at nine and twelve months. Looking for a spoon the baby has been playing with, and which is suddenly dropped, occurred in less than half Gesell's subjects at six months, but at nine months in all of them. Bayley gives turning the head after the spoon when it falls as a seventh-month test, and definitely looking for it as a ninth-month test. Linfert and Hierholzer's percentages for this test are 48 at six months, 92 at nine months, and 100 at twelve months.

Bayley, and Linfert and Hierholzer include a number of tests of visual reactions in their scales, which Gesell does not have. One of Bayley's (7) tests for the first month is momentary regard of the dangling red ring which is used in her reaching and grasping tests, and at two months credit is given for a prolonged regard of the red ring. At two months credits are given for coordinated eye following of a small red light moved in the horizontal, vertical, and circular directions. Linfert and Hierholzer (122) dangle a nine-inch, bright pink translucent ball two to four inches from the baby's eyes, and a dark blue glazed ball. At one month 62 percent of the subjects noticed the pink ball, 52 percent followed it with the eyes when it was moved in an arc from ear to ear, and 14 percent followed it with the head. The percentages for these reactions to the blue ball at one month were 58, 48 and 20. At four months 90 percent noticed the pink ball, and 76 percent the blue ball, 66 and 68 percent followed the respective balls with the eyes, and 36 and 26 percent followed them with the head. At six months the percentages were 96 for noticing both balls, 82 and 76 for following with the eyes, and 64 and 56 for following with the head.

At three months Bayley (7) gives credit if the subject turns the eyes to each side at an angle of at least 30 degrees, to fixate the small red light as it is moved slowly toward the center of vision. Her other eye tests for this age are turning the head freely to look about, and horizontal following of a pencil. At four months her eye tests are showing awareness of a strange situation or room, following a spoon by turning the head when it is slowly moved sidewise out of sight about two feet away from the eyes, and inspection of his own hands by the infant. At five months she gives credit if the child turns his head to look for the source of a sound, and shows eye-and-hand coördination in reaching. At six months credit is given if the baby is able to discriminate strangers, judging by such reactions as staring, frowning, withdrawal or crying. Bayley begins a mirror test at seven months. Gesell (65) also uses this test, but does not make it clear exactly what reactions should be expected at each age level, until the eighteenth month, when he says the child will often reach behind the mirror to try to grasp his own image. Bayley gives credit at seven months if the child makes approach movements or tries to manipulate his own image, at eight months if he smiles at his own image, and at ten months if he plays with his image by laughing, patting, banging, playful reaching, leaning toward it, and so on.

Bühler's (23) tests of eye reactions for the first month are fixating the examiner's glance, and focusing on a small bright object held about a foot away from the eyes. According to Bühler, at this age a child will turn his head in the direction of a sound, but his eyes usually remain staring ahead. In the second month the child is tested for the social smile; for moving the eyes in all directions looking for the source of a sound; for horizontal following of a bright object; for reacting to the sudden disappearance of the examiner's face by staring after it or crying, crinkling the brow or screwing up the mouth, and for a frightened or negative reaction to a mask held about a foot and a half from the child's eyes. The tests for the fourth month are active looking about when moved to a strange part of the room; a positive reaction to a light, by which Bühler apparently means turning the eyes to and looking at a small flashlight when it is turned on while the child is in partial darkness, and watching an object which he is grasping and moving with his own hand. At five months the child should look searchingly in the direction in which he has dropped a toy, or from which it has been taken away from him. At eight months a hand mirror is held about ten inches in front of the child's face, and he passes the test if he smiles at his reflection and "regards it with interest." He is also brought into a strange situation or some familiar object is altered in appearance, and he passes the test if he makes negative, expressional movements. In the thirteenth and fourteenth months the child is tested to see if he reaches after the reflection of a cracker in a mirror. In the fifteenth, sixteenth and seventeenth months, the child should show more interest in a picture of a figure than in a color card when they are presented successively, and should look questioningly at the examiner when he sees his own image in a mirror; in the next three months he should look behind the mirror when shown his reflection. In the last three months of the second year, the child should show signs of interest or pleasure when the examiner puts a mask over her face near enough for the child to reach it, and he should call a picture of a nurse, "mamma," "dolly," or "nurse," or should point to the figure when the examiner says "show me mamma."

Figurin and Denisova (57) make one of the few statements found in the literature as to the distance at which a baby can follow moving objects with the eyes. According to them, the child can follow objects moved horizontally at a distance of six and a half meters from the eyes, in the third month, and in the twelfth month he can follow a bird or an airplane which is in his field of vision. Turning the head in response to the voice is developed by boys in the third to fourth months, and by girls in the fourth to fifth months, these authors state. They also state that a negative reaction to a mask does not appear until the middle of the fifth month, but they require screaming as a sign of the negative reaction, while Bühler accepts turning away or facial grimacing.

Kuhlmann (109) includes eye reactions in his test scale. At three months the infant passes if he follows with no marked incoordination a bright object or a candle in a darkened room, moved to the right and left and back, up and down and diagonally, two and a half feet from the eyes; and if the head and eyes, or eyes alone, turn toward a bright object moved into the marginal field of vision from the rear.

Brainard (20) reports that his daughter, at ten weeks of age, fixated on a hand moving two meters away from her eyes in an arc of ninety degrees in a strong light. She lost the hand at a distance of three meters, and did not fixate at all on objects four meters away. When lying on her back, her eyes followed an object moving in an ellipse half a meter above the body to points directly above either arm. He suggests that eye-hand coördination develops when the child can sit up, because of the better view in the sitting position. At first her eyes followed but did not direct her hands in reaching, and Brainard believes that eye-hand coordination develops through the accidental meeting of eye and hand stimulations. He kept a record of the number of times that the hand touched an object at the same moment that the eyes fixated on it. He found no cases of this in the first month. It occurred 10 times in the second month, 20 in the third, 50 in the fourth, 200 in the fifth, and 600 times in the sixth month. The baby first noticed her hands on the third day of the eleventh week, and about this same time she began to lift her head when excited.

Hetzer, Beaumont and Wiehmeyer (82) have made an elaborate study of reactions to light and color stimulations during the first seven months, on 140 infants, ten at each age level tested. The tests were made with the infant lying under a wooden case which allowed room for moving. There were three holes in the box in a line over the infant's eyes and a fourth hole through which the illumination for the colored-yarn tests was introduced. This study charts what the authors call the impulsive movements, which cannot be explained by the simple stimulus and reaction pattern. These impulsive movements last until the eighth month, and have disappeared by the ninth month. They state that the length of the reactions to the stimulations they used, increases until the third month, and then steadily decreases. Nine-month-old infants were so indifferent to the stimuli that it was not possible to continue the experiment to that age. In the fourth and fifth months most of the reaction time was devoted to "looking around." They follow Bühler's interpretation of spontaneous movements, and divide the reactions observed into negative, neutral and positive responses. In the first two months, over 50 percent of the movements were negative and the remainder neutral. The positive reactions began in the third month and in the seventh month made up 82 percent of the responses. After the fourth month there are no longer any negative responses to the light. The negative reactions disappear before the neutral ones. These facts they interpret to mean that the child dislikes stimulation by a weak flashlight, but that by the fifth month he does not mind the light and can control his system to withstand it. In the third month the child begins to meet the stimulations actively by staring at the light. The earlier looks lack the tension of staring and are interrupted by impulsive eye movements and irritated looking and turning away from the light. The final stages of active behavior show looking at the light, feeling it as if feeling the way tactually, turning the head or the whole body again and again toward the light, and reaching for the light with the hands. In the fifth month, the child is still exclusively looking at the light, and in the seventh month 78 percent of the responses took the form of reaching toward it.

The responses to red, green, yellow and blue wool took the same course as those to the light, though the positive reactions were a trifle slower in developing, but reached 90 percent of the total responses in the fifth month, and were 100 percent after that. The grasping reactions for the colors developed more slowly than for the light. They were 5 percent in the fifth month, 18 percent in the sixth, and 30 percent in the seventh month. The authors suggest that it is possible that the contrast of the colors with the white walls of the room may have made them a stronger stimulus than the light, or that the strangeness of colors as stimuli may account for the greater percentage of active reactions. The light stimulations were presented five times, the colors only once each. They found no change in reactions to the light on repeated stimulations. The results for the colors were tabulated according to the number of reactions to each color, and no significant differences were found except a slightly less response to the green than to the other colors. This is borne out by the number of negative reactions in the first months, as well as by the positive reactions in the later months. This experiment can hardly be called an investigation of vision nor yet of eye reactions, but since the stimulations used were visual, it has been reviewed here. It seems rather to be a statistical count of the increase of specificity of responses with increasing age, as shown by movements of the body, especially by the head and eyes.

Beaumont and Hetzer (9) made a similar investigation of 70 children from nine months to one year and eleven months of age. From nine months to twenty-one months, a cardboard covered with a bright-colored paper was presented to the child. The children showed little interest in this test and attentive interest seemed to occur only when spots of light were reflected on the card. From nine months to eighteen months of age, they were given a card on which were pasted irregular geometric figures in the four primary colors. This was checked by presenting a plain gray card also. The reactions of the younger children to both cards were handling, touching, scratching, knocking, rubbing, and putting in the mouth. In the first quarter of the second year, there was a change from handling to looking at the cards, and by eighteen months of age 100 percent of the reactions were what the authors call "receptive contemplation." The authors assume that this change in the character of the response marks the beginning of interest in colors. From fifteen months to two years of age, the children were presented successively with four cards on which were pasted a cut-out of a woman, a cut-out of a cup, and cut-outs of two meaningless but simple designs. The authors state that the reactions of the 20 subjects to whom these tests were given are somewhat retarded, as all came from poor homes where they received poor care and practically no training. The younger children showed no differences in their reactions to the meaningful and to the nonsense pictures. In the eighteenth month a few of the infants recognized the picture of the woman, from the nineteenth to the twenty-first months 40 percent recognized the woman and 30 percent the cup, and in the last three months of the year 80 percent recognized the woman and 70 percent the cup, judging by linguistic response or pointing at the observer's request or spontaneous naming, the latter not occurring until the last three months. The authors conclude that the understanding of pictures and the linguistic function develop at the same time. Before understanding of the pictures began, the length of time devoted to looking at both cards was the same; when the babies began to understand the pictures the time spent looking at the meaningless designs decreased sharply. Gesell's (65) normative items indicate that in the children he used for fixing the age levels of the responses, the ability to name colors is just beginning at two years of age. It should be remembered that the ability to name colors correctly does not necessarily coincide in time with the ability to distinguish them. The use of the names of colors, whether used correctly or not, occurred in less than half the infants. These infants were shown a card with rectangular shapes of red, white, blue, and yellow, and less than 20 percent named one color correctly.

We have seen that there is no agreement in the literature as to the age at which infants discriminate between colors. Peiper (158) believes that some sort of discrimination is made shortly after birth, even by premature infants. Irwin's (93) tests with colors on neonates were inconclusive, and he and a number of other authors have pointed out the difficulty in presenting colors so that the stimulation is the color alone, not different degrees of brightness. Staples (184) has made a study of color discrimination on 262 subjects under two years of age. Atlas papers in red, yellow, blue, and green, with a known brightness and saturation, were shown the children on an illuminated field. Twenty-three infants under five months of age, with an average age of eighty-seven days, were tested, and judgment of discrimination was the length of time the color was looked at, as compared to the time spent in looking at the field lighted with gray. The author concludes that the sensation of color, as distinct from gray, may be experienced by the end of the third month. At this age, however, there were no significant differences in response to the different colors. The older children were tested in the same way. The responses observed lead her to conclude that the four colors, red, yellow, green, and blue, were clearly seen and were experienced as distinctly different sensations by infants of twelve months of age and most certainly were by those of fifteen months. Differences in responses to the different colors were seen from six months of age on, with the differences most marked from six to twelve months. Red was the most effective stimulus, next yellow, then blue, and last green.

Johnson (99) in her discussion of color discrimination, deals chiefly with studies on children over two years of age. She states that a child of sixteen or eighteen months of age may select an object by color without being able to name the color. She describes Stutsman's study of infants in matching colors, beginning at eighteen months. In the first six months, the color discs were played with indiscriminately, without any attempt to follow the directions for sorting the discs by color. Correct responses began at two years of age and at this time, of the infants who made some correct responses, those for red were always correct, those for blue failed only once, those for yellow were correct only once, and those for green were failed in by all the subjects. Johnson points out that studies on color-naming with older subjects, even with adults, show that discriminating colors by name is a slower response than reading or reciting the names of colors when the stimuli are not present, and concludes that accurate discrimination of colors precedes the ability to name one color after another. She also points out the effect that training has on the ability to name colors. Since differences are perceived before similarities, it is likely that marked differences in shades of the same color look to the young child like different colors.

REACTIONS TO SOUND

There is very little in the literature on infant reactions to sound and the development of auditory acuity after the neonatal period. We have seen that there is a difference of opinion as to whether the newborn infant can hear or not, but there is general agreement, even among those authors who believe that he cannot hear during the first days of life, that hearing is established before the end of the first ten days of life. In the test scales, a number of items are given which attempt to show the appearance of the ability to discriminate the quality of sounds, as shown by different tones of the human voice. In general, the sounds that have been used for testing very young infants have been sudden sharp noises, and there is always the possibility that, with such stimuli, it is the vibrations rather than the sound itself which is reacted to. There are considerable data in the literature as to the age at which infants look in the direction from which a sound comes, but they are not all in agreement. There is also some evidence as to the age at which infants begin to understand simple commands and questions. There is of course a large cortical element involved in the ability to understand words, but it is safe to say that when this ability appears, auditory acuity is established to the point where the baby can hear the different sounds in a word or words sufficiently well to distinguish one auditory stimulus from another. However, the part that facial expression and the general demeanor of the person addressing the infant plays in conveying the desired meaning, has not been investigated so far as we could determine.

Shirley's (180) only observations on the reactions to sounds were those made to the examiner's ringing of a small hand bell out of the infants' reach. The early reactions were looking at the bell and blinking at the sound. Later, the infants began to reach for the bell, and still later to lean forward on the examiner's lap and make great efforts to reach it. The babies were also given an opportunity to grasp the bell, and apparently there were real attempts to ring it. Accidental ringing from shaking the bell occurred first at fifteen weeks, and purposeful ringing at eighteen weeks. An infant's ringing of a bell shows very little about his reactions to sounds, and nothing about auditory acuity, but the appearance of purposeful ringing does seem to indicate that there is some interest in hearing the bell ring. It should be remembered, however, that before the child can indulge this interest, manual skill must have developed to the point where correct manipulation of the bell is possible.

Bayley (7) gives as an eighth-month test, interest in sound production as such, as shown by banging toys, ringing a bell or shaking a rattle. Bühler gives credit for smiling and positive expressional movements to the sound of a bell rung out of sight as a fifth-month test. In the second month Bühler (23) has a test in which the examiner talks to the child in a normal voice for 30 seconds, and then suddenly begins to growl for 30 seconds. "Blinking, distorting the corners of the mouth, wrinkling the forehead, shaking and restless movements of the body, crying sounds of displeasure, weeping, clenching the fists," all are reactions which give the subject credit for passing the test. In the sixth month, Bühler gives a test for distinguishing between friendly and angry speech. The examiner is hidden from the child, who is supposed to respond to the friendly voice with positive expressional movements, and to the angry voice with negative ones.

Kuhlmann (109) tests for a marked start or wink in response to sound, at three months. A telegraph snapper is clicked two inches from the infant's ear at one minute intervals; if there is no reaction to this, the examiner claps his hands behind the infant's ear in such a way that they cannot be seen.

The data on the age at which the infant looks toward the source of a sound are more complete and also, of course, more objective evidence of sound reactions, but even here coördination between control of the neck muscles, eye movements and the auditory response is involved. Decroly (49), in his summary of all the literature on language, gives a brief account of the development of auditory reactions to the voice before definite comprehension begins. In the second month, reactions to the human voice are still diffuse, but differentiation is beginning. Instead of sudden contractions, startles, and flight reactions, neutral reactions begin to appear and some infants distinguish between sound and noise. In the second and third months, flight reactions diminish and positive reactions take their place in the form of turning the head toward the sound; after the third month the eyes, too, are turned toward the source of the sound. After the fourth month the child begins to laugh, hold out his hands and lall to the voice. And after this he begins to imitate sounds by doubling and redoubling syllables which he has already spontaneously sounded. Decroly believes that auditory memory plays a large part in the development of correct speech. At first this memory is immediate and takes the form of attempts to imitate sounds heard. Gradually, as the vocal repertoire increases, deferred memory also enters in, and the child will make corrections in words which he has not just heard, apparently by a kind of process of transfer from the new words he is just learning to the old ones he already knows.

Gesell (65) says that an adaptive motor response to a voice or to the ringing of a bell is established in practically all infants at four months of age. He warns that the stimulus should be presented out of sight, so that the response will be definitely to the sound, not to a visual stimulus. Definite and prompt turning to the sound of a bell develops later, according to Gesell, being observed in about 75 percent of infants at six months. Cooing or laughing on hearing music begins to develop at six months of age and is present in 75 percent of infants at twelve months. He states that at four months of age, babies who will turn toward the sound of a voice frequently will not turn toward a ringing bell. Bayley (7) gives credit at two months if the infant gives evidence of attention to the sound of a voice such as turning the head, vocalization, or cessation of activity. At five months she gives credit if the child definitely turns his head toward the source of the sound of a bell rung out of sight behind him, first at one side then at the other. Bayley gives the percentages of infants she tested who attended to the voice by turning the head when the examiner talked with the infant seated on her lap: first month, 90 percent; second month, 92 percent; fourth month, 98 percent. Bühler (23) gives credit at two months if the child turns the head when a rattle is shaken a foot and a half away, and out of sight. She says that at this age the eyes usually remain staring straight ahead. At three months credit is given if during the sound of the rattle, "the eyes are directed searchingly to all sides." Figurin and Denisova (58) say that turning the head in response to the voice occurs about two weeks earlier than turning it to the source of a sound (nature unspecified). They found that boys developed the reactions in the second or fourth month, and girls in the fourth or fifth month. The differences in the ways different observers gave this test and the ambiguities in their directions for giving credit for the responses, are clearly sufficient to account for the different ages reported at which looking for the source of a sound is found.

Lowenfeld (124) tested 6 infants during the third and fourth weeks and 10 from the second through the eighth months, with five different sound stimuli: a three-tongued clapper; a whistle blown for two seconds, with a one second interval; handclapping with the same duration and interval; a continuous blow on a tuning whistle; and ringing a small bell; also with a one-second interval. He follows Bühler's method of classifying the responses as negative, neutral or positive. To the end of the first month, there were reactions to 68 percent of the stimuli, during the second month there were reactions to 78 percent, and after this the number of reactions remained nearly constant. The negative reactions, which he calls shock or flight reactions, were contractions of the muscles and were generalized over the entire body. During the first month all the reactions were of this character. He distinguishes three degrees of shock, as shown by the violence of the contractions and the body segments involved. The clapper, the whistle and the handclapping elicited reactions of the first degree, while the tuning whistle and the bell did not; to the latter stimuli the largest number of responses were of the third degree. He states that these early reactions to sounds are diffuse and body-wide, because of the immature state of the auditory mechanisms during the first month, and that the strength of the reaction corresponds to the strength of the stimulus.

From the second through the eighth month, Lowenfeld used a one-tongue clapper, blows of one block of wood on another, a tuning whistle blown continuously and one blown with one-second intervals, all of intensity about equal to that of the human voice. The clapper elicited responses of the greatest duration, and the length of the response to all the sounds was greatest during the third month, falling thereafter. During the seventh and eighth months the sounds were too weak to give strong reactions, owing, according to the author, to the fact that infants are developing so rapidly at this time. With increasing age, the differences in responses to the different sounds practically disappeared. During the second month reactions of the arms and hands prevailed; during the third month movements were largely of the head and eyes. After this age, eye movements predominated, with the rest of the body quiet. The author states that the eye movements during the second month cannot be called purposive turning of the eyes toward the sound. Coördination of the eye and ear begins in the third month, and is one of the first signs of consciousness. He suggests that after the fourth month, the eye movements in the direction of the sound are in the nature of searching for the source of the sound. Mouth movements cease after the third month, to reappear in the seventh and eighth months as an opening of the mouth in surprise. Smiling and lalling responses begin in the fourth month. He reports the same predominance of what he terms negative reactions during the first three months, that Hetzer reports in her study of reactions to light; the first appearance of positive reactions in the fourth month; and almost complete disappearance of negative reactions and a great increase in the positive in the sixth month; and 92 percent neutral reactions in the eighth month. He interprets his analysis of the changes in bodily movements as showing that during the fifth month, pleasure and displeasure reactions become established, and that from this time on the reactions without affective quality are in the background, and are almost entirely neutral in character.

Since the data on reactions to sounds are so meager, the few observations in the literature on the ages at which infants imitate sounds will be given here, as well as in the section on the development of language. Bühler (23) gives credit at eleven months, if the child attempts to reproduce such sounds as *mamma, papa, dada, lala* and so on. Gesell (65) requires the ability to repeat more than two words which the child has not been trained to say. Less than 20 percent of infants can repeat in this way at twelve months of age, and less than half at eighteen months, he finds. Shirley gives the ages, as reported by the mothers, at which the infants tested by her repeated words after an adult. The median age was forty-four weeks, and the range from thirty-nine to forty-nine weeks.

There are also some data on the age at which children begin to make adjustments to the spoken word. These data can possibly be taken as a rough indication of the development of auditory acuity to a fairly advanced level, although the ability to translate the sounds into meaningful images is also involved. Bayley (7) gives credit at nine months if the child listens with "selective interest" to familiar words such as *baby, kitty,* and *mama,* and at ten months if the child reacts discriminatively to his own name when a series of names are repeated in the same tone of voice, or if he makes a discriminating response to such questions as "where is the kitty?" Linfert and Hierholzer (122) give the percentages which they found for the name part of this test as 65 at six months, and 100 at nine and twelve months. Gesell (65) says that at nine months slightly more than half of the infants show comprehension or motor adjustment to certain words. This is usually the result of training or of accident, he says.

It is clear that there has been no adequate investigation of the development of auditory reactions and acuity. Even most of the data which we have included here do not strictly belong under that heading. It is true that the subjective factors are of great importance in judging reactions to auditory stimuli, but this is equally true of the infant's responses to all forms of stimulation.

ADJUSTMENT FOR THE SOLUTION OF PROBLEMS

By the solution of problems is meant that behavior which is directly aimed at or achieves a goal which is of immediate concern to the infant, and which requires adjustment of the body or of the environment. No studies of the consecutive development of the ability to solve problems were found in the literature. But when the various data in the literature involving the solution of problems are gathered together, they present an interesting picture of progressive adjustment to the environment, beginning with certain simple reflex acts in which the body or parts of it are adjusted and progressing in an orderly manner, which clearly illustrates the cephalo-caudal direction of development, to the ability to adjust the environment to gain an immediate goal. This is not a hard and fast category, however, and especially in the case of hand activities it is difficult to say to what extent the infant is engaged in solving a problem or simply showing the tendency mentioned by Halverson to respond to the presence of an object within sight and reach by reaching, grasping and manipulative activity. In general we include the type of behavior which is commonly called *adaptive* in the literature, in so far as this behavior involves a relationship between two things and is aimed at the solution of a problem which meets an immediate need or want of the child. We have omitted items such as the simplified form board and piling blocks into a tower, where the problems exist for the adult but not for the child. Much of the material on the solution of problems has already been reviewed, and we shall not repeat it in detail here, but simply summarize it, without reference to authors, from the point of view of development of problem-solving. We have purposely avoided entering into a discussion, at this point, of the age at which awareness that the behavior is aimed at the solution of a problem appears.

At birth the adjustments which the infant makes are entirely concerned with the functions for maintenance of life, breathing and nourishment, and occur whether all the elements in the situation are appropriate or not. When placed prone, the newborn infant will turn his head to free the nose for breathing, and when the lips, cheeks, tongue or inside of the mouth are touched will make sucking movements. It takes a long time for the reflex sucking movements to become specific to the feeding situation and, at the same time, since they are necessary for the taking of nourishment, it is legitimate to include them as one of the

earliest adjustments of the body to meet a need. These two reactions appear to be the only specific responses of the newborn
to external stimulation, which are adapted to meeting the need
of the infant.

Sucking is the first adjustment made toward solving the problem of getting nourishment. Bühler (23) states that the next
step is turning the head toward the nipple when held in the
nursing position, which occurs at one month of age. At two
months of age the infant seeks the nipple with restless movements
of the head and pursing of the lips. Bühler says that until five
months of age, the mouth is opened only on contact with the
nipple, and in this month the infant begins to open his mouth at
the sight of the bottle or of a spoon, if he is fed with one. In
this month, also, the adjustment of the environment for feeding
occurs, in that the child now begins to hold the bottle with his
hands while nursing; and at six months the child will put the
nipple in his mouth himself. Brainard (20), in his observations
of his own daughter, found some of these reactions at earlier
ages. At nine weeks there was an attempted adjustment for
feeding, the hands and feet moved and the fingers opened and
closed, and moved toward the mouth; at ten weeks there was
no reach for the bottle, but the nipple was put into the mouth
when the bottle was put in her hands. According to Bühler the
child does not begin to feed himself with his hands until the
eighth month. Shirley (180) reports earlier ages for feeding reactions in which the child adjusts the environment. The median
age for trying to drink from a cup used as a toy was twenty-
seven weeks, and the mothers reported that the babies held their
cups for actual drinking at ages ranging from twenty-six to
forty-six weeks, held their bottles for nursing at from fourteen
to forty-five weeks of age, and held spoons for eating at from
sixteen to forty-five weeks of age. Gesell's (65) norms indicate
that eating with a spoon without much spilling is not established
until two years of age.

The development of the adjustments an infant makes in getting
a desired object have been taken up in detail, from another point
of view, under the development leading to erect posture and

locomotion, and reaching, prehension and manipulation. Looking at stationary objects and following a moving object with the eyes, appear before the first random reaching, and it is not until after the later reaction has developed that coördination of eye-and-hand movements occur. The first reaching is done from the shoulder, and muscular control of arm-and-hand movements moves gradually from the shoulder to the finger tips. In early reaching, the head and mouth, as well as the arms, often move toward the object. Bühler (23) states that it is not until the seventh month that adjustment of body posture to assist reaching occurs. Prehension is fully developed in its adult form by one year of age, or very shortly thereafter. Looking for a toy that has just fallen begins in the sixth month. Crawling after objects does not occur until later; the median age for making some progress on the stomach found by Shirley (180) was thirty-eight weeks, and for creeping forty-five weeks. All the literature describes the struggling efforts made by the infant before he is able to make progress, which suggests that efforts toward locomotion may involve some of the elements of problem solving. Manipulation of the object after it is obtained is largely random during the entire first year of life. The exceptions are the adjustment for eating listed above, and a few simple adjustments of the object, such as shaking a rattle or a small hand bell to make it ring. Shirley found no purposive attempts to open a series of simple boxes, each containing an object that rattled, as a stimulus to solve the problem, during the first year. Several of the test scales give unwrapping a cube loosely folded in a paper as an adjustment that begins in the ninth month. According to Gesell (65), this adjustment is not established until eighteen months, and credit is given if the cube is shaken out, as well as for a purposive unwrapping. Bühler (23) has a test which definitely requires the solution of a problem, but the necessary adjustment is one of the body, rather than of the object. A toy in which the child is interested is placed behind a 19-by-11-inch glass plate, and at ten months of age he should be able to reach around the plate and get the toy.

Some of the test scales include obtaining an object by pulling in a string which is attached to it. Bayley (7) gives credit at eight months if the infant, in his efforts to reach a ring, scoops or pulls the string attached to the ring and so secures the ring, and at ten months if he "pulls the string adaptively with a directed effort to secure the ring."

Richardson (169) has made a careful study by exact standardized procedure of the development of the ability to secure an object out of reach by pulling in a string which is within reach. The experiment was modeled on Kohler's investigation of the problem-solving behavior of chimpanzees, and was suggested by his statement, which she quotes, "experiments of this kind can be performed at the very tenderest age." Sixteen infants were tested at monthly intervals from the twenty-eighth through the fifty-second weeks of age. The subjects were seated at a table, at the edge of which a grill was set up. The lures were bright-colored toys, small enough to be pulled through the openings in the grill. The toys were set up behind a screen, and were presented one at a time, attached to a heavy eighteen-inch string which came to the edge of the grill. Three single-string situations were first presented and, if the subject solved these, either with or without the grill in place, four multiple-string situations were presented in this order: three perpendicular parallel strings; three oblique parallel strings; three converging strings; and an attached roundabout string and a direct, unattached string.

Some of Richardson's conclusions are given in full:

At 28 and 32 weeks the grill was one of the main factors that prevented the securing of the string and the pulling in reach of the lure. Successes when the grill was removed were frequent. The interference that the grill offered was chiefly mechanical but partly visual. From 44 weeks on, the influence of the grill was negligible.

Between 28 and 44 weeks the infants displayed (a) a rapid development in adaptive response to the situation; (b) a dropping-out of the less adaptive forms of behavior. At 28 weeks, in the situation with the grill, the lure was pulled in reach in 3 per cent of the presentations, at 44 weeks in 100 per cent.

Relatively abrupt drops for the group in the median time required to bring the lure in reach appeared at 40 and 44 weeks.

Five types of perceptive attitude, representing different levels of maturity, were inferred from the total behavior during the securing of the string and pulling in of the lure: a. Interest in the string rather than in the lure. b. Interest in the lure and apparently accidental contact with the string. c. Awareness of both lure and string without evident purposive utilization of the string. d. Experimentation. e. Definite utilization of the string as a means to bring the lure in reach.

She states that with the grill in place there were relatively few successes that were not of the last type. These conclusions apply to the single-string situations. There were apparently no successes with the multiple-string situations until thirty-six weeks of age. Combining all the tests, there was no improvement with age in pulling the attached string first. At some ages the number of cases was small, and the emotional factors seemed to be greater in this part of the test than in the first part. Richardson concludes that the selection of the string to be pulled first seemed to depend on "(a) the visual pattern presented at the moment, with the lure considered as the dominating feature; (b) on the pre-existing tendencies to reach in a given direction or with a given hand; and (c) on the presence or absence of more general disturbing factors."

Richardson describes an experiment of Karl Bühler's on his own daughter, with a piece of rusk attached to a string. In the ninth month, the baby reached directly for the rusk without appearing to notice the string. She then made several correct solutions in succession, but the success was temporary. "Not until the end of the tenth month was the situation completely and permanently mastered so that the string was always looked for and pulled, no matter in what direction it lay."

In the second year, adjustment of the body to solve a problem reaches the point where the child can walk, climb and get up and down without support to reach a goal. At the same time manipulative adjustment of the environment is increasing to the point where the child can first open and later close boxes to get something inside them, and can manipulate correctly a variety of toys. Bühler (23) places walking with support while holding something as thirteenth to fourteenth-month tests; walking alone to the examiner to get a toy or a cracker, and picking up something while standing alone, as sixteenth to eighteenth-month tests;

carrying an object while walking alone, and climbing on a box to get a cracker, as eighteenth to twentieth-month tests; and climbing upon a chair and standing on it to reach a cracker as a twenty-first to twenty-third-month test. Gesell's (65) two normative items for climbing illustrate the progress from adjustment of the body to adjustment of the environment. At eighteen months of age, less than half of the infants will climb upon a chair to reach a basket they are interested in, which is held directly over the chair. At twenty-four months practically all children will move a chair from one place to another, in order to use it to climb upon to get something they want. Gesell states that the method of turning an uncorked glass bottle upside down to get a candy pellet which is inside it, is not established until eighteen months of age, and that at twelve months infants frequently try to get the pellet by thrusting their hands inside the bottle. From fifty-four to seventy-four weeks of age, Shirley (180) gave her subjects a glass, screw-top jar with a doll inside. Only six of the 22 infants succeeded in unscrewing the jar by seventy-four weeks of age, and only three in screwing it up. Four of these tried to get the doll out by pulling with their hands, and two tried turning the bottle upside down. During this period Shirley continued some of the box tests used in the last half of the first year, this time demonstrating the method of opening. There was progressive increase in the number of successful openings and closings of the boxes during the period; the closing was in every case more difficult than opening. The rattling lures inside the boxes were taken out and played with, but the chief interest was in the problem of getting the box open and closed. The progressive reactions to the boxes were: no reaction; passive play; random play; accidental opening, which decreased with age; and unsuccessful and successful attempts to open the boxes, which increased with age. One of Bühler's tests for the nineteenth to twenty-first months is reaching an object by means of a stick. The child is given a drumstick to play with, then a toy is placed on a chair on a level with the crib, just out of arm's reach, and the child should try to push the toy toward himself with the stick.

It is clear that investigations like that of Richardson's with larger numbers of subjects, at different ages and using a variety of problems, offer a fruitful field for studying the behavior of children, even during the first two years. Ability of infants to solve problems, with the exceptions of Halverson's exact studies of the development of the ability to prehend objects, appears to be an untouched field for investigation. Such studies, if systematically carried on, might do much to dispel the fog which at present surrounds the nature and extent of the intellectual functioning of infants. Johnson (99) gives an excellent, brief summary of the work on problem-solving that has been done with young children. She records nothing with subjects as young as two years of age. The summary which is given here does not exhaust every test in the scales which might be assumed to involve an immediate problem for the infant, but those which have been omitted do not add anything substantial to this very sketchy outline.

LANGUAGE

The development of the ability to express ideas and communicate with others by the spoken word has long been of special interest to students of child behavior. The literature on the subject is considerable, and a complete review of all that has been written, even since 1920, would place an undue emphasis upon this phase of development, at the expense of other behavior patterns equally important for the understanding of growth processes. The literature has been read and those studies summarized here which make a contribution to the development of language from its beginnings in the early vocal sounds of the infant. Much of the literature deals with the ages of appearance of the different parts of speech and grammatical forms, and the size of vocabularies at different ages. The most important of these studies will be summarized to give a general picture of what is known today of the course of language acquisitions, after the appearance of the first words. In spite of the large amount of literature on the subject of early language, the same lacks exist in this field that are found in studies of other behavior patterns: many studies simply trace the reactions observed on one or two subjects; there are few studies made by objective scientific procedure, on groups of subjects large enough to make generalizations and conclusions reliable; most of the studies are concerned with the age of appearance of the different steps in language development, rather than with the consecutive tracing of the steps themselves, their relations to one another and to the total growth pattern; studies of the prelanguage stages of vocalizations are especially meager.

There are other special difficulties in generalizing as to the course of language development, which have been accentuated by the method of recording reactions in terms of age levels. Decroly (49) points out the uncertain factor introduced by the fact that children in different countries learn languages which differ widely in phonetic and grammatical difficulty. He concludes, from his recent and complete survey of the literature, that there are differences, in different languages, in the ages at which the ability to use a language in the adult form appears, and that for the few languages for which infant development has been studied, it appears that progress in English goes on at earlier ages than progress in any of the others.

Another difficulty in the study of language development is the extremely important rôle of the environment in learning to speak. In general, it is agreed that children of the lower economic classes develop linguistically later than those of the upper classes. Hetzer and Reindorf (83) state that most of the studies have been made on upper-class children, and quote Stern's estimate that lower-class children are as much as eight months behind. They compared the vocal progress of two groups of children, and conclude that as long as vocalizations are instinctive or meaningless, there is no difference between the two groups, but that the accelerating influence of a superior environment begins at the very beginning of speech proper. Their superior group of subjects kept a steady lead all the way through the study of from three months to one year. This lead was most marked when the attention was fixed on the age of first appearance of a certain step forward, and least when on the ages at which 75 to 100 percent of both groups had established a reaction. In other words, the underprivileged infants catch up with the privileged in a surprisingly short time.

They found that the upper-class children developed much more unevenly than the lower-class, and suggest that perhaps, for their groups at least, the environment of the lower-class children was much more uniform than that of the upper-class. The greatest retardation among the lower-class children was found in the size of the vocabulary, and this is one of the items most largely studied on groups of children from favored environments. Gesell and Lord (66) compared the language development of 11 children from the upper and 11 from the lower socio-economic stratum, and found that the greatest difference in the language habits of the two groups was in the amount of conversation, which was greater among the children from homes of the upper level. They also found that restraint and inhibition in spontaneous speech was greater among the children from homes of lower level than among those from the upper. McCarthy (126, p. 308) says on this subject: "The consistent and striking differences between socio-economic groups probably are true differences which probably do not disappear, since the army intelligence test data revealed similar occupational-group differences in intelligence as measured by a verbal test." She also points out the need of further research in various fields of language development, especially in the prespeech stages.

The literature is in general agreement that the first sounds of the newborn infant are the overt elements from which speech develops, that vocalizations are used as means of communication before words proper are used; that comprehension appears before the use of words; that the normal child has a repertoire of a very few words by one year of age, that development is slow in the first months of the second year, but that toward the end of that year a great increase in the speed of progress appears; that words are first used in a generalized sense, and that their use for specific meanings is a developmental process; that name words appear first, verbs and adjectives later, relational words still later, and pronouns are just beginning to be used by the most advanced children by the end of the second year; that the first words have the force of a phrase or sentence, and combinations of words do not begin for sometime.

There are a number of theories as to the way speech develops from the early vocalizations. In general, two opposing points of view appear: one, that learning goes on by a very gradual process of building up the complex from the simple; the other, that the original phonetic equipment of the individual is very large, and that learning takes place by a process of adjusting and eliminating the sounds used, to the language learned. For example, Foulke and Stinchfield (60) state that the newborn infant has a limited vocabulary of sounds expressive of emotions—anger, fear, love.

Speech is developed in response to the growing need for expressional outlets. Inner states and external stimuli combine to arouse responses which eventually develop into articulate language, as the child finds that by this means he can satisfy his needs more quickly and more satisfactorily. The social stimulation which he receives is thus very important.

Gregoire (71), on the other hand, believes that the sound repertoire of the young infant is phonetically great and that a particular language evolves by the elimination of some sounds. The first sounds the infant makes are uncoördinated, and precision is gained gradually. In the beginning, the infant tries hard to express himself without awareness of trying to use words. He usually ends by crying. Later, about the ninth month, the combination of syllables begins. This sounds in its rhythm like an imitation of adult speech, and in the tenth month he begins to imitate the rhythm of the language of his country. Before the question can be decided we must have more exact, complex, and phonetically correct records of all the sounds made by infants, from the time of birth to the appearance of speech. McCarthy (128) says: "Obviously, it is quite impossible to take down the sounds as they are made by the infant in writing, in shorthand or in a phonetic system." She suggests two types of permanent records which could be made for a scientific study of the pre-speech sounds of infants: a graphic representation of the physical equivalents of the sounds made, and an audible sound record, such as dictaphone or phonograph records. The first method, with some such device as an electric-photographic record, is undoubtedly the most accurate, but the expense involved is so great that no research center has so far been able to undertake such a study.

The behaviorist interpretation (145) of the development of language is that the vocal habits of young infants become language habits by a process of association of sounds with arm, hand and leg activities, and then become substitutable for them. Watson (206) describes an experiment on one infant which illustrates the way this association comes about. An infant, six and one-half months old was allowed to nurse for a moment, and then the bottle was taken away from him. When the infant whimpered and cried, the experimenter said *da* and then gave the bottle back. After a few repetitions of this, the baby said *dada* instead of crying when the bottle was taken away, and it was then immediately given back.

Since it is impossible, within the scope of this work, to summarize all the literature on the development of language, Decroly's (49) excellent study, just published posthumously, is freely used, as also McCarthy's summary (126), and the *Twenty-eighth Yearbook* of the National Society for the Study of Education (145).

Decroly (49) states that there are three stages in progress toward spoken language: (1) the cry, (2) the babble or lallation, and (3) the transition from babble to imitation and expression. The cry is the sounds produced by the larynx. It has been interpreted as positive and negative emotional sounds, and as without emotional or intellectual significance, as a reflex effect which helps oxygenate the blood and is produced by the passage of air across the vocal cords. He says that crying is a preparation for language, in the sense that most of the organs used in language are involved in crying. McCarthy (126) quotes Major as expressing the same point of view: "What one means then by saying that language has its beginnings in these reflex cries is that much of the physical apparatus which is used in later speech activities is involved in the early reflex cries." This is the point of view adopted by the most careful workers at present, although Bühler (23, p. 25) believes that there is probably an affective element in crying, even at first. She says: "Even on the very first day screaming occurs in many situations which have a negative aspect." She also says, however:

The screaming which occurs from the very first day, is, at the start, a highly undifferentiated behavior. It is always closely connected with displeasure and other negative emotions, and, so far as it has meaning, it can be interpreted as negative.

That cries soon become expressive is recognized by all authors who have written on the subject. Decroly says that from the second to the fifth weeks a progressive differentiation in cries occurs, until the organic condition of the infant can be recognized from the character of the cry. These cries may be compared to verbal interjections, since they serve to communicate hunger, fatigue, wet, pain, and, later, a desire for change of position or a wish to be picked up. Cries of joy appear later than simple discharges of sounds of discomfort, which may be due, according to Decroly, to the fact that the cry has a biological significance in conveying the need for attention.

The Hoyers (89), who made a detailed study of the development of speech on their own child, say that the first sounds made immediately after birth were cries of great force, a long-drawn-out and very open *â*. They interpret this as an undifferentiated cry of displeasure, and state that it showed no change or shades. By the eleventh day, changes in the cry had begun as a periodic narrowing of the sounds to *nânânânâ*, but there was still no indication of any affective expressional differentiation. By the twenty-first day, a hunger and a pain cry could be clearly distinguished, and differentiation went on, especially in intonation, until the reason for crying was communicated with great precision. They observed that the *â* characteristic of hunger was given on other occasions also, and conclude from this that cries express a quantity, rather than a quality, of displeasure, in this case the maximum. They state that there was no further development of crying.

Decroly (49) states that the babble, the next stage of development, usually has no expressive value, but results from modifications of tension of the vocal cords, induced by the organs of articulation, the palate, tongue, lips and the changing force of respiration, which serve as obstacles to the sound. It is possible that the sounds are an expression of pleasure. He says that the mouth is the most precocious and delicate reactive agent of the sensori-motor mechanisms, and therefore a great variety of sounds are produced of varying intensity and duration.

Decroly states that the period of lallation, or babbling, begins very young, according to some authors. He believes that, on the average, it appears toward the end of the second month. Although this period comes later than the period of cries, the two overlap and the infant mixes the two types of vocalization, playing with his vocal organs and using them as a means of expression at the same time. The earliest sounds in babbling are among those which occur in the cries. The first sounds which predominate are *e* and *m* and especially the gutturals, *g, k, r*. At this stage, the influence of the sounds which the child hears is secondary to those he himself produces, as is shown by the fact that he makes many sounds he never hears and that exist in no language. Gregoire (71) also states that the young infant makes sounds which exist in no language, and believes that the dorsal position of the infant influences some of the sounds he makes—they occur because they are the easiest to produce in this position.

This seems to be the same stage which the Hoyers (89) call that of *quiet sensation sounds*. They observed these on their own child for the first time at one month and twenty days of age. They describe these sounds as bilabial, and blowing through the partially opened lips. At the end of the second month a new sound develops, which is made by changes in the intensity of expiration and a more or less passive mobility of the articulatory organs, the tongue and the lower jaw. A group of *ğ* sounds are especially common at this time; they are very varied, sometimes produced far back and sometimes well forward, depending on the casual position of the tongue and palate. In the third month, these sounds are often long drawn out, and a vocal stress or change of inflection ("arsis") is often added to them. The open *m* also becomes more frequent. These authors believe, with Decroly, that these sounds are a mild form of pleasurable expression. These sounds disappear toward the beginning of the sixth month, as expressions of quiet affective states, according to the Hoyers.

The next period, Decroly (49) calls the period of transition to imitation and language. The first imitations are of sounds which are the most frequent in lallation, *ma, pa, ta, da,* and these syllables redoubled. These sounds gradually come to have meaning to the child, and become associated with an object, an act or a desire, partly because they are like real words and partly because adults help the infant make the association by using them to the child. He believes there is a certain tendency for certain sounds to link up with certain kinds of meanings, and presents an interesting table of sounds which, from a review of all studies, seem to be linked with certain groups of objects or ideas. Some investigators have carried this theory much further than Decroly, suggesting, for instance, that one reason *mama,* or a very similar word, means *mother* in so many languages is that it is one of the very first doubling of syllables which occurs in all languages. Other authors disagree with this pointing out exceptions, such as the Slavic languages, in which *mama* means *father.* Decroly's middle position, that there is a tendency for certain sounds to become linked with certain meanings and that the adults' talk to the infant influences this, seems a tenable hypothesis. He points out, however, that this is in no sense the spontaneous creation of an individual language which investigators used to believe could occur. He, and most other writers, now state that a child never invents a language, but always learns to speak the language or languages spoken by the adults about him and learns no words which he does not hear. Delacroix (50) gives a few apparently authenticated instances of older children who invent a language of their own, but he believes that these are not true cases of invention, as the child can always talk and understand the adult language first. He states that the early sounds which come to have meaning for the child are not made-up words, but are simply emotional interjections.

According to most authors, babbling sounds become expressive in the sense that certain sounds become associated with certain classes of meaning, sometime between the sixth to the ninth or twelfth months. Imitation of sounds is going on at the same time as babbling and lallation, though it begins later and comprehension is essential to it. It is difficult to separate imitation and lallation, since the first sounds imitated are those which are within the vocal capacity of the infant, and these are the same sounds which he uses in babble play. The distinction appears to occur at the point at which the infant begins to associate certain groups of sounds with classes of meanings. Differentiation seems to go on during this period, in a way similar to the differentiation of cries from the generalized birth cry to variations which can express clearly to the adult the organic state of the infant. The difference appears to be one of level, rather than of process; the cries become expressive of physical condition or proprioceptive stimulation, and the babblings become expressive of the infant's relation to his environment as they differentiate. Before going on from this point to the appearance of the first actual words, it is necessary to review what is known about the development of language comprehension, since it is perfectly clear that the first words appear, not as imitations of pure sounds, but as definite attempts to communicate, and communication involves comprehension as well as expression.

Decroly (49) traces the development of understanding from the early reactions leading up to it. In the first month, the crying of an infant can be stopped by talking to him, the meaning of the words making no difference, only the tone. Singing, music and other sounds have the same effect; the stronger the noise, the easier it is to obtain the reaction. Under the discussion of hearing, we have seen that it is generally recognized by all investigators that the human voice is one of the very earliest sounds attended to by the infant. Later, differential reactions occur; among these are turning to the source of a sound and, later, motor adjustments on command or question. Waving bye-bye, playing pat-a-cake, and so on, are other reactions. These are learned through adults' making motions for the baby while giving orders. The baby does not understand the words, but is influenced by the intonation or sound of a particular word. Decroly compares understanding at this period to that of a good hunting dog. Gestures are understood before words and, when they are accompanied by words, it is natural that the words become associated with the gestures. It is difficult to tell the exact moment when an infant begins to understand words spoken without gestures and without an exaggerated intonation, but this can be tested for from the eighth month on by familiar questions. Understanding is always of things within the infant's capacity and experience, as it is for everyone, and it becomes more exact gradually from association of familiar gestures, intonations and objects with the words and the repetition of the same words in situations which interest him. Decroly points out that in training infants, words should always accompany acts rather than precede them. At first words are understood only when spoken by those familiar to the child, and then gradually when spoken by others. Concrete words are understood before abstract words. There is an interval between comprehension and speech. Comprehension comes first, but it is always of whole phrases, while the first speech is single words used as whole phrases.

The Hoyers (89) state that even during the first week of life, they observed that their child reacted to being spoken to by looking at the speaker, but that it is not certain that it was the sound that caused the reaction, as the child appeared attentive only when the speaker's face was held very close to the child's face and, on occasion, even very loud sounds failed to rouse the infant. By the end of the second week, the child stopped crying if spoken to and, at the end of the fourth, singing had a soothing effect. In the last half of the second month, the child began to turn and look in the direction of the source of sounds. On the twenty-fourth day of the second month, he began responding to the voice by making a sound himself; this was accompanied by movements of the arms and legs, and looking "intensely" at the speaker. During the third to the fifth months, these reactions increased, and sounds accompanied by smiles were frequent and developed into laughter. They state that during the third month the sound responses, especially to such sounds as *an*, *g* and *a*, are adequate imitations, but that imitation disappears at the end of the month, not to reappear until the eighth month.

Guillaume (73) also says that comprehension comes before speech, and that at first the intonation and cadence are important in conveying the meaning. In the eighth and ninth months, certain sounds begin to stand out for the child and bring a whole series of reactions, indicating that the meaning is generalized, not precise. Schaefer (174, 175) distinguishes between the earlier period of understanding, in which he says that it is not the sounds, but the intonations and the accompanying gestures and tones which are reacted to, and the stage of "pure language understanding." The latter, he believes, is always the result of training, apparently what most authors call the association of certain sounds with gestures and situations, until the sounds alone will call out the reaction. He says that the beginning of pure language understanding cannot be determined, as the child may have understanding before he is able to show it, and that the cases which seem to show an early age for it are undoubtedly those in which training has occurred. He experimented on "drilling language complexes" into one infant during the tenth month. Familiar objects and motions, taken from the child's spontaneous play, were used. The child acquired responses to nine drilled directions, and acquired three others spontaneously. He was able to distinguish between *banz* and *Schrank*. His conclusion from this experiment seems to be that in the ninth month, pure language understanding occurs only after systematic purposive training, and that even at this age what appear to be reactions indicating understanding of words, are really reactions to the accompaniments of speech, unless the infant has been trained. This training usually occurs accidentally anyway, and takes about three months to result in understanding.

The next stage in language development which Decroly (49) distinguishes, from his review of all the available data, is one of imitation of spoken language. Children learn any language they hear spoken about them, and they learn it by imitation. Within very narrow limits, a child cannot invent language for himself. At first a child can imitate only certain sounds. He alters these frequently, and little by little improves his language until he arrives at all the sounds and articulations of his native language.

He does not imitate exactly the order of sounds in a word or of words in a sentence. His repetitions are always more exact than his expression. Auditory stimuli are the chief element in eliciting imitation of language. The first words spoken are those using the sounds the child has already spontaneously used in babbling. The first words which occur are redoublings, repeating vowel sounds; next are syllables with the same vowels and consonants; then those with different vowels. These become words, those which are taught infants everywhere in the world by those around them. The next step in imitation is when the child begins to imitate new sounds. Mistakes are corrected, as auditory memory becomes stronger and more exact. A progressive elimination of mistakes occurs, with a selection of movements which bring about a sound similar to the child's memory of it. Then comes a stage of deferred imitation, when the child begins to use words not on immediate imitation and apparently also not by association. This is the moment at which the vocabulary begins to grow and the child begins to form phrases and sentences.

Decroly says that there is a difference of opinion as to whether imitation can precede comprehension or not. The consensus of opinion seems to be that imitation usually begins about the beginning of the ninth month, though it may appear later in some children, and a few authors claim to have observed it earlier. The Hoyers (89) state that at nine months their child easily repeated the sounds which he made spontaneously, but could not imitate new syllables although he tried hard and watched the lips of the speaker; in the tenth month he was able to imitate new syllables, but the reaction disappeared and did not reappear until the end of the eleventh month. Decroly concludes that auditory differentiation must precede speech and is a necessary element in imitation, and that development of comprehension and auditory perception are inseparable. He says that words do not have a purely tonal or musical interest for the child, and that he distinguishes only those to which he gives a meaning. Therefore, imitation cannot precede understanding, for function must not only be within the capacity of the individual, it also must serve some individual need or interest.

Decroly (49) points out that imitation of natural sounds and calls of animals is very common among infants, and that it is commonly encouraged by adults, but that it also occurs spontaneously. These onomatopoetic sounds take on the force of words and come to be used as names for the objects imitated. They are usually alike for the children of the same country and language, but practically the same sounds are found for some animal names in languages differing widely and in nations greatly separated. Delacroix (50) says that onomatopoetic names are common at this stage, but that in spite of the tendency to imitate sounds, it is not certain that these names do not come from adults. Decroly concludes, from all the studies he has reviewed, that there is some evidence that babies whose babblings are meager talk late, although there are a few records of cases where words are said correctly by infants who have not passed through the transition stage.

Decroly's (49) next stage, during which of course, imitation is still going on, is that of the use of the spoken language for the expression of ideas or concepts. He points out that this is the stage at which most studies of language development begin, but that the mechanisms involved are already highly complex and show variations in their functioning, with varying circumstances. Language usually begins toward the end of the first year, and the first words are those already used in imitation. These words are almost identical for all children and for all languages, and are made up of labial and dental consonants and the vowel *a*, *mama*, *papa*, *nana* and so on. He points out the close relation of the articulations involved in these sounds with feeding and the sucking reflex. The use of a word to express a meaning comes about either because a sound accidentally made by the child becomes expressive of a need and so acquires the value of a word (papa), or because a word long understood is finally reproduced. These first words never have an exact meaning to the child, but always express a need or a desire, and the word means all the acts involved in different situations, according to the immediate affective state of the child.

At this stage the pronunciation is never correct. The syllable which appears to carry the word meaning for the child is the one that is spoken, except for the simplest words, which are made up of doubled syllables already in the child's vocalization vocabulary. Diphthongs are said by some investigators to appear late, and consonants are confined to the gutterals and dentals which are being used in babble. The difficulties of recording exactly the sounds made, result in a difference of opinion as to those which do exist at any one stage. Holmes (88) reports on the record of the words of one infant for the first twenty-one months, by the symbols of the International Phonetic Association. He says that the first word occurred at one year of age, although a word was imitated unintelligibly at seven months. At eighteen months there were no intervocalic consonants. The few two-syllable words which occurred were said as if they were two words with a distinct break between syllables. He says that the final *k* was used but not *g*, and that the English *r* occurred only once. Guillaume (73) says that in the beginning of speech, an entire adult sentence is shortened to one word or to a syllable or a vowel, and that just as the reproduction of sound is not precise, so the meaning is not. The Hoyers (89) say that after imitation starts, intonation is rendered surprisingly well and accurately, and that the accent is almost always correct. Very often the unaccented syllables in a word are omitted. Sometimes the syllables preceding or following the stressed syllable are shortened to a single syllable and sometimes other familiar syllables with the same rhythm are substituted for them. In speaking single words, the vowel carrying the sound is usually accurately reproduced and the unaccented vowels are usually fairly accurately reproduced. The infant groups the consonants used into two distinct groups: those which are well rendered are, *k*, dental explosive sounds, *b, p, w* and nasal sounds; and those which are rendered, but not accurately, are the vibrants and composite consonants containing vibrants. These are also the sounds which are most frequently omitted. The Hoyers were interested primarily in lallation in making their study, but these remarks seem to apply to the earliest words as well.

Next the word comes to indicate objects and acts. It then

ceases to be purely affective and acquires an intellectual significance. It is used to indicate and differentiate. At about eighteen
months the child begins to realize that objects have names, and
at this point the increase in vocabulary begins. Next the child's
language begins to resemble that of the adult. The age at which
this occurs varies with the individual, and the phase often begins
suddenly.

At first the isolated words which make up an infant's language
have the force of whole sentences, since they represent a total
situation or affective state, that is, their meanings are complex
and changing. All investigators agree that the great majority of
these first isolated words are nouns. But Decroly (49) believes
that it is a mistake to make grammatical distinctions at this age,
since one word is used to express a total situation including the
objects, the actions and their affectional relation to the child.
Keneyres (104) also stresses this point. He says it is wrong to
talk of a noun stage at the beginning of speech, as at this time one
word expresses action, quality and place as well as name. The
grammatical differences in different languages cause differences in
the ages at which the same language skill in different languages
appears, although the infants may be at exactly the same developmental stage. Grammatical forms and words of relation are used
before they are understood; therefore the investigator should be
very cautious in drawing conclusions as to intellectual processes
from language responses.

The next stage shows the beginning of combination of words,
two or more being used together. Usually one word carries the
central idea and the other or others serve to define and emphasize it. Sometimes the combination has the force of a single sentence, sometims of a whole series of statements. The most common form of the complete sentence at this period is one composed
of a subject and predicate, though the grammatical form and the
intended meaning still have very little connection with each other.
In general, the combination of more than three words is rare
until near the end of the second year. Sentences in the adult sense
of the word are not used until the child is old enough to understand relational and grammatical words. This is a gradual devel-

opment, taking place as the child's experience enlarges, so that more and more exact shades of meaning need to be expressed. The intent or meaning of the sentence is always the important element, and form and inflections follow meaning. At the end of the second year, the average infant is just beginning to use phrases and short sentences, inflections are still largely absent, and the word order in the phrases has not yet become conventional. There is of course great variation in the language equipment of different children at two years of age. Apparently by this age the period of accelerated learning has begun, the vocabulary is increasing rapidly, and varied forms of expression are beginning to be used.

Decroly (49) goes on from this point with his summary of the data, but since individual variations are so great and progress is beginning to take the form of refinement in construction, greater accuracy in pronunciation, word sequence and word differentiation of meaning, the details he covers will not be given here. The literature seems to suggest that the normal child, in an environment where language plays an important rôle, is at the beginning of his third year approaching the point of adult skill in his verbal reactions, and that range of expression and skill in construction progress coincident with the widening experience of the individual. The extent of the accuracy of pronunciation at two years of age seems to be strongly influenced by the environment. Language is still almost completely concrete, and relational words and abstract words are still absent. Since language is the method of expressing intellectual concepts and is a symbolic function, it is extremely difficult to fix the point at which speech mechanisms proper have reached their adult form. Decroly constantly emphasizes the fact that language cannot progress beyond the experience of the individual child, and must grow out of that experience. As he implies, the development of skill in use of language as an expressive tool does not necessarily go hand in hand with the development of speech mechanisms proper. The bulk of the literature on the development of language deals with the period after the first word has appeared, and is concerned with the growth in intellectual concepts as shown by growth volume and grammatical complexity of language.

Shirley (180) did not test for vocal responses during the first year of life of the 24 babies she examined, but the examiner made notes of the vocalizations which occurred spontaneously. The examinations lasted only one hour and were held fortnightly; therefore she reports a wide range in the time of noting the first appearance of different items. Even so, she obtained a rough sequential picture, which held more or less for all the babies, of the development of speech. Some vocalization other than crying was noted in practically all the babies during the hospital period; a grunting sound appeared at a median age of six days. During the first three months, the spontaneous vocalizations noted were syllabic, an initial consonant followed by a vowel and sometimes closed by a consonant, such as *goo, boo, hm, aak,* and so on. The median age for this reaction was eight weeks. A few weeks later, a second syllable was added, *ungoo, elow* and so on. Vocalization became a social reaction sometime between the second and the sixth months. Expressive sounds similar to adult speech were noted at a median age of thirty-six and one-half weeks. From the fifth month on, each baby repeated the same syllable several times in succession. There was little variety in the repertoire of one baby, each one repeating the same sounds for the whole examination period and often for several weeks. At about ten or eleven months of age the babies began combining two or more dissimilar syllables, and jabbered these words in conversational tones. They then combined these syllables into groups of words, and talked in sentences as far as inflection and emphasis go. This type of vocalization was carried over and mixed with early comprehensible speech.

The median age for the first comprehensible word spoken in the examiner's presence was sixty weeks. Most of the mothers reported that their babies had a vocabulary of two or three words at one year. The first word used was usually a noun, and with these words appeared imitative words such as *bow-wow,* which seemed to be copied from parents or brothers and sisters. Only 19 babies were tested during the second year. Thirteen of these were using pronouns by the end of the year. Phrases such as *good boy, hat on, all gone* appeared at a median age of one hundred and one weeks, and at the same age sentences such as *I don't want to, I want it, This broke,* appeared. There were marked individual differences in the amount of vocalization and the ages of appearance of the different stages, but considerable consistency in the sequence. Grunting and playful babbling preceded the use of comprehensible words. Nouns, verbs, adjectives and adverbs occurred as first words, and pronouns not until long after. Combination of words into phrases and sentences appeared late in the second year.

Shirley found some slight evidence that early vocalization is held in check by rapid motor progress, and that babbling is a type of play resorted to when the baby has nothing better to do or when the novelty of a new type of motor activity has worn off. This impression is supported by the figures for the average and median number of utterances at the median ages for development of new motor traits, and the intercorrelations between developmental scores on fine motor, locomotor and vocalization items at various ages, and also by the examiners' observations of a lull in vocal play for a week or two before and after a new motor skill was established. Shirley's developmental scores of vocalization were only slightly related to her locomotor scores, were somewhat related to her scores for fine motor coördination, and were very closely related to the babies' scores on the Minnesota Preschool Test scale. She also found that a number of words were common to the vocabularies of many of the babies, and suggests that this indicates a community of ideas even at this early age.

The test scales include a number of vocalization items for infants under two years of age. These items, however, do not give a picture of the successive stages in the development of language, but simply serve to indicate the ages at which certain types of vocal responses may be expected, at least in the majority of children from an average American environment. Gesell (65) gives as a fourth-month item established for about three-quarters of the infants, simple sounds of vowel combinations. At six months less than 20 percent say *da-da* or some unmistakable equivalent,

and at nine months three-quarters do. Bayley (7) gives credit
on her scale if, during the ninth month, the infant says *da-da*
or successive repetitions of sounds equivalent to *da-da* or *ma-ma*.
Linfert and Hierholzer (122) found that 25 percent of the babies
they tested said *mama* or *dada* at six months, 94 percent at nine
months, and 91 percent at twelve months. Gesell found that at
nine months less than half the infants say one word in addition
to *da-da* or *ma-ma* and less than 20 percent say two additional
words. At twelve months practically all infants say three words,
about three-quarters say four, and less than 20 percent say five,
by eighteen months three-quarters say five words. Bayley
gives credit if the infant says two words spontaneously during the
examination at twelve months; this is in addition to her test for
the same month in which the infant is credited if he imitates
"several words, as mama, dada, baby, etc." Linfert and Hierholzer found that 47 percent of the infants they tested said more
than one word at nine months, and 64 percent at twelve months.

Gesell (65) places comprehension of, or motor adjustment to,
certain words as established in over half of the infants at nine
months. At this age the same number will wave bye-bye, or say
it or *hello*. Linfert and Hierholzer (122) give 20 and 56 respectively as the percentages they found for saying bye-bye at
nine and at twelve months. Gesell (65) says that less than 20
percent of the infants can repeat simple words on hearing them
at twelve months, and slightly less than half at eighteen months.
Bayley (7) gives credit for attempts to imitate words at twelve
months. Linfert and Hierholzer found that 6 percent of their
subjects were able to imitate *kitty* and *baby* at twelve months,
clearly and well. Gesell's other language tests apply to the *second*
year. At eighteen months, less than half can name one object in
a simple picture, and less than 20 percent can name two pictures,
can combine two words appropriately or significantly, and are
beginning to ask in words for things at table. At twenty-four
months, about three-quarters can name five to seven pictures, and
less than half eight to nine pictures; three-quarters can combine
two words appropriately or significantly; less than 20 percent use
pronouns; three-quarters can understand two prepositions, over

half three, and less than 20 percent four or five; less than half can grasp the idea of repeating instead of answering simple sentences and can repeat them, and over half are asking in words for things at table.

Bayley's (7) other language tests for the first year are credit for any vocalization in distinction to crying, and for a definite response such as turning the head, vocalizations, cessation of activity to the sound of the human voice, at two months; at four months credit is given if the infant responds to social stimulation with vocalizations; at six months credit is given if the child vocalizes eagerness while reaching for toys, and for vocalizations of pleasure and displeasure; at seven months if he says several well-defined syllables during the observation period and if he vocalizes satisfaction in obtaining an object or end for which he has striven; at eight months, if he gives vocal expression to recognition of his mother when she has been out of sight; at nine months credit is given if "during the observation period," the child vocalizes in an interjectional manner and if he listens with "selective interest" to familiar words; at ten months if he reacts to his own name or to a simple question like *where is the kitty* in a discriminating manner. In the second year she gives credit for talking in an expressive jargon, in the thirteenth month. Naming one object is a seventeenth-month test, naming two a nineteenth-month test, and three a twenty-first-month test. Naming one picture is an eighteenth-month test, naming three a twenty-first-month test, and understanding two prepositions is a twenty-fifth-month test.

Linfert and Heirholzer (122) say that 90 percent of the infants they tested attended to the voice at one month, 92 percent at two months, and 98 percent at four months. At six months 65 percent recognized their own names when they were spoken in a list with others, and 100 percent did at nine and twelve months. According to the reports of the mothers, 54 percent were asking for things by pointing or by naming objects at twelve months of age.

Kuhlmann (109) gives as a twelfth-month test repeating such syllables as *ba, dada, man, mama, papa,* and the spontaneous frequent combination of two or three syllables and trying to repeat with some success what is said. At eighteen months the child should be able to use some words clearly, such as *mamma, baby, yes, no, cat,* and so on, or to understand questions with gestures. At twenty-four months he should be able to obey commands, such as *catch the ball, throw it back, put the ball on the table.*

Bühler's (23) test scale, which was developed on German infants, includes few language tests. At two months she tests for reactions of displeasure when the examiner, who has been speaking to the child in a normal voice, suddenly changes to a growling tone, and for cooing sounds, occurring spontaneously. At three months she tests for a cooing or smiling response to the prolonged gaze of the examiner. At six months the child should respond to a sudden change from a friendly to an angry voice, by a change from positive to negative "expressional movements," and should attempt to imitate the sound of a drawn out and repeated guttural *re-re-re* spoken by the examiner. At eleven months the child is given credit for attempts to produce sounds similar to the examiner's pronunciation of such syllables as *mamma, papa, dada, lala.* In the third, and through the fifth months of the second year, the child should be able to obey a command such as *give it to me*; however, she provides for accompanying the command with an appropriate gesture. In the next three months, he is tested for understanding a direction not to touch something. In the last three months he should be able to carry out directions such as to put a watch to his ear, or to show the watch to the examiner. She gives no tests for vocalizations beyond the early cooing ones, and these tests for comprehension appear to be placed at rather advanced ages, compared with the reactions found in American children.

Figurin and Denisova (58) include some language tests in their scale, developed on Russian children. They state that at one month infants begin to smile in response to adults talking to them. They also state that until the end of the first month, the child makes no sounds except those of crying or sounds during restless movements. He then begins to make sounds while quiet. These are usually guttural, short sounds made in response to stimulation. Later he will coo for long periods without any stimulation. During the early cooing, the child usually uses only hard vowels, then he makes guttural sounds, next he combines the two. The next step is the use of the lips and the softer vowels in vocalizing, and later in the first year he repeats *sh* and *th*.

There is also a large body of literature on the development of vocabulary and grammatically correct speech, and of the sentence. Nice has made a number of studies on American children. He suggests (147) four stages in the development of the sentence: (1) single words; (2) early sentences; (3) three or four-word sentences; (4) complete sentence of from six to eight words. The first stage, which is common to nearly all children, lasts from four to nine months. In the early sentences verbs are not inflected, the less essential words are omitted, there is an excess of nouns, and from 20 to 60 percent of the sentences are incomplete. The three or four-word sentences appear at from thirteen to twenty-seven months of age, with the average at about seventeen and one-half months of age. The fourth stage is characteristic of the more advanced children of three years of age. In another study (146), he suggests that the single-word sentence may be divided into a period of slow growth and a later one of rapid vocabulary development. In a study (148), of the vocabularies of 28 children, he found that at one year of age the number of words used by 28 children varied from one to 24, with an average of 7; at 18 months, 53 vocabularies varied from one to 523 words, with the average still at 7, and at two years they varied from 5 to 1,212 words with an average of 328.

Blachly (12, 13) has summarized the published studies of the size of vocabularies at eighteen months of age, and added the data collected from her own observations of 51 children. The average number of words for the boys she studied was 59 at eighteen months, for girls it was 78 and for both, 69. Combining the reports of sixteen vocabularies published by others, gave the average words for 4 boys as 72, and for 12 girls as 105, with a combined average of 97.

Foulke and Stinchfield (60) kept a complete record of the speech development of 4 infants from the age of appearance of the first word to the end of the twenty-second month. The first word appeared in one infant at seven months of age. One infant began to talk in the eighth month, with conscious meanings attached to the words. At eighteen months, he used very plain speech for his age and three-word sentences. At the end of the twenty-second month, he had a vocabulary of 403 words, having learned 187 in that month. Another infant used 27 sentences in a twenty-four-hour observation period, confused *me* and *I*, and had a total vocabulary of 50 words.

Bloch's work is on French children and has been extensively used by Decroly in his summary. His studies were made on his own three children. The youngest (16) began to talk at seventeen months. She learned a word and repeated it constantly, practicing on it and confining herself largely to the words she was hearing. If a word disappeared for a time, when it reappeared it was pronounced not as before, but according to the level of pronunciation of the new words then being used. The acquisition of vocabulary of all three children was very slow at first; only a few words were learned in several months. One of the girls used only *papa* and *mama* for six months; at nineteen months she began to learn new words and knew twenty-four by the twenty-first month. After this slow period, he found one in which they learned so rapidly that it was difficult to count the acquisitions, and words were used without knowing their meanings. Vocabulary and grammar were correct before pronunciation. One-word sentences (15) were used first. Grouping words began when the vocabularies began to grow rapidly. He states that the use of word groups is a great step forward, as it shows the ability to differentiate words and give each a fairly exact meaning. The early groups were without expression of relation, or grammar, and were like the single-word sentences. The sentence is a complicated tool, of which the child does not become master without great and continued effort. The ability does not come through imitation, but involves continuous conscious effort. This effort carries him from the stage where he can understand and express only the main elements in a sentence, quite rapidly, to the stage where he can express varied ideas without any of the grammatical tools which serve the adult. Later, when the grammatical forms are used, the child often ignores

them in a spirit of economy, but he is quite well aware he is
doing so.

Gregoire (71) whose work was also on French children, states
that at eighteen months the child knows only a few words, and
at three years he knows several thousand, can use complex sentences, has command of inflections and can use language to communicate all his thoughts, needs and desires. The proportion of
nouns is large in the early stages of speech, decreasing to about
the thirtieth month. There is a corresponding increase in the percentage of verbs, adverbs and pronouns with age. Conjunctions
and prepositions appear late and show only a slight increase with
age. Sex differences, he believes, are slight and disappear when
mental age is kept constant.

Boyd (19) has made a study on English children of a large
number of sentences spoken by children during every-day, unse-
lected conversation. The sentences used at two years of age were
statements, 79.9 percent; questions, 2 percent; commands, 17
percent; exclamations one percent. The number of words per sentence at this age was 3.3. The percentages for the different parts
of speech were nouns, 49.2; pronouns, 2.7; adjectives, 13.6;
prepositions, 2.4; verbs, 22.3; adverbs, 7; conjunctions, 1.1;
interjections, 1.5. The number of prepositions, conjunctions, articles and auxiliaries used at two was only 3.4 percent of the total
number of words, as compared with 25 percent at three years.
Four further characteristics of the sentences used by the two-
year-olds were: (1) the frequency of elliptical construction; (2)
the amplification or repetition of a remark as first made; (3)
inversion of the usual order of words, which put the idea or object
first in mind as the first word in the sentence; (4) the very frequent omissions of grammatical inflection.

Stern (184) distinguishes five stages in the development of
language: (1) babble and imitation of sound forms, which we
have already covered; (2) one-word sentences; (3) awakening
of the consciousness of the object of speech; during this period
the vocabulary shows a great increase, questions as to the names
of things appear, one-word sentences are outgrown, and the vocabulary increases, first by nouns and then by a large addition of

verbs; (4) complete mastery of uninflected speech; (5) the period of the outgrowing of the purely "paralactic" sentence. He suggests that the infant passes from a name stage to an action stage in language, just as he does from a concrete to an abstract stage. We have seen, however, that a number of investigators point out that the first nouns are used to convey action, quality and total complexes of ideas within the child's experience, and that it is not, therefore, safe to draw conclusions as to the intellectual concepts underlying early speech.

Decroly (49) gives a summary table of much of the available literature, giving the proportion of nouns used at different ages, which indicates that there is a great preponderance even as late as the middle of the second year, and that verbs are just beginning to be used at that age, but that the other parts of speech are not far behind verbs in appearing. This summary does not show any marked differences in the proportion of nouns and verbs used at the same age by children learning different languages. Decroly gives considerable data on the appearance of the use of tenses, a mastery which must undoubtedly be easier in English than in most other languages for which development has been studied. At first verbs are used in the present indicative, the infinitive and imperative appear soon after, and the past and future and participles later; in general, past and future are usually expressed first by the use of auxiliary verbs, even in tenses which are inflected without them. There is a large increase in adjectives shortly after that in verbs, and investigators are of the opinion that the first adjectives are used in a personal affective sense to express pleasure and dislike. Adverbs appear in the young child's vocabulary in the next largest proportion, although exact concepts of time, space and other relational ideas are hardly developed by the end of the second year. The use of pronouns is just beginning at the end of the second year.

The use of *I* has been the subject of much speculation, as a number of authors take the point of view that its appearance indicates the first consciousness of self. Decroly points out that the child usually refers to himself by name or as *baby* before he uses *I*, but that this is probably due to the fact that those around him use these words in speaking to him and he can learn only those words which he hears, that is the use of his own name for designating himself for several months before the use of *I* may not indicate a lack of consciousness of self, but may simply be the result of the imitation which governs the rest of his early speech reactions. Articles are entirely absent in early speech, even after the child uses fairly complicated sentences, and if they occur are part of the word itself, according to Decroly, but he does not summarize any of the literature in English on this point. Prepositions apparently appear later than all the above classes of words—not until after the end of the second year. Conjunctions appear late also, in connection with the development of subordinate and secondary clauses.

Decroly gives an interesting résumé of the irregularities occurring in early speech, stating that in general a child's understanding is ahead of his expressive ability, since his intelligence is advanced over his command of the tools which its expression requires. Sensory or perceptual ability lacks refinement and is not sufficiently differentiated, and words are used as totals. Motor habits for the organs of speech are not yet established. Attention is in general necessary for expression and it is still not strong, sustained or understood. External motor and perceptual stimuli are still too weak for the infant to have an exact reproductive memory. The assistance which memory and understanding are to expression is still restricted by the fact that the number of ideas is greater than the number of words, and the speed of thought is greater than that of speech. These lacks or weaknesses bring about speech irregularities which are similar for all children everywhere. Parts of words are elided, especially the last consonants, often the first one, and often, also, the second of two succeeding consonants; this suppression effects several syllables in a polysyllable. One consonant is often substituted for another and less frequently one vowel for another. Economy of effort brings about a repetition of the easier sounds in a word, for others which are more difficult; these may be considered similar to the substitution just mentioned. Several words are often contracted into one. The place of sounds or syllables in a word is often inverted. Sounds in a word are often separated as if they made up more than one word, or are combined with the beginning of the next word. These mispronunciations often result in a single sound being used for a number of different words, and in familiar sounds being used for those not yet established.

Decroly also mentions a number of meaning irregularities in the use of words, besides these early ones which we have already covered. Children use a word to indicate other objects or acts which have a certain analogy to the correct meaning of the word, i.e., *mama* for a picture of any woman. Action words have a very wide meaning for the child, *give* for example may be used to mean both give and take. Words learned are used in new ways, as analogies of sound or sense suggest. Words are often used to mean their opposites, and certain sense similarities are sometimes expressed by the same word. Decroly's example of the latter is one word for heavy, hard and difficult. He also mentions the formation of a verb from a noun to indicate the use of the object, and the formation of nouns by the reverse process; and a variety of other grammatical inaccuracies resulting from the extension of familiar processes to new words, such as the inflection of ir-regular verbs as if they were regular, the use of auxiliary words together with the correct inflection or termination, addition of prefixes and suffixes by analogies with other words in which these are correct, and so on.

McCarthy has made the most careful and scientific studies of the speech of young American children and has developed her methods after a careful analysis of those used by other investi-gators. In a study (127) of language development of the pre-school child, she analyzes by careful procedure the sentence formation of 140 children between eighteen and fifty-four months of age. Although only two of her age levels fall within the scope of this study, her results will be summarized here since they are based on the most complete and accurate data available as to the development of this phase of language. Consecutive verbal re-sponses were recorded for each subject, exactly as they sounded to the examiner, during home visits, and only the comprehensible responses were analyzed. These responses were analyzed according to the length, the function of response in relation to environment, the complexity of sentence structure, and according to the parts of speech used, considering both the total number of words used and the number of different words used. Each of these analyses was studied in relation to chronological age, sex, mental age, parental occupation and age of the child's associates. The author was also able to make some observations on bilingualism. She found that, as indicated by the mean length of response, the hearing of a foreign language in the home does not seem to be a serious handicap to the child's linguistic development.

All the types of analyses showed a marked and consistent difference between the upper and lower occupational groups which persisted, although to a lesser extent when mental age was held constant. There was also a tendency for the girls to be advanced over the boys, as shown by all the types of analyses. The percentage of comprehensible sentences increased rapidly with age, as did the mean length of the sentences, with the increase more rapid at the younger age levels. Similar trends were found when the length of response was related to mental age. The children who associated with adults showed a much greater mean length of response than those who associated with other children. Fifty responses were secured from each subject and the time required to obtain these showed very little change with increasing age. The responses were divided into three types, "adapted information," "questions" and "answers." There was a marked increase in the number of responses of these three types with increasing age, but a relative decrease in the emotionally toned responses with increasing age. Analysis of the adopted-information category of responses showed that naming decreased with age, and remarks associated with the situation increased. There was a much higher proportion of adapted information and of questions at all ages among the children of the upper occupational groups than among those of the lower. There was a relative decrease with age in the proportion of responses that were functionally complete but structurally incomplete, and an initial increase in the proportion of simple sentences. The simple sentence with a phrase appeared late, but then showed a marked increase. The compound-complex sentence appeared late and was rare, even at the upper age levels. Omission of the verb was the most frequent type of omission, especially among the younger children. McCarthy comments that this is consistent with the predominance of naming among the younger children, and the large proportion of nouns found in nearly all studies. The subject was the next element in a sentence most frequently omitted, which occurred more often while the percentage of verbs in the vocabulary was increasing.

Decroly (49) states that all evidence indicates that language development is not regular. Growth is at first slow, then rapid and finally reaches a fairly fixed plateau, as measured by the size of the vocabulary. After two years of age, this curve seems to follow closely mental development as shown by curves from mental-test measurements. Language retardation is the rule among children who are backward mentally, and among those with retarded or abnormal auditory or motor development. Decroly believes that in general it can be said that language retardation is associated with motor difficulties, but that there are cases where environmental influences are so peculiar that development may take a very irregular course. He also discusses the normal environmental differences which appear to be associated with differences in language development. Besides the influence of learning different native languages and of high and low economic status, which have already been mentioned, he states that sex differences in favor of the female are generally recognized as existing, especially in age at talking and size of vocabulary, but that these appear to disappear with increasing age. Some authors have found that first children show a more rapid development than the younger children in a family. Studies on twins seem to indicate that language development is retarded, probably because communication between them is socially satisfying at each developmental stage and the stimulus to improve in order to communicate with those who are advanced beyond them is not so great as with a single child. He also devotes considerable time to the subject of bilingualism and concludes that a number of factors enter into progress made when two languages are learned at once, but that in general when English is one of the languages it shows a marked advantage over the other.

He also states that most of the detailed studies showing the association between language and motor development have been made on abnormal children, which makes it difficult to give precise evidence on the correspondence between normal development in the two fields. Two other studies were found which touch upon the relation of language development to development in other fields. Johnson (100) states from records of spontaneous conversation of children under three, in a nursery school, that vocal equipment is most frequently used while the children are engaged in motor activities. The sounds occurring were shouts, grunts, squeals and various or characteristic word responses to situations accompanying action. There was a tendency to employ markedly rhythmic terms and syllables or words with a regular beat or cadence. Phrases were repeated over and over again. Elation and satisfaction from new and varied uses of vocal equipment were shown. Questions were asked largely to establish social contact, not to get information. The subject matter of the conversations referred largely to the immediate personal activities and conversation. The language reactions and bodily activities seemed to be rhythmically related. The other study is by Hull and Hull (90), on the parallel learning curves of an infant in vocabulary and in voluntary control of the bladder. They found that the difficult early stages of talking of one infant coincided exactly with a plateau in the curve for bladder control, and that learning to talk seemed to interfere with the voluntary control of the bladder.

Summary

The literature on the development of human behavior from the time the umbilical cord is healed to the end of the second year, in spite of great unevenness and large gaps, gives a picture of the enormous growth and increasing complexity in behavior that takes place. During this period development progresses from the point where the infant is practically helpless, able only to perform the simple reflex acts concerned with the necessary visceral and respiratory functions for the maintenance of life and a few other reactions to external stimulation, to the point where some behavior patterns have reached the adult level of skill and most others are approaching that level. It is necessarily difficult to give a brief picture which would summarize clearly such complex and varied growth. The difficulty is increased by the way studies of the period have been made. The development of some patterns has been quite accurately worked out, while that of others has been very meagerly studied. With few exceptions, patterns have not been traced from the reactions occurring at birth to the fully developed form, and different investigators have studied the neonatal period and the later period. The method of tracing the emergence of differentiated reactions from total behavior is just beginning to be used, and the bulk of the literature is still concerned with but a single stage in the development of any one pattern, the appearance of a specific type of reaction, rather than with all the progressive steps leading up to and including the particular skill itself.

The postneonatal development of the special senses, with the exception of vision and hearing, has not been investigated in any systematic or scientific way. It seems probable that the controversy over the functioning of taste and smell mechanisms during the neonatal period might be resolved if the development of these senses in later infancy were studied. The literature on vision and eye reactions is large, but as yet we have no objective knowledge of the nature of the visual images of young infants, of the enlargement of the field of vision, of growing precision in focusing, or of the appearance of color discrimination. There is some evidence of a relation between the ability to sit up and an enlargement or an increased precision in vision. The visual mechanisms are apparently sufficiently developed by about one year of age so that development after that age may be largely in the nature of increasing skill from practice and an enlarging environment. In general, the visual skill of the young infant appears to be greater than was formerly thought, at least as far as fixation and following are concerned. Shirley (180) states that the development of vision and of the visual mechanisms go hand in hand and that both are complete by about two years of age, at which time a child can probably see all that an adult can. The literature on the development of reaching and prehension suggests that there is a relation between the perception of small objects and their manual control, but the point has not been studied, and the most that can be said at present appears to be that not until about one year of age does an infant prehend a small object without looking at it. Reactions to early visual stimulation with lights and bright objects indicate that the first responses are more or less undifferentiated movements of the whole body or of large segments, and are of a character which has led some investigators to call them negative-flight or dislike reactions. With increasing age, there is a limitation of the spread of the reactions and their apparently negative character disappears, leading these same investigators to believe that a tolerance or adjustment to strong visual stimuli develops with age and is fairly well established by about six months of age. There is also some evidence that the ability to distinguish familiar objects when pictured is not established until about the middle of the second year.

The literature on hearing is not so full as that on vision, but the results, at least for later infancy, are somewhat less obscure, since the relation between the comprehension of speech and the ability to speak is recognized as important. The first reactions to sound are of the same generalized character as those to visual stimulation and the same interpretations of their negative affective quality have been made. In the second month, apparently, sound stimuli become sufficiently localized so that the infant begins to turn the head and eyes in the direction of a sound. The literature is in general agreement that the human voice is reacted to specifically earlier than other sounds. The quality of sounds, as indicated by apparently pleasurable reactions, begins to be distinguished toward the middle of the first year. After that the ability to distinguish the meanings of certain total sounds, or some of their components, apparently appears, but the most careful investigators of the stages in the development of the ability to speak, point out that gesture and body movements appear to be the dominating factors in this discrimination. Imitation of sounds begins in the second half of the first year and is shown by interest in manual manipulation as well as verbal responses. By one year of age the child can repeat simple verbal sounds with fair accuracy, and from this age on auditory acuity, as measured by increasing accuracy in verbal responses, apparently develops slowly at first, and then more rapidly. It should be remembered, however, that in judging auditory acuity from verbal responses, control over the mechanisms for sound production is an important factor, and that as yet no technique for separating the two has been developed.

Motor development has been studied chiefly under two categories: postural control, and reaching and prehension. Postural control begins with control over the neck and shoulder muscles, progresses down the spine, with apparently a distal progress in limb control going on at the same time but slightly more retarded. There is variance in the reports of the ages at which the various stages of motor control, up to and including erect posture and walking, occur, and comparatively little work has been done dealing with the whole sequence. Shirley (180) suggests an interesting classification of different stages, with the related skills developing in each. The rest of the literature fits in, in general, with her observations, but it should be remembered that she studied only a small group of children and then for only an hour fortnightly, so that many of her details may need revision. The ability to creep, make progress on the stomach, and sit up, is developing at the same time that increasing skill toward the assumption of an erect posture is going on. None of the stages appear to emerge suddenly, but are the result of slow, progressive increments in strength and controlled reactions. Some of the literature mentions an exaggeration of movements which accompany the first apparently voluntary attempts to achieve a specific motor control. These movements appear to be greatly in excess of those necessary and spread more or less over the whole body, recalling vividly the total body reactions of the very young infant to specific external stimulation. Such detailed accounts as exist of progressing control of the particular act also suggest that increasing motor control takes place by a process of growing specificity and narrowing of the reactions to the particular body segments which can perform them most economically and efficiently, similar to the growing specificity which has been well established for reactions to specific stimulation. There is also some evidence indicating that in the earliest stages of the appearance of a new skill, a lull or lessened activity in skills which are already established takes place. This tendency appears to be more marked in unrelated skills than in those which are more closely related, that is progress toward sitting alone and toward creeping appear to go on simultaneously without interfering with each other, while a new stage in either may bring a temporary lull in verbal play or hand reactions. In the same way increasing skill in creeping and progress toward erect posture and walking with support, go on at the same time, and one skill is not given up when a newer and more difficult one appears. Even after walking has begun, an infant under stress will resort to creeping in order to gain a goal more quickly or simply, or in spontaneous play.

Investigations of the development of reaching and prehension are numerous, and a number of recent ones carried out by Halverson have worked out the details of the steps rather fully. The evidence indicates that the shoulder muscles are the first to come under control and that development takes place distally from the shoulder to the finger tips. Reaching toward objects appears before prehension, but accuracy and sureness are not established until after objects can be picked up and manipulated. Very small objects are not perceived and prehended until later than larger ones. Early prehension is palmar, and thumb opposition is the first use of the digits to appear. The grasp gradually moves out from the palm to the finger tips, and by one year of age the adult method of prehension is established. Halverson mentions the fact that the earlier type of palmar grasp is resorted to, even after this age, under emotional stress or when the motor adjustments involved are awkward or especially difficult. Adjustment of the body to assist in reaching is first a leaning forward of the body when sitting, although facial grimacing and mouth movements often accompany the earliest attempts to reach. Obtaining objects which are out of reach appears to act as an incentive to bodily adjustments to assist reaching, which involve attempts to creep and to assume an erect posture, and the presence of an object within reach appears to serve as a stimulus to reaching and grasping reactions which are almost, if not entirely, reflex in character. Shirley found that in the third and fourth months development of the reaching and grasping functions was going on almost to the exclusion of development along other lines, although progress in control of the upper trunk muscles is also going on at this time. Random movements, like those in the earliest reaching, occur for many months after accurate reaching is established, when an object or person causing pleasurable excitement appears before the child. This waving of the arms in the direction of the object is often accompanied by reaching or excited waving of the legs.

The cephalo-caudal direction of motor development, corresponding to neural development, is generally mentioned by all investigators of the progressive stages of any one phase of such development. However, among investigators of behavior this process is frequently referred to as if it included progressive development down the legs. Cephalo-caudal development, however, includes only the head, neck and trunk muscles, and the most careful observations show that, although control of the legs may progress distally just as that of the arms does, it does not necessarily take place after or as an extension of true cephalo-caudal development. An infant's use of his feet, as shown by grasping with the toes, pushing and creeping, appears to be well developed before, or at least by the time, the lower trunk muscles are sufficiently under control so that he can sit alone. It seems probable that some development of the legs is going on at the same time that the development of arm and hand reactions are taking place. The fact that the infant cannot stand or walk until after the development of the trunk is complete, may be due, not to immaturity of the neural mechanisms so much as to lack in length and strength of the lower extremities and lack of coordination of all the various mechanisms necessary to maintain balance and support weight in the erect posture.

One of the aspects of motor development which is only beginning to be studied, and which may throw considerable light on growth processes, is the presence at the reflex level of a number of motor reactions which are shortly lost. There is adequate scientific evidence at present to establish the presence of holding the head erect, sitting, crawling and stepping movements at or very shortly after birth, and that the reflex grasp is present at birth has long been known. Evidence on grasping is more complete than that on the other reactions and indicates that the reflex disappears as voluntary grasping develops and becomes established. Chaney and McGraw (21) found reflex stepping movements in newborn infants, and Shirley (180) began testing for these movements early in infancy. The reports of these two studies appear to show that reflex stepping occurs under suitable conditions until the child is able to walk. Nothing is known of the mechanisms governing the reflex reactions as compared to the emergence of the same patterns in a purposive or controlled form, and even the recognition of the reflex reactions is new. The careful tracing of the patterns from the reflexes present at birth to their controlled form, with special attention to the disappearance of the reflex reaction and the first form of the purposive reactions, would seem to offer a fruitful method of investigating total behavior patterns and the possible processes underlying them.

Since the purpose of behavior development is, for the organism, adequate adjustment to the environment for the support of life independently, the course of development of reactions which are in the nature of adjustment for the solution of problems, would seem to be a particularly interesting field for investigation. Studies of development in these terms are, however, very few and inadequate, and any information we have on the subject is drawn largely from observations on the development of specific patterns. At birth the only adjustments of which the infant is capable are simple visceral and respiratory reflex reactions, reflex sucking movements which enable him to take nourishment, and turning the head to free the nose for breathing when lying prone. It is possible that the reactions which regress, or change later, to the human form, such as the labyrinth and tonic-neck reflexes, and those which disappear at the reflex level about the time that they emerge in a purposive form, are atavistic hang-overs which served organisms lower in the phylogenetic scale in the same way that the meager adjustive repertoire of the newborn infant serves the human organism. The first adjustments which appear after birth are those to the feeding situation, and are first adjustment of the body and later the ability to hold a bottle and put the nipple into the mouth, and then to drink from a cup and hold it. These reactions appear long before any other adjustments of the environment for the solution of problems. Meanwhile, adjustments of the body for other purposes than feeding are slowly appearing, such as bending forward the body to extend the reach, some sort of struggling progression to reach lures, turning from unpleasant contacts and objects, and so on. According to Bühler (23), pushing away an unwelcome object and then trying to grasp and restrain it are among the earliest attempts to control the environment, starting in the fourth month. Late in the second half of the first year, the child begins to pull objects toward him by attached strings, to feed himself with his hands, and to try to imitate useful acts connected with his own person, such as pulling off his clothes, putting on a bonnet and so on, but his chief method of meeting situations which present a problem is still largely adjustment of his own body. He moves after things he wants and to escape from things that are unpleasant. It is not until the second year, apparently, that any extensive use of the environment for the solution of problems begins. After a child can walk, he begins to climb, and will first climb onto furniture to get desired objects, and later begin to move furniture about to get it into the desired position for climbing. The ability to open and close boxes to get objects and to manipulate any but such toys as rattles, does not appear until well along in the second year. The literature is replete with speculations as to the time intellectual processes begin and conclusions as to the emergence of intelligence. Testing for the appearance and methods of solution of problems, which are clearly such to the child, would appear to be a method of gathering objective data on the early functioning of the intellectual faculties. It is curious that the material used in testing infants is almost completely lacking in situations calling for a problem the solution of which has meaning for the subject.

Information on the development which takes place during the second year of life is meager and unsatisfactory, compared with data for the first year. It is confined almost entirely to the results obtained in formulating test scales, and covers the performance of complex tasks of increasing difficulty, rather than the progressive development of total behavior patterns. The one exception to this is the studies of the development of language during the second year. It is true that this is one of the most striking skills for which mastery is beginning during the period, but the available data indicate that marked advances in motor control, such as skill in climbing, running and management of the body in walking and manipulation of the environment are also going on during the period. Visual and auditory acuity also seem to be increasing, as shown by the appearance of the ability to recognize and discriminate pictured images and increasing accuracy in verbal responses. Studies have not been made by methods, however, which throw any light on the relative rôles of progressive maturity of the neural mechanisms and the varied practice furnished by a widening environment and accumulating experience. As behavior becomes more complex and as several different mechanisms are coördinated in the performance of a single act, it becomes more and more difficult to classify stimuli and responses as belonging primarily to one behavior pattern, and to distinguish between responses which are part of the fundamental behavior equipment necessary to every individual for the maintenance of life, and those which are the result of individual environmental or innate intellectual differences. In order to obtain behavior data sufficient to arrive at hypotheses of underlying growth processes, such classifications and distinctions are necessary. Before they can be made, more studies are needed which trace a single pattern from its beginning to its adult form, which cover large enough groups so that the common developmental elements can be distinguished, and which furnish data on the correlations between development in different fields. A beginning has been made in such studies for the first year, but nothing was found which threw any light on any of these points during the second year.

There is a general assumption in the literature that the kind of observation and tests which have been made for early infancy furnish at least a rough measure or forecast of intelligence. Most of the items tested for, however, are simple adjustments and reactions which appear to be common to all normal development, and data are yet insufficient to draw even any tentative conclusions as to the relation between normal development and future intelligence. Furfey, Bonham and Sargent (62) have reported on the correlations obtained for a scale of seventeen responses given to 62 newborn infants. The coefficients for the relation of the seventeen responses to one another

proved to be zero after certain interrelations involving specific parts of the nervous system had been eliminated. These results suggest that there is no mental integration in the newborn. Integration takes place during the first postnatal month and can be reasonably supposed to be conditioned by the maturation of the nerve tracts.

These authors do not give the data on which they base the statement that integration takes place during the first postnatal month, and it seems quite possible that it may grow in the same uneven but gradual way in which development of a single pattern appears to take place. Shirley (180) believes that she found some evidence of a relation between the first phases of postural control and walking. This seems a reasonable probability since, from the developmental point of view, one pattern, not several, is involved. Other authors, however, have assumed a relation between the age of appearance of walking and later intellectual ability. Although the point has never been studied objectively, the evidence presented by all the literature seems to suggest that there is nothing in this theory. Clearly it appears only reasonable that some genetic and developmental relation must exist between the different behavior patterns and their developmental course, but nothing was found in the literature giving any grounds for even tentative statements, at present, as to what these relationships may be. We can say only that development of any one pattern appears to be progressive and gradual, with probably latent periods, if not actual regressions, during which some other pattern is developing at an accelerated rate, and that development of one pattern does not go on to the exclusion of others, but that all are progressing simultaneously at different rates, with vastly different ages for maturity and with different periods of accelerated growth. By the end of the second year, the special senses are probably practically, if not entirely, at the adult level of maturity; motor development appears to be mature within the limitations of the small size and infant proportions of the body parts; and the individual has reached a stage of development where he is beginning to make adjustments for the solution of his own problems and to understand and use adult symbols for concrete objects. The intellectual functions are somewhat developed, as shown by the difficulty of tasks performed and the complexity of reactions. The rôle of the individual environment has already become a very important factor in development, as shown by the studies of the relation of language development to economic status and the evidence from the speed and ease of learning different languages. We have omitted all mention of emotional reactions and development from this survey, except as they were necessary to the understanding of certain studies. The literature, however, indicates that by the end of the period under discussion, social adjustments have begun, although the individual is still centered in his immediate environment and needs.

PART V

SUMMARY AND CONCLUSIONS

V

SUMMARY AND CONCLUSIONS

THE FOREGOING summary of the literature, since 1920, on the behavior of human infants during the fetal period and the first two years of postnatal life, presents in condensed form a great mass of data from which it is impossible to assemble a clear and conclusive picture of the total growth pattern or of the fundamental processes underlying it. The difficulties to be overcome and the problems to be solved before such a picture can scientifically be constructed are numerous, and many of them have already been touched upon here. In general, they appear to be of two kinds: first, those of gathering complete data by uniform, comparable and sufficiently objective methods so that results are free from interpretations made in terms of preconceived theories; second, the more fundamental one of gathering sufficient data on human subjects on the correlation between neural structure and its development, and behavior and its development.

Up to about 1920, the study of young infants was confined almost entirely to observation of a single baby for a fairly long period, with the emphasis upon the time at which different skills appeared. There were also a few investigations of specific patterns on larger groups of infants by careful scientific procedure. The great impetus to investigation of infant behavior which can be noted from about that date, seems to be due to two main sources: the development of scales for measuring intelligence, and the normal growth increments to be expected with increasing age in older children; and the great advances in the biological sciences, notably neurology and physiology.

Norms have been obtained by observation of the behavior of groups of babies and simple tests at stated age periods from birth on, which have proved useful in clinical practice as guides in judging the normality of individual infants. In general, these scales have been made from tests on much smaller groups of infants than are considered adequate for norms for older children; the subjects have been examined at intervals too infrequent to obtain a picture of the course of behavior growth, and the published scales do not report the exact methods used in giving the examinations or the exact kind of responses to be credited with sufficient accuracy to make the scales useful to others than their authors. Since these scales are primarily concerned with specific performance in relation to chronological age, patterns are not followed from their inception to their fully developed form, which greatly increases the difficulty of generalizing from the results, and even of comparing one scale with another. A more fundamental weakness of this method of studying infant behavior is that adequate criteria for selecting the significant items in growth increments, and for judging their relation to one another and to probable future growth are completely lacking and will be until the detailed course of each pattern and its relation to the total growth pattern has been worked out. From the point of view of this discussion, test scales and infant norms are significant only in adding something to the picture of infant behavior which is at present so incomplete and so little organized that all data are valuable.

The great recent advances in the biological sciences and the breaking down of the sharp line between psychology, and neurology and physiology which they have brought about, give promise of the accumulation of data which will eventually prove adequate for charting the development of behavior and the processes whereby it takes place. Methods of studying behavior and its specific patterns have made great strides in objectivity, in accuracy and in the quantity of results. As the literature shows, however, there is still a break between the fetal, the neonatal, and later periods of development, which introduces many questions and problems in interpreting data. Shirley's (180) consecutive study of 25 infants from birth, in spite of certain limitations in methods and equipment, has made an excellent beginning in bridging this gap. Bühler (23) has also contributed something, but her numerical results are presented in the form of a scale and her general discussion is so interpretive that much of great value in her continuous observations has undoubtedly been lost to other investigators. Halverson's work (76, 77, 78) at the Yale Psycho-Clinic has contributed the most complete data as yet published on the development of a specific pattern, reaching and prehension. Decroly's (49) posthumous volumes on the development of language present a similar picture of that pattern, but his data are drawn largely from a painstaking assembling of all the literature on the subject, rather than from a first-hand study by a uniform and scientific method. The literature also contains many reports of exact investigations of certain patterns at different age periods, but as the appearance of a certain degree of skill in the pattern is taken as the criterion for the ages for beginning and stopping the studies, they serve to fill in details at certain points, rather than to contribute to an understanding of total growth processes. The work at Ohio State University, if continued into the postnatal period, promises to furnish invaluable data on the differentiation and development of specific patterns from birth on. Tilney's work at the Neurological Institute of New York including, as it does, the correlation of structure and function on a phylogenetic series of animals, and the work of the Normal Child Development Clinic on the behavior development of a large number of infants from birth and of the effect of exercise upon development during infancy as shown in a study of a series of twins, appear to be the first attempts to cover all phases of the investigation of behavior as a coördinated unit.

The field to be covered is obviously so vast that all data are valuable. But investigation seems to have reached the point where progress would be more rapid if there were a greater degree of uniformity in methods among different investigators and centers. Some of the simplest methodological problems (for example the exact age covered by the term *neonatal*) are still left undecided, or are met differently by different groups. Each country and each center appears to follow out its own line of investigation and its own point of view, too little influenced by the work of others in the field. And above all, so little is known of the exact nature of the correlation between behavior and the development of neural structures, and so many investigators appear to work independently of even this little knowledge, that theoretical considerations unfounded on scientific evidence still play a large part in producing incomparable and confusing results. However, progress is being made and a few fundamental principles as to the development of neuromuscular and glandular activity of the human organism seem to be sufficiently established to furnish working hypotheses which may well govern investigation for some time to come.

Evidence from biology and neurology have established the fact that in its broad outline the development of neural structures follows the same course and operates under the same laws for all animal life. It is, therefore, the accepted practice to make analogies from the correlation of structure and function on animals, near man in the phylogenetic scale, to man himself. The acceptance of this principle has led to most of the marked advances in the formulation of theories of human behavior based on sound biological evidence. It is also generally accepted that the development of behavior follows, or is coördinate with, the development of neural structures. There are sharp differences of opinion as to the processes by which this mutual development takes place, especially as to the relative rôles of the environment and the innate neural matrix in controlling development. But whichever point of view is adopted, it is accepted that normal behavior serves to adapt the organism to its environment and that development goes on until the adult level of adaptation of the species is reached. It is also generally accepted that postnatal growth is merely a continuation of prenatal growth, and that birth itself brings no changes in the processes governing development. The acceptance of this point of view has led to abandoning the old distinction between instinct and learning, and both are now recognized as parts of a continuous process of development, occurring, if not brought about, through the interaction of the environment and the organism. The behaviorists retain something of the general concept of instincts, in that they postulate a minimum of unconditioned behavior which functions almost immediately at birth without, so far as was revealed in the literature, offering any suggestion that this minimum may be the result of conditioning in utero. In fact, they more than any other school, seem to ignore fetal behavior as an essential part of development. The Gestalt school of psychologists, while denying instincts, postulate a fundamental organization of the nervous system which serves to give the organism a certain very simple adaptation to the environment from the beginning. Among the experimental psychologists, the problem has shifted from one of instinct versus learning to one of maturation versus learning. Some, like Gesell,* hold that the maturation of neural structures brings about behavior growth, apparently practically independently of practice or the environment. Others adopt the point of view that appears to be generally held by the neurophysiologists that growth in structure and its use are interdependent, each reacting upon and stimulating the other, but that a certain degree of maturity of the neural tracts must exist before functioning occurs.

In general, the evidence for the all-or-none points of view is drawn from young organisms after the fetal period, and is based on investigation of some one pattern or arranged situation for a short age period, so that conclusions are made from what appears to be inadequate evidence and without taking into consideration all the possible variables. However, all the existing evidence seems to point to the conclusion that maturation is essential to growth in function, although it seems too early to state positively that it alone is responsible for development, or to decide whether growth or practice is the primary influence in development. The most careful workers seem to incline to the view that the two are but different faces of a total process, and that it is impossible to make too sharp a distinction between them. The evidence on behavior and Tilney's results (189, 191, 192) on myelinization of neural fibers suggest that one of the difficulties in the controversy has been the general assumption that growth takes place at all periods in exactly the same way, and that investigation of structure and function with special reference to the extent of neural organiza-

* See for example "The developmental morphology of infant behavior patterns," *Proc. Nat. Acad. Sci.*, 1932, Vol. 18, No. 2, pp. 139-143; "Maturation of infant behavior pattern," *Psychol. Rev.*, 1929, Vol. 36, pp. 307-319; "Maturation and the patterning of behavior," *Handbook of Child Psychol.*, 2d rev. ed., 1933, pp. 209-236.

tion at the time may reveal that this assumption is false. Tilney believes he has shown that, although reactions can be elicited before myelinization has occurred, in most instances myelin will have developed before the pattern reaches full maturity. Minkowski has traced the reactions to plantar stimulation from their earliest appearance in utero to the adult form, giving the level of cortical and subcortical control probably dominating at each stage. On the behavioral side, what is known of the tonic-neck and labyrinth reflexes, and Chaney and McGraw's work on the early walking, crawling and sitting reflexes, suggest that a similar scale of reaction and level of neural domination may be traced through the development of possibly all patterns.

Hilgard (86) has made a study of learning and maturation on two groups of ten children, two to three years of age, for the skills of buttoning, cutting with scissors and stair-climbing. While her subjects are older than those covered by this discussion, her conclusions are suggestive for younger infants. She says:

After the 12 weeks of practice, the practice group exceeded the performance of the control group on all the tests, but one week of practice by the control group was sufficient to bring the scores of the control group and the practice group to similar levels. The rapid relative gains of the control group are interpreted to mean that factors other than specific training contribute to the development of these three skills, factors which may be partly accounted for by maturation and partly by general practice in related skills. There is evidence from the learning curves of the practice group in buttoning and climbing that improvement is more rapid in the latter part of the training period, consistent with the accelerated learning of the control group at the end of the experiment.

Carmichael (29, p. 34), from a complete review of all the literature on the fetal behavior of animals and man, stresses the probability of the interdependence of growth and learning as follows:

from the moment that growth has begun in the fertilized ovum until senescence or death, development consists in the alteration of existing structures and functions in an organism living in a continually changing environment. That is, it is not possible save for pragmatic reasons to say at any point that growth has stopped and learning has begun, but that the environment plays a part in all "maturation," and maturation plays a part in all learning. The course of this development, however, is apparently almost infinitely complex. It cannot be summarized by any catch-word phrase. But it does seem that the suggestion that . . . even the first receptor-neuromuscular response of the organism is not to be considered in all respects a novel event follows directly from the knowledge that the organism develops in relation to an environment of energies. The processes which have gone on in the organism in order that the first response can occur apparently themselves involve elaborate stimulus-response relationships in narrower environments. . . . Thus it seems probable that the first activity of the total arc is both old and new. The processes that are involved are similar to the processes of its growth in certain respects, but when it acts as a totality new time relations, if not new polarities, are involved. Thus an "organismic" response emerges from more primitive activities. But the function is to be understood completely only if described in terms of the past history of the mechanism concerned and of the present stimulating situation.

These data and opinions suggest that maturation and practice may play different rôles in the development of a pattern at different periods, according to the level of the dominating mechanism, and that in the early stages of growth of a skill, maturation may be the important factor, while after the neural tracts are mature or nearly so, practice may play an equally if not more important rôle. It also seems probable that in order to draw conclusions on a strictly neurological point of this kind, the behavior tested for should be of a fundamental character concerned with an act essential to the normal adaptation of all infants for the common environment, and that the training period should begin before the skill has begun to emerge spontaneously, and should be carried on until the adult level of achievement is reached, with the control subjects under observation for an equal period.

Evidence from human fetal material is very meager. This fact, plus the fact that the fetus has a comparatively simple and very restricted environment to adapt to, makes the available picture of behavior during this period seem clear and simple. It is generally agreed by those who have worked on animals and on human material, that some reactions take place before there is any participation by the nervous system and that the aneural phase gradually and unevenly gives way to a neural phase in which the reactions are diffuse, body-wise and uncoördinated, with any affector segment serving as a reflexogenous zone for any reaction. Gradually responses become less diffuse, with a lessening of the reactions in the segments furthest from the stimulated point. There is evidence of fatigability in the fetal period, as shown by the tendency of responses to become weaker with repeated stimulation, indicating that the inhibitory mechanisms are little developed. The differentiation and organization of responses which occurs before birth, is largely that of the proprioceptive reactions concerned with alimentation and respiration, and responses to specific muscle, skin and tendon stimulation. There is evidence, chiefly from analogy from animal studies, that the effector nerve tracts function before the affector, which tends to support the Gestalt and organismic concepts of growth processes.

Birth, with its change from life in a restricted liquid environment to that in the air with its varied and changing stimuli, brings no marked or sudden access in behavior. Even the special senses, which are probably not capable of stimulation in utero, do not spring into full-fledged use, but responses differentiate slowly from the body-wide, uncoördinated type of responses which occur in utero. The comparative evidence on structure and functioning of the sensory mechanisms supports the hypothesis that maturation and practice go hand in hand, as there is a great acceleration in the deposit of myelin in the sensory tracts shortly after birth.

With the exception of the specific reactions necessary for nourishment and respiration, behavior continues to be body-wide and uncoördinated for some time after birth. Purposive adaptive behavior differentiates slowly and unevenly out of this early mass activity, from the generalized to the specific. There is evidence, established from studies of the animal and human fetal period and of neurological development, that differentation begins as early as the first two weeks of life and continues to proceed in the cephalo-caudal and proximodistal directions. Animal studies have shown that this progression in growth includes the head and trunk, and that development of the appendages occurs concurrently and distally. The literature on human behavior frequently assumes that development of the lower limbs takes place in a continuum after control of the caudal region is established. This is a confusing misreading of the physiological evidence, and the term *cephalo-caudad* should be given its precise meaning, head to tail, not head to feet. There is also some evidence that development takes place anteriorly-posteriorly.

As a controlled response develops from the early mass activity, there is an excess of movements over that necessary to achieve a successful directed act. Controlled reactions develop slowly from this excess random activity, apparently by a process of elimination of the unnecessary movements. Halverson's studies of reaching and prehension furnish an excellent picture, in one pattern, of the progress of this increasing control and elimination. Descriptions of the details of the early stages of other patterns indicate that this same process operates for all, although few patterns have been studied in sufficient sequential detail to work out the various steps of increasing control. The general practice in the literature is to mention that a great excess of movements occurs in the early stages of a new skill, without recognizing the similarity between such movements and the early, general mass activity. Theoretical discussions of the behaviorists claim that control develops through the fact that a chance successful movement, occurring as part of the total mass activity, brings satisfaction or pleasure to the organism and so tends to dominate over the unsuccessful or random movements. Other discussions again suggest the interaction of the environment and the organism —that control develops by a process of increasing maturity in the neural tracts, for which some purposive exercise is undoubtedly necessary and which in turn brings about an increasing specificity in response.

The developmental significance of the group of reflex reactions which are present, before and for some time after birth, but which disappear later, is only just beginning to be recognized. The tonic-neck, labyrinth and grasping reflexes have long been known, and it is generally accepted that they disappear at about the time that the purposive form of these reactions appears. All these reflexes serve a useful purpose to the young of some species in the mammalian scale. The tonic-neck and labyrinth reflexes tend to keep the animal in its normal upright position; the clasping reflex enables the animal to cling to the hairy coat of its mother; the sucking reflex enables the animal to feed, and so on. There is another group of such reflexes in man which is only beginning to be investigated. The presence of crawling and stepping reflexes very shortly after birth has been commented upon by some authors. The work of Chaney and McGraw (31) on a small group of infants under half an hour old and on a large group during the neonatal period, has recently shown that the stepping reflex is so common as to justify the statement that it is normally present at birth, and that there are other postural and locomotor reflexes of an atavistic or animal hang-over nature that are also present. The published results of these authors cover an erect head reflex, a sitting, and a crawling reflex, as well as the stepping, and their unpublished results, a swimming reflex. Like the grasping reflex, these disappear some time after birth, to emerge later in the voluntary form leading to the adult reaction. Discovery of the neural mechanisms which govern these reactions at the reflex level, as compared with those governing the later purposeful or voluntary reactions, would obviously throw light upon the processes by which growth takes place. Here again even such meager data as are available suggest that growth is not a total and uniform neural development, but that control is exercised at different levels at different times for different patterns. It is significant that the unpublished records of Chaney and McGraw's work indicate that as the reflex is lost, there follows a period of random, uncoördinated, purposeless activity similar to the early mass activity, and that the controlled adult form of the pattern appears to develop from this, just as early patterns do.

The sequential studies of the behavior of groups of infants, the studies of the development of a single pattern, and the test items in the scales for successive levels of performance in a skill, all point to the fact that development is gradual and continuous for the totality of behavior, but that single patterns develop at uneven and discontinuous rates. The fact of regression, or latency in growth, of neural tracts has been established, and growth in behavior appears to take a similar course. There is some evidence, in the studies of behavior summarized here, that at the time of the appearance of a new skill there is regression or a latent period in those already fully or partially developed. For example, Shirley (180) noticed a lull in the development of manipulation during the period that her subjects were making rapid progress in the gross motor skills of sitting and creeping. Thompson (190) has made a study of the variations in infant behavior in relation to growth increments, as seen in daily ten-minute observations of the spontaneous and stimulated play of one infant with ten one-inch cubes from twenty-four to seventy-nine weeks of age. She concludes that growth in behavior proceeds fully as rapidly as physical growth.

The growth increment is in different functions on successive days but may be in more than one function on the same day. The behavior growth increment manifests itself in: (1) the greater frequency in one item of behavior; (2) the improved performance of an activity; (3) the appearance of a new activity; and (4) the integration of previous activities. Some items of behavior are permanent, others are transient. Transient behavior may have as great or greater significance concerning the stage of growth as more permanent behavior. When the infant is apparently regressing in behavior, it does not respond in a more immature manner but occupies itself with a functionally more confined repertoire but yet characteristic of its age.

Shirley (181) concludes from the results of her sequential study that there is some evidence that traits emerge suddenly, and states that this lends support to the maturation theory. A careful study of her own published results, however, does not appear to support this conclusion. Her material has been extensively used throughout this summary, and reference to it indicates that her own data frequently illustrate the gradual emergence of traits. This is particularly striking in the carefully worked-out sequence of stages she presents for the development of erect posture and locomotion, and she specifically mentions the details during a period of improvement after the appearance of walking alone. Other investigators also mention the fact that after the appearance of walking alone, creeping is still resorted to as the easiest method of attaining a goal, and that at first walking

appears to be accompanied by a conscious effort and is apparently
voluntarily practiced. The literature on the development of vision
and eye reactions seems to point quite conclusively to a gradual
development. Clearly with any individual, there will be a moment
when an act is for the first time successfully performed, reaching
and grasping a lure for example. But Shirley's own account of
her observation states that this is preceded by a period of random
waving in the direction of an object and that, even after objects
are occasionally grasped, unsuccessful attempts frequently occur.
Halverson (76, 77) has shown that after successful reaching is
established, the movements involved go through a long period
of improvement in preliminary adjustment, aim and economy of
effort and movements, and that the grasp goes through an equally
long period of development from the early palmar grasp to the
adult form of digital prehension. When one stage of a pattern
is studied, or when talking, walking and so on are considered
only from the time of appearance of the first successful performance, as has been so frequently done, it may be possible to assume
that emergence of traits is sudden, but when responses are
observed from birth on, all the evidence seems to point to the fact
that any one response is preceded by various more primitive
stages, and is subject to improvement and to periods of latency
or regression during which it is comparatively little exercised, or
a more primitive form is used.

So far as is revealed in the literature, we do not have adequate
data on the relation between body growth and the development
of skills. It is evident that the strength of the muscles and the
relative proportions of certain bone lengths must play a large
rôle in the development of locomotion, and it seems possible that
for certain patterns physical growth may be as important a factor
as neural development. Gotcu and Variot emphasize the fact that
muscular strength, as well as the ability to coördinate the body
segments involved, is necessary to the emergence of walking. But
in general, the extent to which development along one line is
dependent upon muscular and bone growth is a neglected field.

Almost no work has been done on the interrelation in the
development of different patterns. Gesell (65) makes the state-

ment that the age of walking has a connection with future intellectual development, but does not present his evidence to support this, in normal children. Shirley (180) worked out the sequence of steps in gross motor development, and found that as far as her 25 subjects were concerned, there was very little skipping or transposition of steps in the order of appearance of the different stages, but that a definite sequence held in its general outlines for all the subjects. She also found ratios between the time of appearance of some of the stages leading up to walking and the time of walking. She concludes, however, from her point scores, developmental curves, intercorrelations, and correlations of her data with two test scales that, at the time of emergence of a skill, it is little integrated with other skills, and that integration begins in the second year. The literature on language development emphasizes the interrelation between the development of verbal comprehension and the use of words; and the connection between skill in reaching, manipulation, prehension and eye coordination is generally recognized. But aside from Shirley's work and the general recognition that such patterns as speech and manipulation involve more than one skill, nothing was found in the literature on this important point.

Although the relation between development in different traits has not been studied, the literature indicates definitely that, as we have said above, development of different skills goes on concurrently, and that, although there is apparently a lull in the use of old skills at the time that the new one is emerging, patterns overlap and dovetail into one another. Halverson (77) found that his subjects reverted to an early form of prehension in situations where the reach or grasp was difficult. As we have seen, there is frequent mention of the fact that the appearance of a new order of skill in locomotion does not bring an immediate cessation of the method used before its appearance. The new order appears to be practiced with some degree of consciousness and with considerable excess effort for some time, while the old order is used to achieve an immediate goal, to solve a problem, or under emotional stress. It is perhaps also pertinent to note in this connection that mass activity appears to persist in situations with a strong emotional element, after it has otherwise largely disappeared. All students of total infant behavior mention the fact that pleasurable excitement, or the presence of a desired object just out of reach, elicit body-wide, generalized movements and especially random waving of the arms and legs, up to the end of the first year. These data again suggest that the mechanisms controlling behavior may operate by different methods at different levels of control.

In conclusion, a summary of all the literature on infant behavior indicates that it is impossible as yet to give an adequate picture of the total course of development of single patterns to their adult level, to give the interrelations between the different patterns, or even definitely to state that the evidence conclusively supports any one of the current theories of behavior. The tendency at present is to discard *in toto* the older reflex-arc and behaviorist theories, and to support a Gestalt or organismic concept of growth processes, with great emphasis on the rôle of maturation of the nervous system. A careful perusal of all the evidence and a recognition of the great gaps that still exist in our knowledge of the correlation of structure and function suggest that the pendulum may have swung too far in this direction, and that complete data will eventually show that there is truth in both points of view. The individual is a unit, as is his environment. His nervous matrix may well have a total organization suited to adaptation to the environment, while within that organization a variety of processes may operate to bring about development. With a greater understanding of the way by which specific behavior differentiates from the original mass activity, localization of function, the reflex arc, and practice may prove to play their rôles in development of neuromuscular activity, which has a fundamental unitary activity and integration.

BIBLIOGRAPHY

1. ALDRICH, C. A. A new test for hearing in the new born. *Am. J. Dis. Child.*, 1928, Vol. 35, pp. 36-37.
2. ANGELIS, F. DE. Reflexes of the new-born. *Am. J. Dis. Child.*, 1923, Vol. 26, pp. 211-215.
3. ANGULO Y GONZALES, A. W. The motor-cell columns of the albino rat before birth. *Anat. Rec.*, 1929, Vol. 42, p. 17.
4. ———— The motor nuclei in the cervical cord of the albino rat at birth. *J. Comp. Neurol.*, 1927, Vol. 43, pp. 115-142.
5. ARMSTRONG, E. M., and L. C. WAGONER. The motor control of children as involved in the dressing process. *J. Genet. Psychol.*, 1928, Vol. 35, pp. 84-97.
6. BAUER, J. Das Kriechphänomenon des Neugeborenen. *Klin. Wchnschr.*, 1926, Vol. 5, pp. 1468-1469.
7. BAYLEY, N. Mental growth during the first three years: a developmental study of 61 children by repeated tests. *Genet. Psychol. Monog.*, 1933, Vol. 14, pp. 1-92.
8. BEASLEY, W. C. Visual pursuit in 109 white and 142 negro newborn infants. *Child Develop.*, 1933, Vol. 4, pp. 106-120.
9. BEAUMONT, H., and H. HETZER. Spontane Zuwendung zu Licht und Farbe im ersten Lebensjahr. *Ztsch. f. Psych. u. Physiol. d. Sinnesorg.*, Vol. 113, pp. 239-267.
10. BERSOT, H. Développement réactionnel et réflexe plantaire du bébé né avant terme à celui de deux ans. *Schweiz. Arch. f. Neurol. u. Psychiat.*, 1920, Vol. 7, pp. 212-239; 1921, Vol. 8, pp. 47-74.
11. ———— Variabilité et correlations organiques. Nouvelle étude du réflexe plantaire. *Schweiz. Arch. f. Neurol. u. Psychiat.*, 1918, Vol. 4, pp. 277-323; 1919, Vol. 5, pp. 305-324.
12. BLACHLY, M. E. O. A comparison of the sizes of the vocabularies of fifty children of the same age. *Proc. Okla. Acad. Sci.*, 1923, Vol. 3 (Univ. Okla. Bull., N. S. No. 271), pp. 151-155.
13. ———— Further notes on eighteen-month vocabularies. *Proc. Okla. Acad. Sci.*, 1922, Vol. 2 (Univ. Okla. Bull., N. S. No. 247), pp. 106-108.
14. BLANTON, M. G. The behavior of the human infant during the first thirty days of life. *Psychol. Rev.*, 1917, Vol. 24, pp. 456-483.
15. BLOCH, O. La phrase dans le langage de l'enfant. *J. de Psychol.*, 1924, Vol. 21, pp. 18-43.

16. ——— Les premiers stades du langage de l'enfant. *J. de Psychol.*, 1921, Vol. 18, pp. 593-712.

17. BLOUNT, W. P.   Studies of the movements of the eyelids of animals: blinking. *Quart. J. Exper. Physiol.*, 1927-28, Vol. 18, pp. 111-125.

18. BOLAFFIO, M., and G. ARTOM.   Richerche sulla fisiologia del sistema nervosa del feto umano. *Arch. di sc. biol.*, 1924, Vol. 5, pp. 457-487.

19. BOYD, W.   The development of sentence structure in childhood. *Brit. J. Psychol.*, 1927, Vol. 17, pp. 181-191.

20. BRAINARD, P.   Some observations on infant learning and instincts. *Pedag. Sem.*, 1927, Vol. 34, pp. 231-254.

21. BRUDZINSKI, J.   Un signe nouveau sur les membres inferieures dans les meningites chez les enfants. *Arch. de med. des enfants*, Vol. 12, pp. 745-752.

22. BRYAN, E. S.   Variations in the responses of infants during the first ten days of post-natal life. *Child Develop.*, 1930, Vol. 1, pp. 56-77.

23. BÜHLER, C.   The first year of life. New York: John Day Co., 1930. x + 281 pp.

24. BURNSIDE, L. H.   Coördination in the locomotion of infants. *Genet. Psych. Monog.*, 1927, Vol. 2, pp. 283-372.

25. BURR, C. W.   The reflexes in early infancy. *Am. J. Dis. Child.*, 1921, Vol. 21, pp. 529-533; *Brit. J. Child Dis.*, 1921, Vol. 18, pp. 152-153.

26. CAMERON, H. C.   Suction difficulties of young infants. *Lancet*, 1922, Vol. 1, pp. 936-938.

27. CANESTRINI, S.   Über das Sinnesleben des Neugeborenen (Nach physiologischen Experimenten). Berlin: Springer, 1913. iv + 104 p.

28. CARLSON, A. J., and H. GINSBURG.   The tonus and hunger contractions of the stomach of the newborn. *Am. J. Physiol.*, 1915, Vol. 38, pp. 29-32.

29. CARMICHAEL, L.   Origin and prenatal growth of behavior. *Handbook of Child Psychol.*, edit. by Carl Murchison. Worcester, Mass.: Clark Univ. Press, 1933, pp. 31-159.

30. CASTNER, B. M.   The development of fine prehension in infancy. *Genet. Psychol. Monog.*, 1932, Vol. 12, pp. 105-193.

31. CHANEY, L. B., and M. B. McGRAW.   Reflexes and other motor activities in newborn infants: a report of 125 cases as a preliminary study of infant behavior. *Bull. Neurol. Inst. New York*, 1932, Vol. 2, pp. 1-56.

32. COGHILL, G. E. Correlated anatomical and physiological studies of the growth of the nervous system of Amphibia. I. The afferent system of the trunk of Amblystoma. *J. Comp. Neurol.*, 1914, Vol. 24, pp. 161-233.

33. COGHILL, G. E. Correlated anatomical and physiological studies of the growth of the nervous system of Amphibia. II. The afferent system of the head of Amblystoma. *J. Comp. Neurol.*, 1916, Vol. 26, pp. 247-340.

34. —— Correlated anatomical and physiological studies of the growth of the nervous system of Amphibia. III. The floor plate of Amblystoma. *J. Comp. Neurol.*, 1924, Vol. 37, pp. 37-69.

35. —— Correlated anatomical and physiological studies of the growth of the nervous system of Amphibia. IV. Rates of proliferation and differentiation in the central nervous system of Amblystoma. *J. Comp. Neurol.*, 1924, Vol. 37, pp. 71-119.

36. —— Correlated anatomical and physiological studies of the growth of the nervous system of Amphibia. V. The growth of the pattern of the motor mechanism of *Amblystoma punctatum*. *J. Comp. Neurol.*, 1926, Vol. 40, pp. 47-94.

37. —— Correlated anatomical and physiological studies of the growth of the nervous system of Amphibia. VII. The growth of the pattern of the association mechanism of the rhombencephalon and spinal cord of *Amblystoma punctatum*. *J. Comp. Neurol.*, 1926, Vol. 42, pp. 1-16.

38. —— Correlated anatomical and physiological studies of the growth of the nervous system of Amphibia. VIII. The development of the pattern of differentiation in the cerebrum of *Amblystoma punctatum*. *J. Comp. Neurol.*, 1928, Vol. 45, pp. 227-247.

39. —— Correlated anatomical and physiological studies of the growth of the nervous system of Amphibia. IX. The mechanism of association of *Amblystoma punctatum*. *J. Comp. Neurol.*, 1930, Vol. 51, pp. 311-375.

40. —— Correlated anatomical and physiological studies of the growth of the nervous system of Amphibia. X. Corollaries of the anatomical and physiological study of Amblystoma from the age of earliest movement to swimming. *J. Comp. Neurol.*, 1931, Vol. 53, pp. 147-168.

41. —— The development of the movement of the hind leg of Amblystoma. *Proc. Soc. Exper. Biol. & Med.*, 1929, Vol. 27, pp. 74-75.

42. —— The early development of behavior in the Amblystoma and in man. *Arch. Neurol. & Psychiat.*, 1929, Vol. 21, pp. 989-1009.

43. COGHILL, G. E. The genetic interrelation of instinctive behavior and reflexes. *Psychol. Rev.*, 1930, Vol. 37, pp. 264-266.

44. —— Individuation versus integration in the development of behavior. *J. Genet. Psychol.*, 1930, Vol. 3, pp. 431-435.

45. CORONIOS, J. D. The development of behavior in the fetal cat. *Genet. Psychol. Monog.*, 1933, Vol. 14, pp. 283-386.

46. COTELESSA, M. La motilita riflessa del neo-nato e del lattante. *Lattante*, 1931, Vol. 9, pp. 707-737; Vol. 10, pp. 761-790.

47. DAVENPORT, C. The growth of the human foot. *Am. J. Phys. Anthrop.*, 1932, Vol. 17, pp. 167-211.

48. DE BRUIN, M. Over het verschijnsel van Babinski en soortgelijke reflexen bij zeer jonge kinderen. *Nederl. tijdschr. v. geneesk.*, 1928, Vol. 72, pp. 3002-3027. (*Child Dev. Abs.*, 1929, Vol. 3, No. 143.)

49. DECROLY, O. Comment l'enfant arrive à parler. *Cahiers de la Centrale* (Centrale du P.E.S. de Belgique), Vol. 8, Nos. 1-2, pp. 1-306.

50. DELACROIX, H. L'Activité linguistique de l'enfant. *J. de psychol. norm. et path.*, 1924, Vol. 21, pp. 4-17.

51. DENNIS, W. The role of mass activity in the development of infant behavior. *Psychol. Rev.*, 1932, Vol. 39, pp. 593-595.

52. —— Two new responses of infants. *Child Develop.*, 1932, Vol. 3, pp. 362-363.

53. DUDLEY, D., DUNCAN, D., and E. SEARS. A study of the development of motor coördination in an infant between the ages of 58 and 67 weeks. *Child Develop.*, 1932, Vol. 3, pp. 82-86.

54. EAST, E. W. An anatomical study of the initiation of movement in rat embryos. *Anat. Rec.*, 1931, Vol. 50, pp. 201-212.

55. ECKSTEIN, A., and H. PAFFRATH. Bewegungsstudien bei frühgeborenen und jungen Säuglingen. *Ztschr. Kinderh.*, 1928, Vol. 46, pp. 595-610.

56. FELDMAN, W. M. The nature of the plantar reflex in early life and the causes of its variations. *Am. J. Dis. Child.*, 1922, Vol. 23, pp. 1-40.

57. —— Principles of ante-natal and post-natal child physiology, pure and applied. London and New York: Longmans, Green, 1920. xxvii + 694 pp.

58. FIGURIN, N., and M. DENISOVA. Stages of development of behavior of the infant from birth to one year. Problems of genetic reflexology and infant pedology. Leningrad: Institute for Brain Study, 1929, pp. 19-89. (Unpublished translation.)

59. FORBES, M. H. S., and H. B. FORBES. Foetal sensory reactions-hearing. *J. Comp. Psychol.*, 1927, Vol. 7, pp. 353-355.

60. FOULKE, K., and S. M. STINCHFIELD. The speech development of four infants under two years of age. *J. Genet. Psychol.*, 1929, Vol. 36, pp. 140-171.

61. FREUDENBERG, E. Der Morosche Umklammerungsreflex und das Brudzinskische Nackenzeichen als Reflexe des Säuglingsalters. *München. med. Wchnschr.*, 1921, Vol. 68, pp. 1646-1647.

62. FURFEY, P. H., BONHAM, M. A., and M. K. SARGENT. The mental organization of the newborn. *Child Develop.*, 1930, Vol. 1, pp. 48-51.

63. GALANT, J. S. Über den Fussohlengreifreflex der Säuglinge. *Arch. f. Kinderh.*, 1931, Vol. 92, pp. 304-305.

64. GALEWOOD, M. C., and A. P. WEISS. Race and sex differences in newborn infants. *Pedag. Sem.*, 1930, Vol. 38, pp. 31-49.

65. GESELL, A. The mental growth of the pre-school child. New York: Macmillan, 1928. x + 447 pp.

66. GESELL, A., and E. E. LORD. A psychological comparison of nursery school children from homes of low and high economic status. *J. Genet. Psychol.*, 1927, Vol. 35, pp. 339-356.

67. GILMER, B. VON H. An analysis of the spontaneous responses of the newborn infant. *J. Genet. Psychol.*, 1933, Vol. 42, pp. 392-405.

68. GIVLER, R. C. The intellectual significance of the grasping reflex. *J. Phil.*, 1921, Vol. 18, pp. 617-628.

69. GONZALES, J. DE J. Investigaciones acerca del estado de los reflejos durante el sueño. *Cron. med. quirur. de la Habana*, 1919, Vol. 45, pp. 285-292.

70. GORDON, M. B. Moro embrace reflex in infancy. *Am. J. Dis. Child.*, 1929, Vol. 38, pp. 26-34.

71. GREGOIRE, A. L'apprentisage de la parole pendant les deux premières années de l'enfance. *J. de Psychol.*, 1933, Vol. 30, pp. 375-389.

72. GUERNSEY, M. A quantitative study of the eye reflexes in infants. *Psychol. Bull.*, 1929, Vol. 26, pp. 160-161.

73. GUILLAUME, P. Les débuts de la phrase dans le langage de l'enfant. *J. de Psychol.*, 1927, Vol. 24, pp. 1-25.

74. GUTMAN, M. I. Über Augenbewegungen der Neugeborenen und ihre theoretische Bedeutung. *Arch. f. d. ges. Psychol.*, 1924, Vol. 47, pp. 108-121.

75. HALLER, M. W. The reactions of infants to change in the intensity and pitch of pure tone. *J. Genet. Psychol.*, 1932, Vol. 40, pp. 162-180.

76. HALVERSON, H. M. The acquisition of skill in infancy. *J. Genet. Psychol.*, 1933, Vol. 43, pp. 3-48.

77. —— An experimental study of prehension in infants by means of systematic cinema records. *Genet. Psychol. Monog.*, 1931, Vol. 10, pp. 107-286.

78. HALVERSON, H. M. A further study of grasping. *J. Genet. Psychol.*, 1932, Vol. 7, pp. 34-64.

79. HAYASHI, M. First appearance of reflexes in children. *J. Pediat.* (Tokyo), 1928, No. 343, p. 2150. (*Child Dev. Abs.*, 1929, Vol. 3, No. 454.)

80. HAZLITT, V. The psychology of infancy. New York: Dutton, 1933. viii + 149 pp.

81. HESS, J. H. Premature and congenitally diseased infants. Philadelphia: Lea and Febiger, 1922. xi + 397 pp.

82. HETZER, H., BEAUMONT, H., and E. WIEHMEYER. Das Schauen und Greifen des Kindes. Untersuchungen über spontanen Funktionswandel und Reizauslese in der Entwicklung, *Ztschr. f. Psychol.*, Vol. 113, Parts 1 and 2, pp. 239-286.

83. HETZER, H., and B. REINDORF. Sprachentwicklung und soziales Milieu. *Ztschr. f. ang. Psychol.*, 1929, Vol. 30, pp. 449-462.

84. HETZER, H., and K. WOLF. Eine Testserie für das erste Lebensjahr. *Ztschr. f. Psychol.*, 1928, Vol. 107, Parts 1-4, pp. 62-104.

85. HEUBNER, O. Über die Zeitfolge in der psychischen Entwicklung des Säuglings und jungen Kindes. *Ergeb. d. inneren Med. u. Kinderh.*, 1919, Vol. 16, pp. 1-31.

86. HILGARD, J. R. Learning and maturation in preschool children. *J. Genet. Psychol.*, 1932, Vol. 41, pp. 36-56.

87. HINSEY, J. C., RANSON, S. W., and R. F. McNATTIN. The role of the hypothalamus and mesencephalon in locomotion. *Arch. Neurol. & Psychiat.*, 1930, Vol. 23, pp. 1-43.

88. HOLMES, V. T. The phonology of an English child. *Amer. Speech*, 1926-27, Vol. 2, pp. 219-225.

89. HOYER, A., and G. HOYER. Über die Lallsprache eines Kindes. *Ztschr. f. ang. Psychol.*, 1924, Vol. 24, pp. 363-384.

90. HULL, C. L., and B. I. HULL. Parallel learning curves of an infant in vocabulary and in voluntary control of the bladder. *Pedag. Sem.*, 1919, Vol. 26, pp. 272-283.

91. HUNTER, W. S. Psychology and anthroponomy. *Psychologies of 1925*, edit. by Carl Murchison. Worcester, Mass.: Clark Univ. Press., 1926, pp. 83-107.

92. INGRAM, W. R., and S. W. RANSON. Postural reactions in cats following destruction of both red nuclei. *Proc. Soc. Exper. Biol. & Med.*, 1932, Vol. 29, p. 1089.

93. IRWIN, O. C. The amount and nature of activities of newborn infants under constant external stimulating conditions during the first ten days of life. *Genet. Psychol. Monog.*, 1930, Vol. 8, pp. 1-92.

94. IRWIN, O. C. Infant responses to vertical movements. *Child Develop.*, 1932, Vol. 3, pp. 167-169.

95. —— The latent time of the body startle in infants. *Child Develop.*, 1932, Vol. 3, pp. 104-107.

96. —— The organismic hypothesis and differentiation of behavior. III. The differentiation of human behavior. *Psychol. Rev.*, 1932, Vol. 39, pp. 387-393.

97. IRWIN, O. C., and A. P. WEISS. A note on mass activity in newborn infants. *Pedag. Sem.*, 1930, Vol. 38, pp. 20-30.

98. JENSEN, K. Differential reactions to taste and temperature stimuli in newborn infants. *Genet. Psychol. Monog.*, 1932, Vol. 12, pp. 361-479.

99. JOHNSON, B. J. Child psychology. Baltimore, Md.: Chas C. Thomas, 1932. xii + 439 pp.

100. JOHNSON, H. M. Children in the nursery school. New York: John Day Co., 1928. xx + 325 pp.

101. JONES, H. E. The galvanic skin reflex in infancy. *Child Develop.*, 1930, Vol. 1, pp. 106-110.

102. JONES, M. C. The development of early behavior patterns in young children. *Pedag. Sem.*, 1926, Vol. 33, pp. 537-585.

103. JUARROS, C. Aportacion al conocimiento de algunos problemas planteados por el estudio del signo de Babinski. *Siglo medico Madrid*, 1930, Vol. 85, pp. 689-694.

104. KENEYERS, E. Les premiers mots de l'enfant et l'apparition des éspèces de mots dans son langage. *Arch. de Pychol.*, 1927, Vol. 20, pp. 191-218.

105. KHERSON. Ontogenesis of plantar reflex. (In Ukrainian with German summary.) *Ber. wiss. Forschungs-inst., Odessa*, 1927, Vol. 3, pp. 68-74.

106. KOFFKA, K. The growth of the mind: an introduction to child psychology. (Trans. by R. M. Ogden.) New York: Harcourt, Brace; London: Paul Kegan, 1924, xvi + 383 pp.

107. —— Mental development. *Psychologies of 1925*, edit. by Carl Murchison. Worcester, Mass.: Clark Univ. Press, 1926, pp. 129-143.

108. KÖHLER, W. Some tasks of Gestalt psychology. *Psychologies of 1930*, edit. by Carl Murchison. Worcester, Mass.: Clark Univ. Press, 1931, pp. 143-160.

109. KUHLMANN, F. A handbook of mental tests: A further revision and extension of the Binet-Simon scale. Baltimore, Md.: Warwick and York, 1922. 208 pp.

110. Kuo, Z. Y. Ontogeny of embryonic behavior in Aves. IV. The influence of embryonic movements upon the behavior after hatching. *J. Comp. Psychol.*, 1932, Vol. 14, pp. 109-122.

111. Lambanyi, R., and C. Pianetta. Recherches sur le reflexe buccal. *Rev. de Psychiat. et de Psychol. Exper.*, 1906, Vol. 10, pp. 148-154.

112. Landau, A. Über einen tonischen Lagereflex beim älteren Säugling. *Klin. Wchnschr.*, 1923, Vol. 2, pp. 1253-1255.

113. Langworthy, O. R. The behavior of pouch-young opossums correlated with the myelinization of tracts in the nervous system. *J. Comp. Neurol.*, 1928, Vol. 146, pp. 201-247.

114. ——— Development of behavior patterns and myelinization of tracts in the nervous system. *Arch. Neurol. & Psychiat.*, 1932, Vol. 28, pp. 1365-1382.

115. ——— The differentiation of behavior patterns in the fetus and infant. *Brain*, 1932, Vol. 55, pp. 265-276.

116. ——— Relation of onset of decerebrate rigidity to the time of myelinization of tracts in the brain-stem and spinal cord of young animals. *Contrib. Embryol.*, 1926, Vol. 17, p. 125.

117. Lashley, K. S. Basic neural mechanisms in behavior. *Psychol. Rev.*, 1930, Vol. 37, pp. 1-24.

118. ——— Mass action in cerebral function. *Science*, 1931, Vol. 73, pp. 245-254.

119. ——— Studies of cerebral function in learning. Vol. 7: The relation between cerebral mass, learning, and retention. *J. Comp. Neurol.*, 1926, Vol. 41, pp. 1-48.

120. Lashley, K. S., and D. A. McCarthy. The survival of the maze habit after cerebellar injuries. *J. Comp. Neurol.*, 1926, Vol. 6, pp. 423-432.

121. Laughton, N. B. Studies on the nervous regulation of progression in mammals. *Am. J. Physiol.*, 1924, Vol. 70, pp. 358-384.

122. Linfert, H. E., and H. M. Hierholzer. A scale for measuring mental development of infants during the first year of life. *Studies in Psychol. & Psychiat.*, Catholic Univ. of Am., 1928, Vol. 1, pp. 1-33.

123. Lippman, H. S. Certain behavior responses in early infancy. *Pedag. Sem.*, 1927, Vol. 34, pp. 424-440.

124. Löwenfeld, B. Systematisches Studium der Reaktionen der Saüglinge auf Klänge und Geräusche. *Ztschr. f. Psychol.*, 1927, Vol. 104, pp. 62-96.

125. Lucas, P. W., and B. H. Pryor. Physical measurements and physiologic processes in young children. *J. A. M. A.*, 1931, Vol. 97, pp. 1127-1132.

126. McCARTHY, D. Language development. *Handbook of Child Psychol.*, edit. by Carl Murchison. Worcester, Mass.: Clark Univ. Press, 1931, pp. 278-315.

127. McCARTHY, D. Language development of the preschool child. Minneapolis, Minn.: University of Minnesota Press, 1930. 174 pp.

128. ——— The vocalization of infants; Part I: Studies; Part II: Methods of recording. *Psychol. Bull.*, 1929, Vol. 26, pp. 625-651.

129. McGINNIS, J. M. Eye-movements and optic nystagmus in early infancy. *Genet. Psychol. Monog.*, 1930, Vol. 8, pp. 321-430.

130. McGRAW, M. B. From reflex to muscular control in the assumption of an erect posture and ambulation in the human infant. *Child Develop.*, 1932, Vol. 3, pp. 291-297.

131. MAIER, N. R. F. The effect of cerebral destruction of reasoning and learning in rats. *J. Comp. Neurol.*, 1932, Vol. 54, pp. 45-72.

132. MARQUIS, D. P. Can conditioned responses be established in the newborn infant? *J. Genet. Psychol.*, 1931, Vol. 39, pp. 479-492.

133. ——— A study of activity and postures in infants' sleep. *J. Genet. Psychol.*, 1933, Vol. 42, pp. 51-69.

134. MINKOWSKI, M. Sur les modalités et la localisation du réflexe plantaire au cours de son évolution du foetus à l'adulte. *C. r. du Cong. des. méd. aliénistes et neurologistes fr.*, Geneva, 1926, Vol. 30, pp. 301-308.

135. ——— Sur les mouvements, les réflexes, et les réactions musculaires du foetus humain de 2 à 5 mois et leurs relations avec le système nerveux foetal. *Rev. neur.*, 1921, Vol. 37, pp. 1105-1118, 1235-1250.

136. ——— Neurobiologische Studien am menschlichen Foetus. *Hdbh. d. biol. Arbeitsmeth.*, 1928, Abt. 5, T. 5B, H. 5, pp. 511-618.

137. ——— Über Bewegungen und Reflexe des menschlichen Foetus wahrend der ersten Halfte seiner Entwicklung. *Schweiz. Arch. f. Neurol. u. Psychiat.*, 1921, Vol. 8, pp. 148-151.

138. ——— Über die elektrische Erregbarkeit der fötalen Muskulatur. *Schweiz. Arch. f. Neurol. u. Psychiat.*, 1928, Vol. 22, pp. 64-71.

139. ——— Über frühzeitige Bewegungen, Reflexe und muskuläre Reaktionen beim menschlichen Fötus und ihre Beziehungen zur fötalen Nerven- und Muskelsystem. *Schweiz. med. Wchnschr.*, 1922, Vol. 52, pp. 721-724, 751-755.

140. ——— Zum gegenwartigen Stand der Lehre von den Reflexen in entwicklungsgeschichtlicher und der anatomisch-physiologischer Beziehung. *Schweiz. Arch. f. Neurol. u. Psychiat.*, 1924, Vol. 15, pp. 239-259; 1925, Vol. 16, pp. 133-152, 266-284.

141. —— Zur Entwicklungsgeschichte, Lokalisation und Klinik des Fussohlenreflexes. *Schweiz. Arch. f. Neurol. u. Psychiat.*, 1923, Vol. 13, pp. 475-514.

142. MORO, E. Das erste Trimenon. *München. med. Wchnschr.*, 1918, Vol. 65, pp. 1147-1150.

143. MYERS, G. C. Evolution of an infant's walking. *Pedag. Sem.*, 1922, Vol. 29, pp. 295-301.

144. NAKAOJI *et al.* The pupillary reflex in infants. *J. Pediat.* (Tokyo), 1928, No. 339, p. 337. (*Child Dev. Abs.*, 1929, Vol. 3, No. 165).

145. NATIONAL SOCIETY FOR THE STUDY OF EDUCATION. *Twenty-eighth yearbook:* Preschool and parental education. Bloomington, Ill.: Public School Publishing Co., 1929. 875 pp.

146. NICE, M. M. A child's vocabularies from fifteen months to three years. *Proc. Okla. Acad. Sci.*, 1926, Vol. 6, Part II, pp. 317-333.

147. —— Length of sentence as a criterion of a child's progress in speech. *J. Educ. Psychol.*, 1925, Vol. 16, pp. 370-379.

148. —— On the size of vocabularies. *Am. Speech*, 1926, Vol. 2, pp. 1-7.

149. PARKER, R. H. The elementary nervous system. Philadelphia: Lippincott, 1919. 229 pp.

150. PARKER, G. H. Smell, taste, and allied senses in the vertebrates. Philadelphia: Lippincott, 1922. 192 pp.

151. PAVLOV, I. P. A brief outline of the higher nervous activity. *Psychologies of 1930*, edit. by Carl Murchison. Worcester, Mass.: Clark Univ. Press, 1931, pp. 207-220.

152. —— Lectures on conditioned reflexes. (Trans. by W. H. Gantt.) New York: International Publishers, 1928. 414 pp.

153. PEIPER, A. Beiträge zur Neurologie der jungen Säuglinge. *Monatschr. f. Kinderh.*, 1931, Vol. 49, pp. 265-271.

154. —— Beiträge zur Sinnesphysiologie der Frühgeburt. *Jahrb. f. Kinderh.*, 1924, Vol. 104, pp. 195-200.

155. —— Sinnesempfindungen des Kindes vor seiner Geburt. *Monatschr. f. Kinderh.*, 1925, Vol. 29, pp. 236-241.

156. —— Sinnesreaktionen des Neugeborenen. *Ztschr. f. Psychol.*, 1930, Vol. 114, pp. 363-370.

157. —— Über die Helligkeit und Farbenempfindungen der Frühgeburten. *Arch. f. Kinderh.*, 1926, Vol. 80, pp. 1-20.

158. —— Untersuchungen über den galvanischen Hautreflex (psychogalvanischen Reflex) im Kindesalter. *Jahrb. f. Kinderh.*, 1925, Vol. 107, pp. 139-150.

159. PEIPER, A., and H. ISBERT. Über die Körperstellung des Säuglings. *Jahrb. f. Kinderh.*, 1927, Vol. 115, pp. 142-176.

160. PONDER, E., and W. P. KENNEDY. On the act of blinking. *Quart. J. Exper. Physiol.*, 1927-28, Vol. 18, pp. 89-110.

161. PRATT, K. C. The effects of repeated auditory stimulation upon the general activity of newborn infants. *J. Genet. Psychol.*, 1934, Vol. 44, pp. 96-116.

162. —— The effects of repeated visual stimulation upon the activity of newborn infants. *J. Genet. Psychol.*, 1934, Vol. 44, pp. 117-126.

163. —— Note on the relation of temperature and humidity to the activity of young infants. *Pedag. Sem.*, 1930, Vol. 38, pp. 480-484.

164. PRATT, K. C., NELSON, A. K., and K. H. SUN. The behavior of the newborn infant. *Ohio State Univ. Stud.*: Contrib. Psychol., 1930, No. 10.

165. RABINER, A. M., and M. KESCHNER. Theory of the mechanism for the Babinski toe phenomenon. *Arch. Neurol. & Psychiat.*, 1926, Vol. 16, pp. 313-318.

166. RANSON, S. W. Rigidity caused by pyramidal lesions in the cat. *J. Comp. Neurol.*, 1932, Vol. 55, pp. 91-97.

167. RANSON, S. W., MUIR, J. C., and F. R. ZEISS. Extensor tonus after spinal-cord lesions in the cat. *J. Comp. Neurol.*, 1932, Vol. 54, pp. 13-33.

168. RASMUSSEN, V. Child psychology. Vcl. I: Development in the first four years. London: Glyldendal, 1920. xv + 166 pp.

169. RICHARDSON, H. M. Growth of adaptive behavior in infants: an experimental study at seven age levels. *Genet. Psychol. Monog.*, 1932, Vol. 12, pp. 195-359.

170. RICHTER, C. P. High electrical resistance of the skin of newborn infants and its significance. *Am. J. Dis. Child.*, 1930, Vol. 40, pp. 18-26.

171. RIPIN, R. A study of the infant's feeding reactions during the first six months of life. *Arch. Psychol.*, 1930, Vol. 8, pp. 1-44.

172. ROLANDO, F. I riflessi del neonato normale. *Pediatria*, 1931, Vol. 39, pp. 645-650.

173. SANFORD, H. N. The Moro reflex as a diagnostic aid in fracture of the clavicle in the new-born infant. *Am. J. Dis. Child.*, 1931, Vol. 41, pp. 1304-1306.

174. SCHAEFER, P. Beobachtungen und Versuche an einem Kinde in der Entwicklungsperiode des reinen Sprachverständnisses. *Ztschr. f. pädag. Psychol.*, 1922, Vol. 23, pp. 269-289.

175. —— Die kindliche Entwicklungsperiode des reinen Sprachverständnisses nach ihrer Abgrenzung. *Ztschr. f. pädag. Psychol.*, 1921, Vol. 22, pp. 317-325.

176. SCHALTENBRAND, G. The development of human motility and motor disturbances. *Arch. Neurol. & Psychiat.*, 1928, Vol. 20, pp. 720-730.

177. SCHALTENBRAND, G. Normale Bewegungs- und Lagereaktionen bei Kindern. *Deutsche Ztschr. f. Nervenh.*, 1925, Vol. 87, pp. 23-59.

178. SHERMAN, M. The differentiation of emotional responses in infants. *J. Comp. Psychol.*, 1927, Vol. 7, pp. 265-284; 335-351.

179. SHERMAN, M., and I. C. SHERMAN. Sensori-motor responses in infants. *J. Comp. Psychol.*, 1925, Vol. 5, pp. 53-68.

180. SHIRLEY, M. The first two years: a study of twenty-five children. Vol. I: Postural and locomotor development; 1931, Monograph series No. 4, xv + 227 pp.; Vol. II: Intellectual development; 1933, Monograph series No. 7, xvi + 513 pp. Minneapolis, Minn.: Univ. of Minnesota: Instit. of Child Welfare.

181. ——— A motor sequence favors the maturation theory. *Psychol. Bull.*, 1931, Vol. 28, pp. 204-205.

182. SIMON, T. Questionnaire for the observation of a young child from birth to two years of age. (Trans. by M. L. Reymert.) *Pedag. Sem.*, 1920, Vol. 27, pp. 200-204.

183. SMITH, M. E., LECHER, G., DUNLOP, J. W., and E. E. CURETON. The effect of race, sex and environment on the age at which children walk. *Pedag. Sem.*, 1930, Vol. 38, pp. 489-498.

184. STAPLES, R. The responses of infants to color. *J. Exper. Psychol.*, 1932, Vol. 15, pp. 119-141.

185. STERN, W. Psychology of early childhood up to the sixth year. (Trans. by A. Barwell from 3rd edition.) New York: Holt, 1934. 557 pp.

186. STOLTE, K. Der Babinskische Fussohlenreflex. *Jahrb. f. Kinderh.*, 1933, Vol. 139, pp. 163-164.

187. SWENSON, E. A. The active simple movements of the albino-rat fetus: the order of their appearance, their qualities and their significance. *Anat. Rec.*, 1929, Vol. 42, p. 40.

188. ——— The simple movements of the trunk of the albino-rat fetus. *Anat. Rec.*, 1928, Vol. 38, p. 31.

189. TAYLOR-JONES, L. A study of behavior in the newborn. *Am. J. Med. Sci.*, 1927, Vol. 174, pp. 357-362.

190. THOMPSON, H. The growth and significance of daily variations in infant behavior. *J. Genet. Psychol.*, 1932, Vol. 40, pp. 16-36.

191. THOMSON, J. On the lip-reflex (mouth phenomenon) of newborn children. *Rev. Neur. & Psychiat.*, 1903, Vol. 1, pp. 145-148.

192. TILNEY, F. Behavior in its relation to the development of the brain. Part II. Correlation between the development of the brain and behavior in the albino rat from embryonic states to maturity. *Bull. Neurol. Inst. New York*, 1933, Vol. 3, pp. 252-357.

193. TILNEY, F. Genesis of cerebellar functions. *Arch. Neurol. & Psychiat.*, 1923, Vol. 9, pp. 137-169.

194. TILNEY, F., and L. CASAMAJOR. Myelinogeny as applied to the study of behavior. *Arch. Neurol. & Psychiat.*, 1924, Vol. 12, pp. 1-66.

195. TILNEY, F., and L. S. KUBIE. Behavior in its relation to the development of the brain. Part I. *Bull. Neurol. Inst. New York*, 1931, Vol. 1, pp. 229-313.

196. TRACY, H. L. The development of motility and behavior reactions in the toadfish (*Opsanus Tau*). *J. Comp. Neurol.*, 1926, Vol. 40, pp. 253-360.

197. TROEMNER, E. Reflexuntersuchungen an einem Anencephalus. *J. f. Psych. u. Neurol.*, 1928, Vol. 35, pp. 194-198.

198. VALENTINE, C. W. Reflexes in early childhood. Their development, variability, evanescence, inhibition and relation to instincts. *Brit. J. Med. Psychol.*, 1927, Vol. 7, pp. 1-35.

199. VARIOT, G. La prélocomotion chez le jeune enfant avant le marche bipède. *Rev. scient.*, 1927, Vol. 65, pp. 70-74.

200. ———— Présentation de deux frères chez lesquels le début de la marche bipède a coincidé avec une taille de 80 cent. *Bull. et mem. de la soc. d'anthrop. de Paris*, 1927, Vol. 8, pp. 13-15.

201. VARIOT, G., and P. GOTCU. Le début de la marche bipède chez le jeune enfant, dans ses rapports avec l'âge et la taille. *Bull. et mem. de la soc. d'anthrop. de Paris*, 1927, Vol. 8, pp. 17-23.

202. ———— La marche bipède chez le jeune enfant dans ses rapports avec le poids de naissance, le poids actuel, la dentition, l'alimentation et le sexe. *Bull. et mem. de la soc. d'anthrop. de Paris*, 1927, Vol. 8, pp. 23-30.

203. WADA, T. An experimental study of hunger in its relation to activity. *Arch. Psychol.*, 1922, Vol. 8, pp. 1-65.

204. WAGGONER, R., and W. G. FERGUSON. The development of the plantar reflex in children. *Arch. Neurol. & Psychiat.*, 1930, Vol. 23, pp. 619-633.

205. WARDEN, C. J. Notes on a male infant. *J. Genet. Psychol.*, 1928, Vol. 35, pp. 328-330.

206. WATSON, J. B. Behaviorism. New York: People's Institute Publishing Co., 1925. 251 pp.

207. ———— Psychology from the standpoint of a behaviorist. Philadelphia: Lippincott, 1919. ix + 429 pp.

208. WEISS, A. P. The biosocial standpoint in psychology. *Psychologies of 1930*, edit. by Carl Murchison. Worcester, Mass.: Clark Univ. Press, 1931, pp. 301-306.